ROMEO & JULIET: THE STUDY GUIDE

Francis Gilbert

Francis Gilbert

All rights reserved. This book contains material protected under International and Federal Copyright Laws and Treaties. Any unauthorized reprint or use of the original material written by Francis Gilbert is prohibited: these sections of the book may not be reproduced or transmitted in any form or by any means, electronic or mechanical, including photocopying, recording, or by any information storage and retrieval system without express written permission from the author / publisher.
This edition first published in 2014 by FGI publishing:
www.francisgilbert.co.uk;
fgipublishing.com
Copyright © 2014 Francis Gilbert
FGI Publishing, London UK, sir@francisgilbert.co.uk
British Library Cataloguing-in-Publications Data
A catalogue record for this book is available from the British Library
ISBN-13: 978-1501001338
ISBN-10: 1501001337

Dedication
I dedicate this book to Michael Whyte whose passion for this play always makes me want to read it again.

Acknowledgments
First, huge thanks must go to my wife, Erica Wagner, for always supporting me with my writing and teaching. Second, I'm very grateful to all the students and teachers who have helped me write this book.
Also by Francis Gilbert:
I'm A Teacher, Get Me Out Of Here (2004)
Teacher On The Run (2005)
Yob Nation (2006)
Parent Power (2007)
Working The System: How To Get The Very State Education For Your Child (2011)
The Last Day Of Term (2012)
Gilbert's Study Guides on: *Frankenstein, Far From The Madding Crowd, The Hound of the Baskervilles , Pride and Prejudice, The Strange Case of Dr Jekyll and Mr Hyde, The Turn of the Screw, Wuthering Heights* (2013)
Dr Jekyll & Mr Hyde: The Study Guide Edition
Romeo and Juliet: The Study Guide Edition (2014)

Contents

Introduction 7
Part I: What You Need To Know 9
Why study *Romeo and Juliet?* 11
   Useful links 12
Story: structure & themes 13
   Love 14
   Hatred: the feud 15
   Fate 15
   The use of time 17
   Useful links 18
   Tasks 18
Contexts 20
   The different versions 20
   Source 1: Brooke's poem 21
   Source 2: Nashe's *Have With You to Saffron Walden* (1596) 22
   Source 3: A Midsummer Night's Dream 23
   Questions 24
   Tragedy 25
Shakespeare's theatre: The Globe 26
   Social, political contexts 27
   Productions of *Romeo and Juliet* 28
   Useful links 29
Shakespeare's language 29
   Shakespeare's imagery 31
   Love imagery 32
   Hate Imagery 34
   Fate imagery 35
   Thou and You 36
   Beware the false friends! 37
   Nouns 37
   Verbs and verb phrases 40
   Adjectives 42
   Prepositions 42
   Adverbs 43
   Regrets 43
   Hence, thence and whence 43
   Hither, thither, whither 44
   Stage directions 44
   Tasks on language 44
Rhythm & rhyme 45
   Exercise 47
Characterisations 49
   Being a man & a woman 50
   The similarities and differences between the characters 51
   Romeo 52
   Questions 57
Juliet 57
   Questions 61

Capulet	62
Questions	64
The Nurse	64
Questions	65
Mercutio	66
Questions	67
Friar Lawrence	67
Questions	69
Tybalt	69
Questions	70
Benvolio	70
Questions	71
Prince Escalus	71
Questions	73
Paris	73
Questions	73
Web links for characters	74
Part II: Activities on the play	75
An explanation of the activities	75
Prologue	75
Act 1, SCENE I. Verona. A public place.	77
Activities 1.1	78
Activities 1.2	79
Activities 1.3	80
Act 1, SCENE II. A street.	81
Activities 1.4	81
Activities 1.5	82
Act 1, SCENE III. A room in Capulet's house.	83
Activities 1.6	83
Act 1, SCENE IV. A street.	84
Activities 1.7	85
Act 1, SCENE V. A hall in Capulet's house.	86
Activities 1.8	86
Activities 1.9	87
Activities 1.10	88
Activities 1.11	88
Activities 1.12	89
Looking back at Act 1	90
Answers	93
Act 2, Prologue	98
Activities 2.1	98
Act 2, SCENE I. A lane by the wall of Capulet's orchard.	99
Activities 2.2	99
Act 2, SCENE II. Capulet's orchard.	100
Activities 2.3	100
Activities 2.4	101
Activities 2.5	102
Act 2, SCENE III. Friar Lawrence's cell.	103
Activities 2.6	103
Activities 2.7	104
Act 2, SCENE IV. A street.	105
Activities 2.8	105

Activities 2.9	106
Act 2, SCENE V. Capulet's orchard.	107
Activities 2.10	108
Act 2, SCENE VI. Friar Lawrence's cell.	109
Activities 2.11	109
Looking Back At Act 2	110
Answers	112
Act 3, SCENE I. A public place.	117
Activities 3.1	117
Activities 3.2	118
Activities 3.3	119
Activities 3.4	120
Act 3, SCENE II. Capulet's orchard.	120
Activities 3.5	121
Activities 3.6	121
Act 3, SCENE III. Friar Lawrence's cell.	122
Activities 3.7	123
Activities 3.8	123
Act 3, SCENE IV. A room in Capulet's house.	124
Activities 3.9	124
Act 3, SCENE V. Capulet's orchard.	125
Activities 3.10	126
Activities 3.11	127
Looking back at Act 3	128
Answers	131
Act 4, SCENE I. Friar Lawrence's cell.	137
Activities 4.1	137
Activities 4.2	138
Act 4, SCENE II. Hall in Capulet's house.	139
Activities 4.3	139
Act 4, SCENE III. Juliet's chamber.	140
Activities 4.4	140
Act 4, SCENE IV. Hall in Capulet's house.	141
Activities 4.5	141
Act 4, Scene V. Juliet's Chamber.	142
Activities 4.6	142
Looking back at Act 4	143
Answers	145
Act 5, SCENE I. Mantua. A street.	148
Activities 5.1	148
Act 5, Scene II. Friar Lawrence's Cell.	149
Activities 5.2	149
Act 5, SCENE III. A churchyard; in it a tomb belonging to the Capulets.	150
Activities 5.3	150
Activities 5.4	151
Activities 5.5	152
Activities 5.6	152
Looking back at Act 5	153
Answers	156
Summary of the whole play	161
Prologue	161
Act 1, Sc I	161

Act 1, Sc II	161
Act 1, Sc III	161
Act 1, Sc IV	162
Act 1, Sc V	162
Act 2, Prologue	163
Act 2, Sc I	163
Act 2, Sc II	163
Act 2, Sc III	164
Act 2, Sc IV	164
Act 2, Sc V	164
Act 2, Sc VI	165
Act 3, Sc I	165
Act 3, Sc II	166
Act 3, Sc III	166
Act 3, Sc IV	166
Act 3, Sc V	167
Act 4, Sc I	167
Act 4, Sc II	168
Act 4, Sc III	168
Act 4, Sc IV	168
Act 5, Sc I	169
Act 5, Sc II	169
Act 5, Sc III	169
Speaking and listening activities	170
Literary Criticism	171
Early critics	171
Nicholas Brooke	171
Feminist criticism	173
Marxist and cultural materialist criticism	173
Queer criticism	174
Tasks	175
Essays	176
Dissecting a sub-standard essay	177
Learning points	182
The scene-based essay	182
The A* essay	183
Preparation and planning	184
Comparing the play with filmed versions & performances	189
Works Cited	191
About the author	192

Introduction

Welcome to *Romeo & Juliet: The Study Guide*. The aim of this study guide is to give students the tools to gain a very good grade at GCSE level and possibly A Level. All the key areas connected with the play are covered: the story, characters, themes, language and imagery.

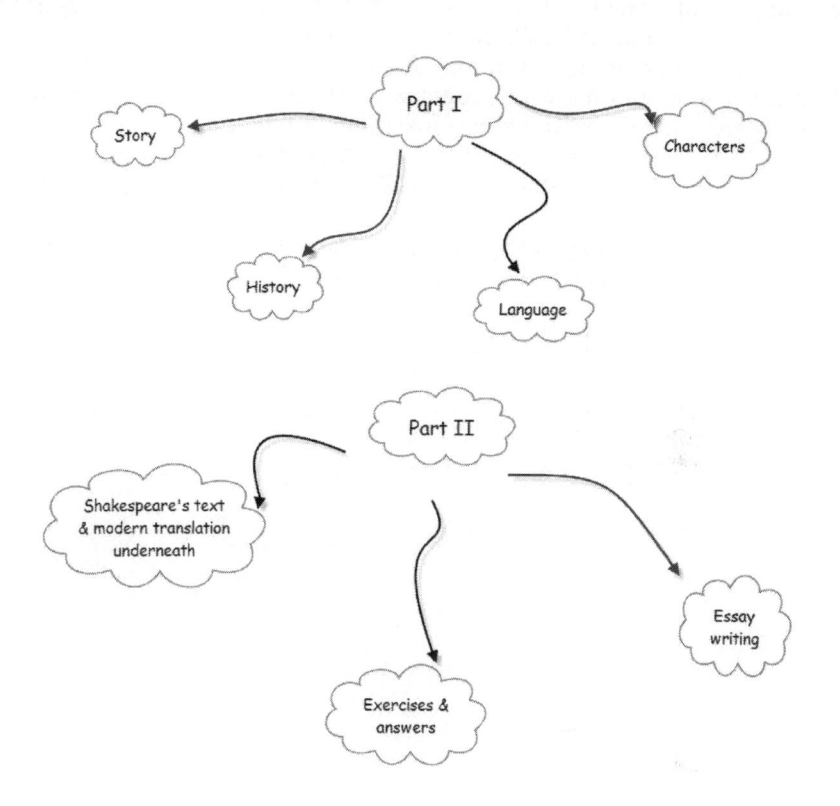

Diagram: Part I branches to Story, Characters, History, Language. Part II branches to Shakespeare's text & modern translation underneath, Exercises & answers, Essay writing.

Figure 1 Outline of the guide: you will be able to find a larger version of this diagram on <u>the Romeo and Juliet Reloaded website here</u>.

Part I of the book explains a number of important things which are very helpful to know about before you read the play: it is useful to think about reasons why people read Shakespeare and *Romeo and Juliet* in particular; it's helpful to know the basic story, what happens in the play; it is also advisable to know about the "background" or "context" to the play. When you try and think about how people felt and thought in

Shakespeare's time, it helps you understand the play more deeply. Knowing a bit about Shakespeare's language, his use of rhythm and rhyme, and the characters can also help you as well.

Part II contains activities on the text itself. If you are reading the e-Book version for Kindle, which is free if you have bought the paperback on Amazon, you will be able to click on the underlined words in the text and go to the relevant resource on the internet: any phrase which is underlined is a weblink. All of the titles of the scenes in Part II are hyperlinked and take you to annotated version of the text, which explains all the difficult words. The diagrams that punctuate the book can also be seen and downloaded in larger versions on Romeo and Juliet Reloaded: the Kindle version provides all the relevant links.

If you want to read the whole text please buy my *Romeo and Juliet: The Study Guide Edition*, which contains all the exercises here as well as Shakespeare's text with a modern translation.

I would appreciate any feedback that readers might want to give, either by commenting on *Romeo and Juliet Reloaded*, or by emailing me, sir@francisgilbert.co.uk.

Question: What do you know about Shakespeare and *Romeo and Juliet* already? Do a spider diagram to illustrate all that you know.

Francis Gilbert 2014

Part I: What You Need To Know

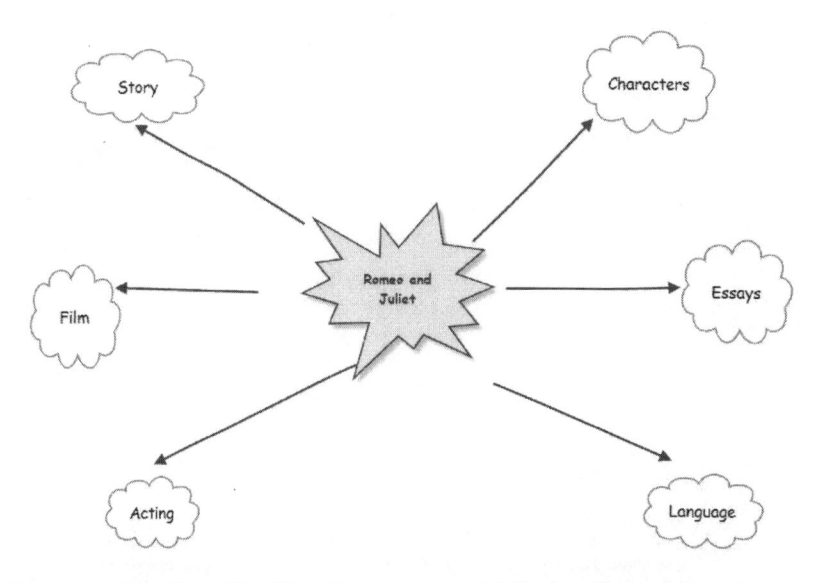

Figure 2 What You Need To Know: you can find a larger version of this diagram on <u>the Romeo and Juliet Reloaded website here</u>

When studying *Romeo and Juliet*, you need to know some basic things: what the **story** is about; who the **characters** are and what they do; you need to understand a great deal of Shakespeare's **language**, though not all of it; you should watch a **filmed version** of the play and should watch performances in the theatre if you get a chance; and you should understand how the play is **acted** out on stage.

How to study Shakespeare

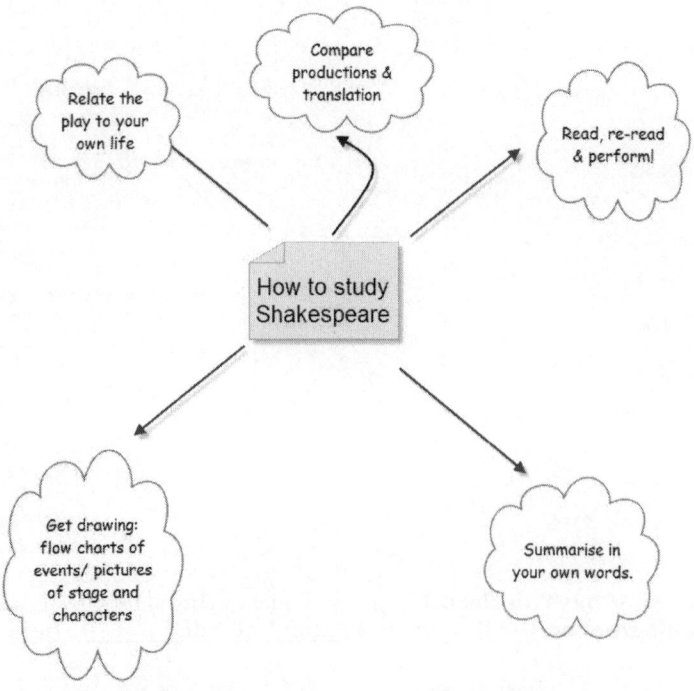

Diagram: Central node "How to study Shakespeare" with branches to:
- *Relate the play to your own life*
- *Compare productions & translation*
- *Read, re-read & perform!*
- *Get drawing: flow charts of events/ pictures of stage and characters*
- *Summarise in your own words.*

Figure 3 How To Study Shakespeare: you can find a larger version of this diagram on <u>the Romeo and Juliet Reloaded website here</u>

Learning Shakespeare is difficult, possibly one of the most difficult things you will ever do at school, because there is so much to learn about. In the flow chart above are some tips that will help you learn the play better: they are all suggestions based on the latest educational research as to what helps people learn, summarized brilliantly in a little book called *Learning & The Brain Pocketbook* by Dommett, Devonshire and Churches (Eleanor Dommett, Ian Devonshire, Richard Churches, 2011). First, it's always a good idea to relate the play to your own life if you can; think in particular about the ideas in the play that relate to your life. This will help you remember the play better and will make it much more meaningful for you. Second, get drawing the key elements of the play: flow charts really help you understand what's going on, and drawings of characters and scenes will help you visualize scenes in your mind. Third, have a go at summarizing key parts of the play in your own words. Fourth, read and re-read the play, performing if you can. Fifth, have a go at comparing different productions of the play that you've watched and compare my translation of Shakespeare's words with his own original words. Have I got the translation right? Can you think of a better translation? This will really help you think about Shakespeare's language, what it means and the effect it has on the audience.

Perhaps above all, you need to have a **positive attitude**, what some psychologists call a "Growth Mindset" towards Shakespeare: if you try hard, you will succeed in understanding his work. Instead of telling yourself that his work is boring, think about it as challenging; instead of saying you can't do it, tell yourself you can with more effort.

Why study *Romeo and Juliet*?

Having taught Shakespeare for nearly twenty five years now, I have been confronted by many students asking: why are we reading this play when it's so difficult? I think it's a question worth answering. When you're clearer about why you're studying Shakespeare, often referred to as "the Bard", it can really help you enjoy his work more and, as a consequence, learn more. In *Doing English* (Eaglestone, 2009) Professor Robert Eaglestone highlights two main approaches to Shakespeare: the "traditionalist" (old fashioned) approach and the "cultural materialist" approach. There are other approaches, but Eaglestone is probably right in saying that these two are the ones that dominate literary criticism (analysis of literature). When discussing the traditionalist approach, Eaglestone claims that most traditionalists have three main arguments for studying Shakespeare: "the artistic (or aesthetic worth) of Shakespeare's plays; the values taught by Shakespeare's plays; the universal appeal of Shakespeare's work" (Eaglestone, 2009, p.64). All three arguments are regularly wheeled out by teachers throughout the globe as reasons for studying *Romeo and Juliet*. It is regularly claimed that it is the greatest love-story ever written; it is often argued that it teaches us invaluable lessons about love, hate and fate; and many claim that the story has universal appeal. Eaglestone writes: "For the traditionalists, Shakespeare's plays are like a star: beautiful, remote, independent of earth and worldly concerns, to be wondered at and admired." (Eaglestone, 2009, p.66)

A cultural materialist critic would reject all three of these claims because a critic of this sort is most interested in studying Shakespeare's text as the material products of very specific cultural conditions; they examine the "contexts" – the social background -- in which Shakespeare's plays existed, and look at the ways in which his plays tell us about the cultural conditions of his time: most often looking at the attitudes towards women, the different social classes and the various institutions that formed the society -- the family, the monarchy, the church etc. They also examine how we view Shakespeare by looking at the "contexts of reading": how different social groups, genders, classes, ethnicities and so on read Shakespeare in the present day. Eaglestone says: "A cultural-materialist critic is principally interested in the way material factors – like economic conditions and political struggles of all sorts – have influenced or even created a text. In turn, they argue that any text can tell us about material conditions." (Eaglestone, 2009, p.66) Brilliant exhibitions and programmes like *Shakespeare's Restless World* (The British Museum) are informed by a cultural materialist approach because they try to piece together what it was like in Shakespeare's time by looking at his texts and other cultural artefacts.

This study guide examines both approaches, even though they are at odds with one another. The traditionalists' approach needs to be looked at because so much Shakespearean criticism embraces their ideas. Furthermore, the traditionalist approach of looking at a text by examining its story, characters and themes can be useful helping students increase their understanding of the play. However, the cultural materialist approach has real validity too: thinking about the contexts in which the play arose is very illuminating and really helps students understand the play better. This is something that many exam boards require students to do. Equally, looking at the ways in which we read Shakespeare now, how different directors and actors have interpreted *Romeo and Juliet* can bring the play alive. The modern translation I have provided is very much informed by a "cultural materialist" approach: traditionalists would be horrified to read the way I have "mangled" Shakespeare's beautiful poetry. But I have found the translation really helps students understand the language and then make their own judgments about the effects of Shakespeare's actual language. The translation is not definitive, it is there as a guide and a help.

Useful links

Professor Emma Smith's lecture on *Why We Should Study* Shakespeare is excellent.

This discussion panel which she was involved with is also very useful.

Question: why do people study Shakespeare and *Romeo and Juliet*?

Story: structure & themes

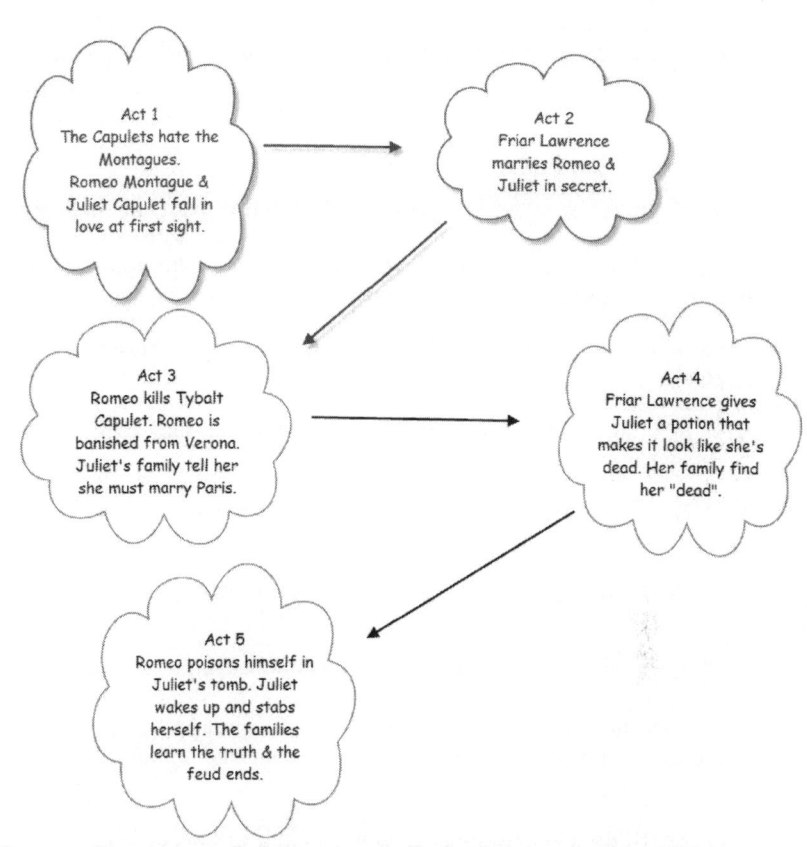

Act 1
The Capulets hate the Montagues. Romeo Montague & Juliet Capulet fall in love at first sight.

Act 2
Friar Lawrence marries Romeo & Juliet in secret.

Act 3
Romeo kills Tybalt Capulet. Romeo is banished from Verona. Juliet's family tell her she must marry Paris.

Act 4
Friar Lawrence gives Juliet a potion that makes it look like she's dead. Her family find her "dead".

Act 5
Romeo poisons himself in Juliet's tomb. Juliet wakes up and stabs herself. The families learn the truth & the feud ends.

Figure 4 Summary of plot: you can find a larger version of this diagram on <u>the Romeo and Juliet Reloaded website here</u>

Above, is the **very basic plot** of *Romeo and Juliet,* which as you can see is based around the story of Romeo and Juliet marrying in secret. There are many different plot-summaries of *Romeo and Juliet* on the internet from the <u>Spark Notes summary</u> (Sparknotes), which is quite formal in tone, to Schmoop's <u>deliberately informal, jokey summary</u> (Schmoop). You can also find my detailed summary which I have put at the end of this book because it is based on the fill-in-the-gaps exercises that punctuate the play text and I wouldn't want you to get the answers first!

Many summaries do not take into account the fact that the plot that Shakespeare constructed is shaped around particular themes or ideas. Above all, *Romeo and Juliet* is a play of "opposites", of contrasts and comparisons. Concepts such as hatred and love, day and night, male and female, old and young are constantly "juxtaposed" (put together with contrasting effect) in the text: a violent scene is followed by a very loving one; a night-time scene is full of imagery connected with light; a scene with only men is followed by an all-female scene; an old character talks to a young character and so on.

In *Romeo and Juliet*, nearly all the major events and speeches in the play are structured around three major themes or ideas: love, hate and fate.

Love

For the "love" theme, we could break down the main events in this way:

> Act 1, Sc 1: Romeo appears to be in love with a woman, Rosaline, but she has consistently rejected him.
>
> Act 2, Sc II: Romeo and Benvolio discover Rosaline is attending Capulet's "masque" which they plan to gate-crash.
>
> Act 1, Sc V: Romeo first meets Juliet at Capulet's "masque"; they fall in love immediately. Rosaline is forgotten.
>
> Act 2, Scs I & IV: Mercutio makes fun of Romeo for being in love with Rosaline.
>
> Act 2, Sc II: Romeo and Juliet agree to marry during the balcony scene.
>
> Act 2, Sc VI: The lovers marry.
>
> Act 3, Sc V: Romeo and Juliet spend their wedding night together. Romeo leaves for Mantua because he's been banished for killing Tybalt.
>
> Act 5, Sc III: Romeo visits Juliet's tomb and kills himself by her body, which he believes to be dead. Juliet wakes and stabs herself to death on seeing Romeo dead.

If you look at the plot this way, you see that the lovers only meet four times -- if you discount the death scene. And yet, these are the scenes which "drive" the whole plot: they are its "engine" without which the whole play would not exist. So how does Shakespeare manage to write such a long and complex play when his love story only occupies five scenes? He does this by setting the love story in a very particular context which adds suspense and drama to the love story. The first major context is Shakespeare's exploration of the theme of "hatred" or the feud.

Task: Do a flow or spider diagram of this **key theme**.

Hatred: the feud

The "feud" (a prolonged and bitter quarrel or dispute) occupies many more scenes in the play:

> Act 1, Sc 1: After joking about raping the Montague women, the Capulet servants become embroiled in a fight with the Montagues because they are making rude hand gestures at each other: biting their thumbs. The two families join in, including the younger and older generations: Tybalt (a young Capulet), Benvolio (a young Montague), Lord Capulet (Juliet's father) and Lord Montague (Romeo's father). The brawl is stopped by the Prince who threatens to execute the next person who starts a fight.
>
> Act 1, Sc V: Tybalt, a Capulet, sees Romeo at the Capulet's party and wants to kill him but is stopped by Capulet, Juliet's father. Tybalt vows to get his revenge on Romeo for this insult.
>
> Act 2, Sc IV: We learn from Benvolio (a Montague) that Tybalt has sent a letter to Romeo, presumably challenging him to a duel.
>
> Act 3, Sc 1: Romeo (a Montague) refuses to fight Tybalt (a Capulet), saying he loves him more than he could know. Mercutio (from neither family but related to the Prince) sees this as cowardice and fights Tybalt instead: he is killed, blaming Romeo because Tybalt stabbed him under Romeo's arm as Romeo tried to intervene, and blaming the feud between the two houses: before he dies he says "plague on both your houses". Romeo kills Tybalt in revenge and is banished from Verona as a result.
>
> Act 5, Sc III: Romeo (a Montague) kills Paris (a Capulet supporter because he was going to marry Juliet). Paris believed Romeo had come to the tomb to vandalize the dead bodies of the Capulets and fights Romeo as result. When the families learn from Friar Lawrence that Romeo and Juliet were married, they decide to end their feud.

The feud provides the backdrop for the play and the reason why the lovers are separated and see each other so infrequently. It provides the play with its menace and violence.

Question: why does the theme of hatred occupy many more scenes in the play?

Task: Do a flow or spider diagram of this **key theme**.

Fate

Fate means "the development of events outside a person's control, regarded as predetermined by a supernatural power". Fate plays an important role in play: a series of unlikely coincidences lead inevitably to the doom of the lovers. They are "star-crossed"; it has been written in their stars that they will die – this is their fate. Let's look at the scenes in which fate plays a role:

> Act 1, Sc II: Romeo is asked to read a letter by a servant of the Capulet's because the servant can't read: he sees that Rosaline is attending the party. This means he goes to the party where he sees Juliet.
>
> Act 1, Sc IV: Romeo has a premonition that he will die as a result of something happening to him that night.
>
> Act 1, Sc V: Romeo sees Juliet for the first time at Capulet's feast. This is his destiny, his fate.
>
> Act 2, Sc VI: Romeo and Juliet marry: a key part of their destiny is fulfilled.
>
> Act 3, Sc I: Romeo happens to meet Tybalt after he has married; Mercutio happens to be there. Mercutio and Tybalt die as a result of this fateful meeting. Romeo calls himself "fortune's fool" (the idiot/clown of fate). He is banished from Verona and Juliet.
>
> Act 3, Sc V: Romeo and Juliet spend their only night together. Juliet has a premonition of seeing Romeo at the bottom of a tomb as he climbs down her balcony. Juliet is threatened with being thrown onto the streets if she doesn't marry Paris.
>
> Act 4, Sc 1: Friar Lawrence offers Juliet the fateful potion so that she can avoid marrying Paris and Romeo can rescue her.
>
> Act 4, Sc III: Juliet takes the potion which will make it look like she's dead for 42 hours.
>
> Act 4, Sc V: The Capulets find Juliet and believe her to be dead.
>
> Act 5, Sc 1: Romeo learns from Balthasar that Juliet is dead. He buys poison from an apothecary, believing he will defy his fate by killing himself.
>
> Act 5, Sc II: Friar John is quarantined in a plague house and cannot deliver Friar Lawrence's letter to Juliet which informs Romeo that Juliet is alive.
>
> Act 5, Sc III: Romeo kills himself before Juliet wakes up. Juliet sees Romeo is dead and kills herself. Their destinies are fulfilled. The families learn of the tragedy and unite, thus fulfilling fate's decree.

Task: Do a flow or spider diagram of this **key theme**.

The use of time

Sunday
- **Morning:** Prince stops fight between Capulets & Montagues; Romeo tells Benvolio of his love for Rosaline.
- **Evening:** Romeo & Juliet fall in love at Capulet's feast; Tybalt sees Romeo gate-crashing & vows revenge; Romeo visits Juliet and they agree to marry on her balcony.

Monday
- **Morning:** Romeo visits Friar Lawrence and plans are made for the wedding.
- **Afternoon:** Friar Lawrence marries Romeo and Juliet; Leaving the wedding Romeo watches Tybalt kill Mercutio & then kills Tybalt.
- **Evening:** Romeo is banished from Verona; Capulet decides Juliet will marry Paris.

Tuesday
- **Morning:** after spending the night together, Romeo leaves Juliet. Capulet tells Juliet she must marry Paris on Thursday; Juliet visits Friar Lawrence and he gives her a potion to make it look like she's dead. Friar Lawrence writes to Romeo.
- **Evening:** Juliet tells Capulet she will marry Paris; Capulet moves the wedding to Wednesday; Juliet takes the potion that makes her look like she's dead for 42 hours.

Wednesday
- **Morning:** the Capulet family discover Juliet's dead body.

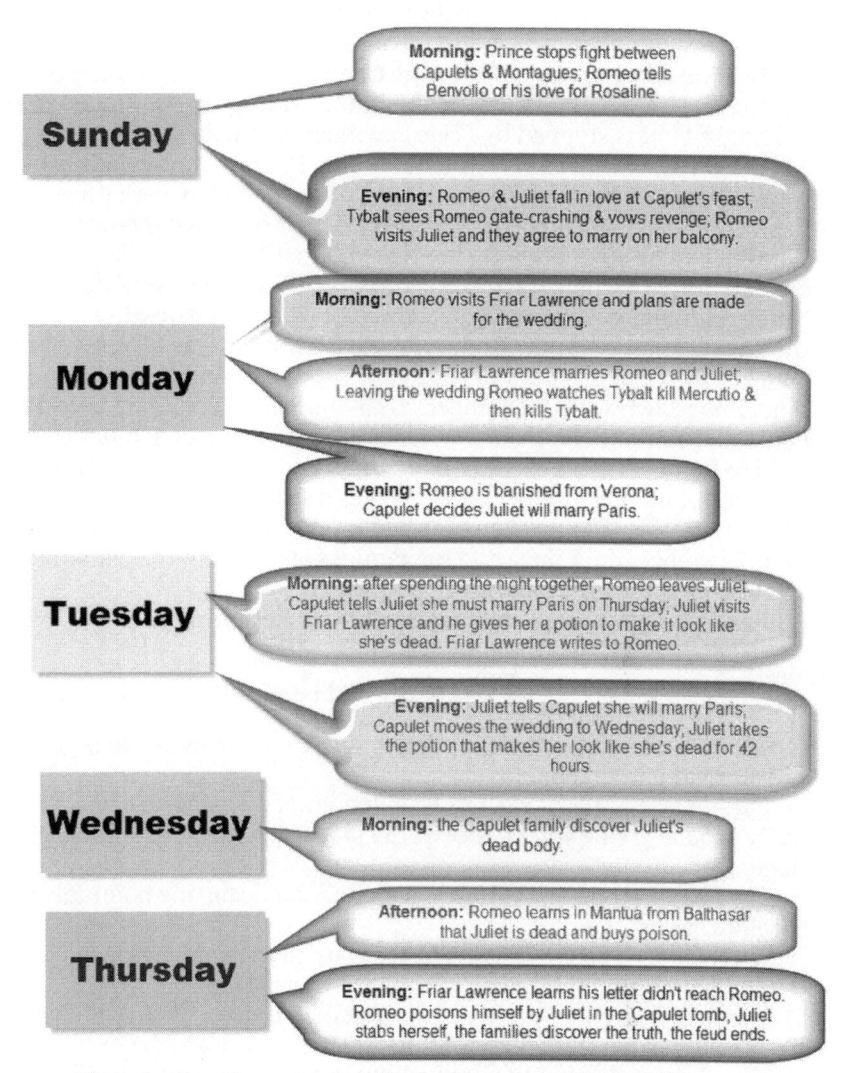

Thursday
- **Afternoon:** Romeo learns in Mantua from Balthasar that Juliet is dead and buys poison.
- **Evening:** Friar Lawrence learns his letter didn't reach Romeo. Romeo poisons himself by Juliet in the Capulet tomb, Juliet stabs herself, the families discover the truth, the feud ends.

Figure 5 Time in the play: you can find a larger version of this diagram on <u>the Romeo and Juliet Reloaded website here</u>

The play takes place in a very tight time-frame with all the events occurring within four days. Time is constantly mentioned in the play; what o'clock it is, whether it is the morning, how long a potion will work and so on. It is worth noting the precise time-scale for the play and seeing how it works in the play because time is a major theme.

Act 1 takes place on **Sunday**: with the feud occurring in the morning as well as Romeo's lovesickness for Rosaline. Romeo and his friends gate-crash Capulet's feast on **Sunday night.** Romeo then visits Juliet that night and plans are made for the wedding on **Monday morning**. The lovers marry in the **early Monday afternoon**. Romeo is leaving the wedding when he revenges Mercutio's death by killing Tybalt in the **early Monday evening**. That **night**, the Prince banishes Romeo from Verona and Capulet makes plans for Juliet to marry Paris. Romeo tries to kill himself but is stopped by Friar Lawrence who tells Romeo to spend **Monday night** with Juliet, which he does. The lovers wake **early on Tuesday morning** and Romeo leaves. Juliet is told by her father, Capulet, that she must marry Paris; she visits Friar Lawrence for a solution and he gives her a potion that will make it appear like she is dead for forty two hours, which she takes on **Tuesday evening**. The Nurse finds Juliet supposedly dead in her bed on **Wednesday morning**. Later that day, Romeo learns from Balthasar his servant that Juliet is dead and has been taken to the Capulet's tomb. At roughly this time, Friar Lawrence's messenger, Friar John, is quarantined in a plague house and can't deliver Friar Lawrence's letter saying that Juliet is not dead to Romeo. On **Thursday evening**, Romeo visits Juliet's tomb and kills Paris, and then himself. Juliet wakes up and seeing Romeo dead, commits suicide. Discovering the dead lovers, Paris and the frightened Friar Lawrence, the Prince and the families learn about the whole story and end their feud on **Thursday evening**.

Task: Do a flow or spider diagram of this **key theme**.

Useful links

David Crystal's summary on his Shakespeare's Words website is good and short and can be found here.

These RSC photos of various productions of *Romeo and Juliet* are really good at giving you an idea of the plot and how it might be seen on stage.

The Sixty-Second Shakespeare is quite a good starting point for the absolute basics:

There's a nice Sixty-Second Shakespeare newspaper article here.

The Schmoop slideshow on the play is worth a look:

The time-line on Robert's page is excellent because it shows all the references to time in the play and the precise trajectory of events:

There's a good essay on time in *Romeo and Juliet* on the Globe Education site.

Tasks

In what ways is the story of *Romeo and Juliet* **similar and different** to stories and situations you have encountered in your life? Brainstorm all your thoughts at first, then write up your findings in a flow-chart or chart, or in a continuous piece of writing.

Draw a flow-chart, time-line, comic strip or map of the **plot** and its different elements. For more on how to do this, see this excellent YouTube presentation by superteacher, Ellie Wood.

Print out a summary of the play from Spark Notes or Schmoop and **highlight them thematically**, giving different colours to love, hate and fate.

If you were modernizing the story of Romeo and Juliet, how would you "modernize" the plot? **Write your "modern" plot** for the play.

In groups of four, prepare a series of **freeze frames** or a **short drama** which illustrates the plot. Write out key words, phrases or lines on pieces of paper and use them to illustrate your freeze frames. This RSC page which has pictures of good productions of *Romeo and Juliet* is a very useful resource for doing this.

Contexts
The different versions

[Diagram: Sources for Romeo & Juliet]

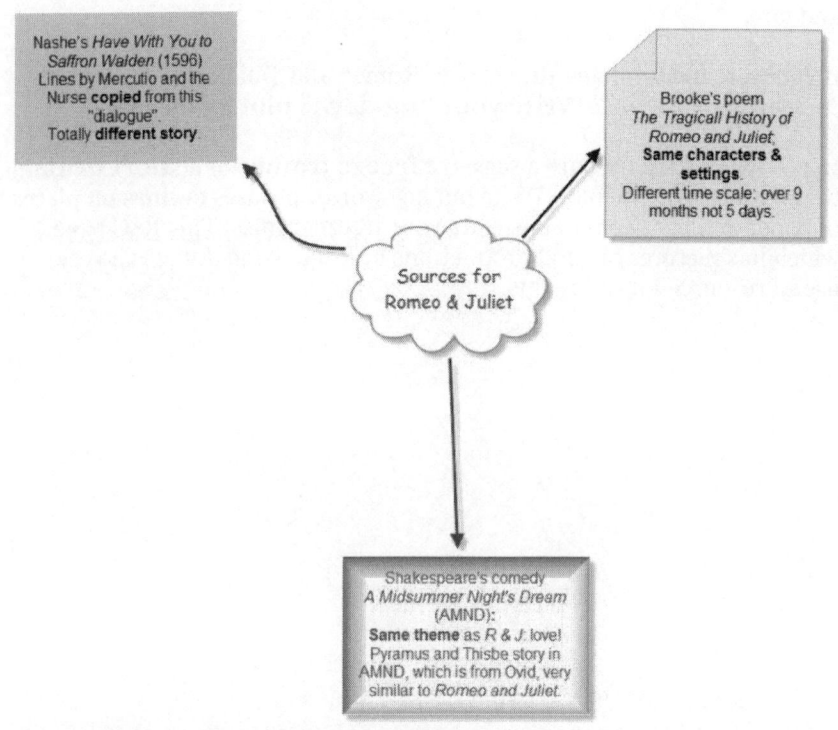

- Nashe's *Have With You to Saffron Walden* (1596). Lines by Mercutio and the Nurse **copied** from this "dialogue". Totally **different story**.
- Brooke's poem *The Tragicall History of Romeo and Juliet*: **Same characters & settings**. Different time scale: over 9 months not 5 days.
- Shakespeare's comedy *A Midsummer Night's Dream* (AMND): **Same theme** as *R & J*: love! Pyramus and Thisbe story in AMND, which is from Ovid, very similar to *Romeo and Juliet*.

Figure 6 Sources for *Romeo and Juliet*: you can find a larger version of this diagram on the Romeo and Juliet Reloaded website here

There are a number of early printed versions of *Romeo and Juliet* from which editors have pieced together the play. There are two "Quarto" versions of the play from 1597 and 1599, which were published during Shakespeare's life-time: Quarto versions are so-called because they were printed on "quarto" sized paper and sold for sixpence. The first Quarto was a "bad" version of the play, almost certainly pirated and sold without Shakespeare's permission and full of mistakes (British Library) while the second Quarto was a better, more accurate version. Other versions followed during Shakespeare's life-time but what is fascinating is that some literary critics feel that there is no definitive version of the play: indeed if you check all the different printed versions, you'll see that "no two are identical" (White, 2001, p.3). It's important to realise that the versions of the play we read now have been "cleaned up" and organised by an editor. Most particularly, the organisation of the play into "acts" and "scenes" has been done by an early editor; there were no such divisions in the first versions of the play. You can learn more about all the versions and see the original printed Quartos at the British Library's website for Romeo and Juliet (British Library) which is a fascinating treasure trove of texts and information. Experts believe that *Romeo and Juliet* was probably performed in the early 1590s based on the available evidence.

Source 1: Brooke's poem

Shakespeare based the play partly on Arthur Brooke's poem: The Tragicall Historye of Romeus and Juliet; his reading of 'Troilus and Criseyde', in *The Workes of Geffrey Chaucer* (1561) and the story of Pyramus and Thisbe. It is Brooke's free translation of an Italian poem by Bandello, published in 1562, which is thought to be the chief source of inspiration for Shakespeare. His poem is very long and generally regarded to be pretty bad, far inferior to Shakespeare's play, but it is interesting to note how the plot is similar to Shakespeare's. Brooke begins his poem with what he calls 'The Argument' which is similar in tone and approach to Shakespeare's Prologue:

The Argument
Love hath inflaméd twain by sudden sight,
And both do grant the thing that both desire
They wed in shrift by counsel of a friar.
Young Romeus climbs fair Juliet's bower by night.
Three months he doth enjoy his chief delight.
By Tybalt's rage provokéd unto ire,
He payeth death to Tybalt for his hire.
A banished man he 'scapes by secret flight.
New marriage is offered to his wife.
She drinks a drink that seems to reave her breath:
They bury her that sleeping yet hath life.
Her husband hears the tidings of her death.
He drinks his bane. And she with Romeus' knife,
When she awakes, herself, alas! she slay'th.

There are a number of significant differences between Brooke's poem and the play. These are some of them:

Literary form: Shakespeare wrote a **dramatic play, a drama,** whereas Brooke wrote a **rhyming poem, poetry**: Brooke's poem is full of **consistent rhymes** but the play isn't consistently rhymed, although it does use rhyme at important moments in the play such as when Romeo and Juliet first meet.
Names: Brooke's Romeus is changed to Romeo.
Setting: The Italian setting of Verona, and most settings such as Juliet's bower (orchard) and market squares etc. are the same.
Ages: Juliet is 16 years old in Brooke's poem and 13-years-old in Shakespeare's play but only a fortnight away from her 14th

birthday.

The use of time: the story stretches over nine months in Brooke's poem, with Capulet's party being part of the Christmas revels and her wedding to Paris fixed for 10th September. Shakespeare's play compresses all the action into four days: time is a very important structural device in the play and a "theme" in itself.

Suspense and Tybalt: In Brooke's poem, Romeus has been married for a while before he encounters Tybalt whereas Tybalt appears at the very beginning of Shakespeare's play and is a menacing presence even when Romeo and Juliet first meet. Shakespeare uses the threat of Tybalt to create suspense throughout the whole play whereas Brooke does not. Brooke's poem takes a long time to build up to Romeus killing Tybalt whereas Romeo in Shakespeare's play kills Tybalt very quickly in a fit of rage.

Characters: There is no Benvolio in Brooke's poem, and Mercutio, who plays a large role in Shakespeare's play, is not so significant. However, Mercutio tries and fails to woo Juliet in Brooke's poem. In Brooke's poem, the Friars are often presented as devious, bad people with strong sexual desires; Friar Lawrence in Brooke's poem is presented as a man with a dark past history. However, in Shakespeare's play, the Friar is portrayed as a good man struggling to do what is right.

Exercise: When you've read the play, it's worth asking yourself: what are the similarities and differences between Brooke's poem and Shakespeare's play: devise a chart which illustrates these similarities and differences. The full version of Brooke's *Romeus and Juliet* can be found here.

Source 2: Nashe's *Have With You to Saffron Walden* (1596)

The writer Nashe wrote a pamphlet which contained a dialogue or conversation which has a number of similarities with *Romeo and Juliet*. The dialogue is NOT the story of Romeo and Juliet but is the representation of a discussion between four friends who refer to well-known stories of the day, including the story and characters of *Romeo and Juliet*, indicating that the love story was already very popular in the wider culture. There are some very telling sections where Shakespeare actually copies Nashe word-for-word. Key similarities include:

Nashe's phrases for **Mercutio** are used in the play, including: Mercutio's calling Tybalt "the Prince of Cats"; using the phrase "rat-catcher"; talking about "fantasticoes" when Mercutio makes fun of Tybalt's desire to be fashionable.

Nashe's phrases for the **Nurse**, including: "dishclout" when the Nurse says that Romeo is a "dishclout" compared with Paris and when the Nurse talks about Mercutio's "ropery".

For more, read the Wikipedia page on the dialogue:
And William Shakespeare, René Weis, 2012 pp. 39-41
   This entertaining article by Ros Barber tries to argue that it was Christophere Marlowe and Nashe who wrote Romeo and Juliet and not Shakespeare. While this is not commonly accepted by most critics, the article is worth reading if you're interested in the connections with Nashe's work and Shakespeare's.

Source 3: A Midsummer Night's Dream

Many critics have pointed out that *Romeo and Juliet* shares a number of similarities with *A Midsummer Night's Dream* (William Shakespeare, René Weis, 2012, p. 41). It should be noted though that *A Midsummer Night's Dream* (AMND) is a comedy and is meant to be funny whereas *Romeo and Juliet* is a tragedy.

   Key similarities are: both stories are about love, and most particularly forbidden love.

   Both plays were influenced by William Addington's 1566 translation Apuleius' comic story *The Golden Ass*. The comic figure of Bottom in AMND who turns into a sexy donkey is very similar to the ass or donkey in Apuleius' poem while Romeo refers to the story of Cupid and Psyche which is a story in Apuleius' poem.

   Ovid's story of Pyramus and Thisbe which is performed as a "play within a play" in AMND is very similar to the *Romeo and Juliet* story: it is about two doomed, unlucky lovers:

> Pyramus and Thisbe have been forbidden to marry and so talk to each other through a crack in the wall. They arrange to meet near a mulberry tree. Thisbe arrives first but runs away after seeing a lion with a bloody mouth, dropping her veil. When Pyramus comes upon the scene, he sees Thisbe's veil on the ground and assumes the lion killed her. He kills himself by falling on his sword in the Roman style, splashing the then white fruit of the mulberry tree with his blood, turning the fruit dark. When Thisbe returns and sees her lover is dead, she stabs herself with Pyramus's sword. When the Gods learn of the lovers' deaths, they honour the lovers by turning the fruit of the mulberry tree dark forever.

In AMND, the tale is told in a very comical fashion by a troop of totally useless actors led by the comical Bottom, who has spent much of the play changed into a donkey. The contrast between the high seriousness of *Romeo and Juliet* and the silly re-telling of the Pyramus and Thisbe story could not be more striking. But the stories are very similar: they are about doomed, "ill-starred" lovers who kill themselves.

   For more, check out these links: The Universal Teacher's website.
   Wikipedia on Pyramus and Thisbe and Educational Portal as well.

Questions

Why do you think Shakespeare used so many **sources** for the play? Why did he use **Brooke's poem** as the main source, do you think? What are the similarities and differences between the Pyramus and Thisbe story and the *Romeo and Juliet* story?

Nowadays, writers try to be "original" but in Shakespeare's day it was apparently acceptable to **copy other people's ideas** and even words. Why do you think this was?

Even before people had seen Shakespeare's play, **Shakespeare's audience** would have probably been very familiar with the story of *Romeo and Juliet* from Brooke's poem, which was popular. How do you think this would have affected their attitude towards Shakespeare's play? Think about the films, you go to where you know the basic story already: e.g. James Bond, Batman, other sequels, or versions of books you've read. How does this affect your attitude towards those films?

Devise a **spider diagram** on all the sources for Shakespeare's play.

Tragedy

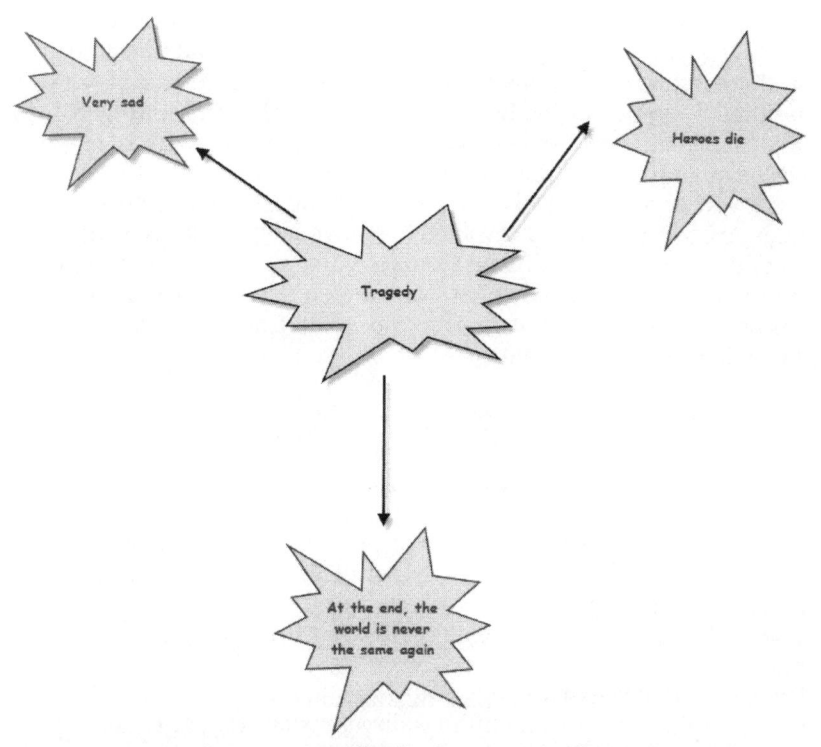

(Diagram: central "Tragedy" star linking to three stars: "Very sad", "Heroes die", and "At the end, the world is never the same again".)

Figure 7 Tragedy: you can find a larger version of this diagram on <u>the Romeo and Juliet Reloaded website here</u>

Definitions of tragedy: 1) very sad event: an event in life that evokes feelings of sorrow or grief; 2) a disastrous event: a disastrous circumstance or event, e.g. serious illness, financial ruin, or fatality; 3) tragic play: a serious play with a tragic theme, often involving a heroic struggle and the downfall of the main character.

Shakespeare called his play "The Most Excellent and Lamentable Tragedy of Romeo and Juliet". The title is very important because it sent clear signals to the audience as to what to expect. It will be "excellent" (i.e. of good quality, very interesting); it will be "lamentable" (i.e. very sad) and it will be a "tragedy". This means the audience knows that the main characters will die.

There's much debate about the nature of Shakespeare's tragedies but it is important to think about the vital ingredients that "made up" a tragic play in Shakespeare's time. The ancient Greek philosopher Aristotle had written in his book *Poetics* that "tragedies" – by which he meant 'serious stories' as opposed to comedies – should contain certain key elements. For Aristotle, a tragedy should show <u>"mimesis"</u>: it should imitate what might happen in real life. It should also have a clear beginning, middle and end, with every story having moments of reversal. Aristotle also said that the heroes in his tragedies should show what he calls "hamartia" which is sometimes translated as a "tragic flaw"; this is contested by Aristotle scholars who suggest that it means "mistake" and that actually Aristotle therefore argues that the tragedy arises from the role of fate rather than a "tragic flaw" (McMannus, 1999). In this sense, Romeo does exhibit "hamartia" because his tragedy arises because of a mistake. Shakespearean tragedy appears to be different from Aristotlean tragedy in that it very definitely involved the death of the main characters whereas Aristotlean tragedy involved the downfall but not necessarily death of the hero. This is difficult for us to grasp now: we rarely go to see films or plays where the main characters are doomed to die horrible deaths at the end (Smith, 2013). Shakespearean tragedy appears to contain a few of these elements:

> A high born person or persons suffer a terrible, violent death;
> Often the tragedy happens because of a fatal flaw in the tragic hero's character;
> The tragedy disturbs or changes the moral order of the world.

Question: what key elements of Shakespearean tragedy can be found in *Romeo and Juliet*? Devise a flow or spider diagram of all the elements that make up a tragedy.

Useful links: the key elements of Shakespearean tragedy are outlined here.

Emma Smith discusses *Romeo and Juliet* here.

Oliver Tapling and Joshua Billings discuss what tragedy means.

Shakespeare's theatre: The Globe

There are no records of any performances of *Romeo and Juliet* before 1660, but experts are almost certain that it was performed by 1597, when the first Quarto was published. They believe that *Romeo and Juliet* was first performed by the Lord Chamberlain's Men at the Theatre with Shakespeare's lead actor, Richard Burbage playing Romeo and the boy actor Robert Goffe playing Juliet (British Library). It is worth considering how the play might have been acted out at the Theatre, which was probably very similar in structure to the Globe, a reproduction of which you can now visit in London or look at here on its website. The way Shakespeare wrote his plays makes much more sense when you see a play at the Globe because you realize that there was virtually no scenery and the only lighting available was daylight. In other words, Shakespeare had to conjure the worlds of his plays through words and couldn't rely on scenery or lighting to do this. As a result, his plays read more like modern day novels which often describe scenes in detail in order to give the reader an impression of the world the characters live in. Many speeches in Shakespeare give many visual clues about what the world looks like: the time of day, the objects that are nearby, the weather and the costumes of the characters. Similarly, Shakespeare wrote very few stage directions but they are all embedded in the characters' lines instead. This is the "dramatic" context of his plays: his plays took place within very specific dramatic contexts and, as a result, they are written for these particular stages.

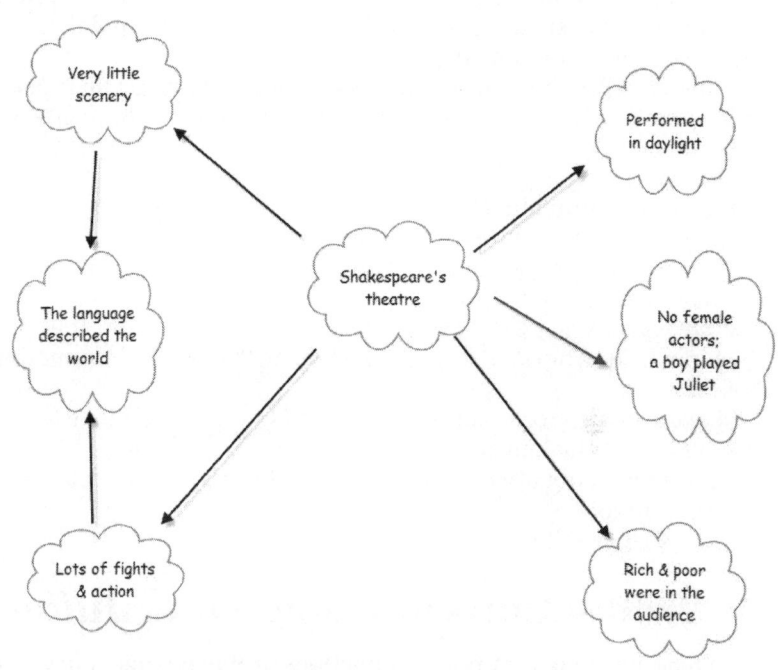

Figure 8 Key points about Shakespeare's theatre: you can find a larger version of this diagram on **the Romeo and Juliet Reloaded website here**

Social, political contexts

The world of the 1590s was one of huge upheaval, danger, excitement and hope. This is reflected in the play; even though the play is set in Verona, Italy, the settings evoked probably share more in common with Shakespeare's England, and London most particularly. It appears that Elizabethan England was a very violent society: there may well have been an epidemic of knife crime during the time Shakespeare wrote the play. Neil MacGregor says in *Shakespeare's Restless World*: "We tend to think of *Romeo and Juliet* as essentially the balcony scene, a play about the romantic tribulations of young love. In fact, it is just as much a play about bands of privileged lads slicing each other to death and the failure of the authorities to control their brawling." (The British Museum)

In addition to the depiction of violent crime, the play explores the ways in which traditional bonds between the generations were breaking down: Capulet's arguments with first Tybalt and then Juliet reveal this. Juliet refuses to marry Paris and thereby tells her parents that she should have the power to choose who she should marry; she is part of a new generation who are rejecting the old rules of their parents, who espoused things like arranged marriages and blood feuds.

Shakespeare's England was also a country riven by disease with many people concerned that they would catch the plague. This is alluded to when Friar John gets trapped in a plague house in Act 5 and thereby can't get his letter to Romeo.

While many of the facts about Shakespeare were made up in the film *Shakespeare in Love*, it is very good at giving a sense of the context of the time.

Further research: This education pack produced by the Oxford Playhouse is good on the issue of knife crime:

James Shapiro's book *1599* is brilliant evoking what it was like to live in Shakespeare's time:

Watch Shakespeare in Love or listen to *Shakespeare's Restless World* which can be downloaded as podcasts here with detailed information about it here.

Shakespeare's Words is Professor David Crystal's website which explores the original meanings of Shakespeare's language.

Shakespeare's Quartos. You can look at the original printed versions of the play here.

Shakespeare's Globe is here.

Productions of *Romeo and Juliet*

There have been many famous productions of *Romeo and Juliet* and the play has been adapted into many different forms: operas, ballets, musicals and so on.

It is one of the few plays where the most famous young actors of the day invariably attempt to star in it. For the purposes of this study guide, I will discuss the directors Franco Zeffirelli (Zeffirelli, 1968) and Baz Luhrmann's (DiCaprio, 1996) filmed versions of the play because they are both excellent and readily accessible. In contrast to studying a novel, where I would recommend reading the book before watching the film because novels are meant to be read, I would recommend seeing at least one or two performed versions of the play before reading it because it is a play. It is meant primarily to be seen, not read.

Useful links

These photos from various RSC productions of the play are excellent at showing what the play is like in different performances.

The BBC's Shakespeare Unlocked is excellent for learning more about many productions of Shakespeare, including scenes from Romeo and Juliet. The BBC's website on Shakespeare is also excellent.

This Teachers's Pack devised by the Royal Shakespeare Company is brilliant on how to bring the play alive as a piece of drama in the classroom and makes great use of the BBC's materials.

This Wikipedia article on the play contains a detailed discussion of famous productions.

The Guardian critic Michael Billington discusses his favourite versions of the play here.

Digital Theatre filmed an acclaimed production of the play for the Globe which can be watched here for a fee.

The Museum of the City of New York blog has a good page which illustrates the old Broadway productions of the play, which really show how attitudes towards the play have changed.

Further research: investigate the different productions of *Romeo and Juliet*, use these RSC photos as a starting point. What different approaches do they take to the play and why?

Shakespeare's language

It takes hard work to really understand Shakespeare's language but there are some things that will make life much easier for you. First, get to know the story of the play and the characters by reading a summary of the play and turning it into a flow-chart where you map out for yourself on a piece of paper what actually happens. The act of doing that "mapping-out" will really consolidate things in your mind. Second, once you know the story fairly well, have a go at watching a performed version of the play; see the words in the context of them being acted out on stage or in a film. However, do be careful about watching a film: be aware that modern versions of the play such as Baz Luhrmann's *Romeo + Juliet* have adapted the play to a modern setting. For example, Shakespeare's characters used swords, while in Luhrmann's film they use guns. Once you've got clear on the story, then you're ready to look closely at the language.

Shakespeare wrote in what is called "early modern English" by linguists. He did not write in old English as many of my students often say! Old English was written from about 0AD-1000 AD; Middle English, which is what Chaucer wrote, was from about 1100-1400. Shakespeare and the Tudor and Stuart period generally (1500-1648) heralds the emergence of early modern English. Many of the words used in Shakespeare are very similar to ours. However, there are a few which are quite different. Shakespeare is doubly difficult because some of these words are very similar to our own but have quite different meanings: these are termed by David Crystal as **"false friends"**; you can learn more about them here or look at my section (below) devoted to them. If you learn the words on the nouns, verbs, adjectives and adverbs list and know them well you should be qualified to read the play and understand a great deal of the language. Most of the other words he employs are relatively easy to work out by either the context of the quote or from their modern English equivalent. This isn't to say that Shakespeare is easy; he definitely is not! He delighted playing around with words, using extended comparisons (metaphors and similes) and this makes his work rewarding but complex.

    Useful links: David Crystal's list of "false friends" in Shakespeare can be found here.

    Crystal's annotated version of *Romeo and Juliet* with many difficult words explained can be found here.

    Crystal's dictionary of all the difficult words in *Romeo and Juliet* can be found here.

Shakespeare's imagery

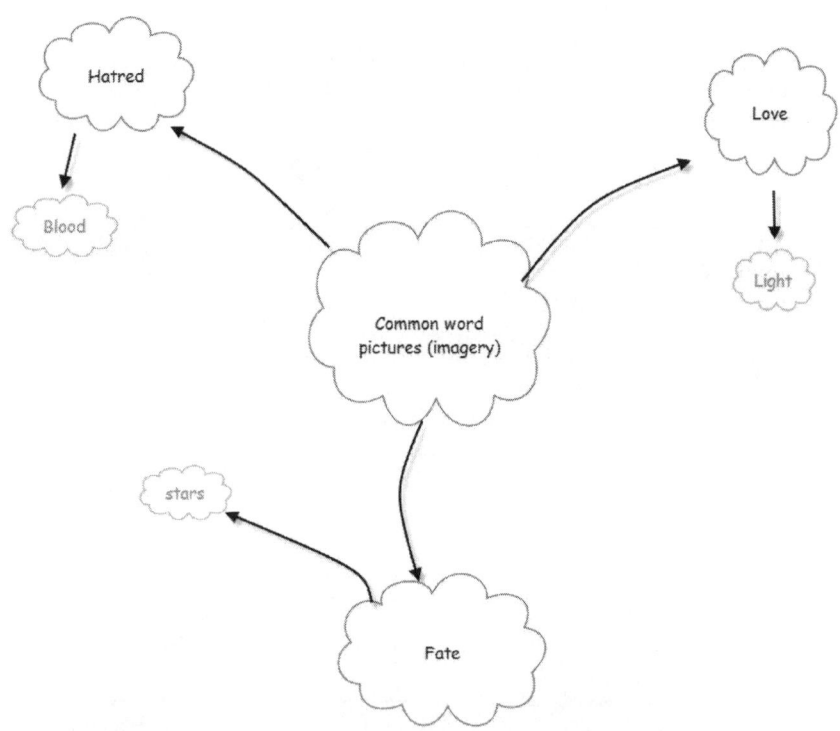

[Diagram: "Common word pictures (imagery)" in center, connected to: "Hatred" (→ "Blood"), "Love" (→ "Light"), "Fate" (→ "stars")]

Figure 9 Imagery in *Romeo and Juliet*: you can find a larger version of this diagram on the Romeo and Juliet Reloaded website here

At its simplest level, imagery means the "word pictures" a writer creates in an audience's or a reader's minds. This means that interpreting the imagery of a text is a very personal thing. To really comment upon the imagery of a text, you need to consider a few things:

What are the most striking word pictures or images in a text for you; what images affect you the most and why?

Think about what the images mean and what they "connote"; the associations that they create in your mind.

Another definition of imagery is all the "poetic devices" in a text: its visual images (word pictures); its metaphors (direct comparisons); its similes (indirect comparisons, i.e. comparisons using "like" or "as"); its uses of personification, alliteration, rhyme, rhythm and so on. This makes imagery a very general thing, which in a way is a good thing because as long you explore the "connotations" of an image, or imagery, you're unlikely to go wrong.

Countless books, articles and academic essays have been written on the imagery in this tragedy so it's impossible to highlight all the points here. For the purposes of this study guide edition, I'm going to focus upon the ways in which the imagery reinforces the **key themes** of the play, because, as with the structure of the play, it is the interplay of the themes and the imagery which is possibly the most striking thing about the play.

Exercise: look at the flow chart at the beginning of this section and try and explain what it is saying in your own words.

Love imagery

[Flow chart showing "Imagery to do with love" at the centre, connected to: Imagery about light (which leads to: Juliet is the "sun"); Abstract imagery (which leads to: "what's in a name?"); Religious imagery (which leads to: The lovers are "pilgrims"); Imagery about birds (which leads to: R & J compare themselves to birds of prey).]

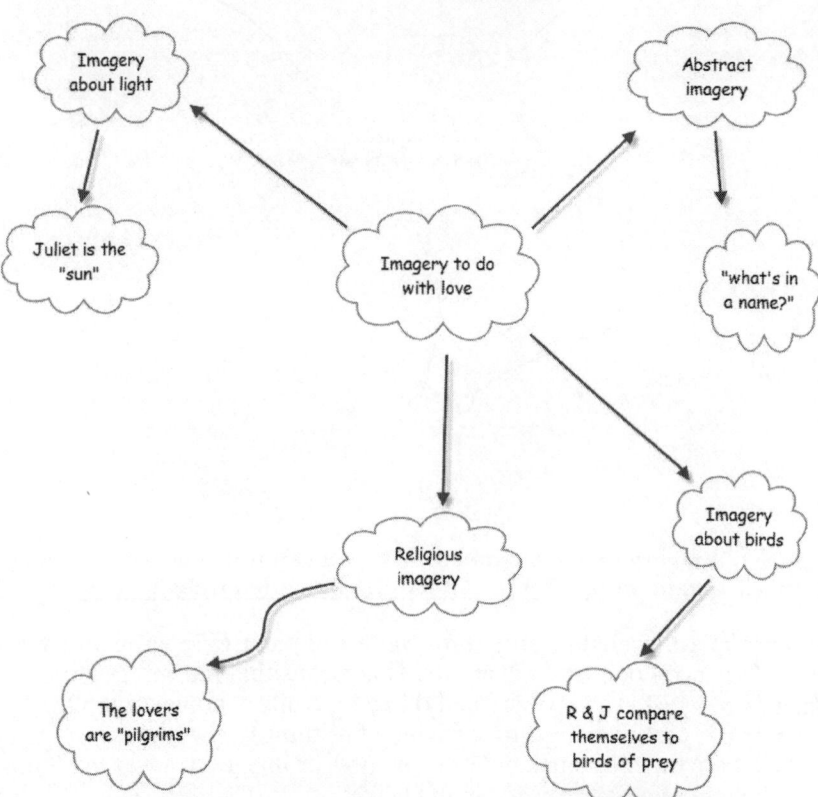

Figure 10 Love imagery in the play: you can find a larger version of this diagram on <u>the Romeo and Juliet Reloaded website here</u>

The two characters who use imagery which infused with love are, of course, Romeo and Juliet. Right from the moment we meet Romeo, he deploys imagery which is connected with love; he is very self-consciously a lover; in other words, he is aware that he is a lover and tries to express this identity in words. He wants to be a "lover". Initially, his imagery about love is full of oxymoron, phrases that are deliberately contradictory (see the section on Romeo's character for this), but when he sees Juliet his imagery becomes preoccupied with the concept of "light". For him Juliet is a shining beacon of light; in such a way, we see how love for him is articulated as "light": Juliet is a brightly burning "torch", a "snowy dove" (Act 1, Sc V), she is the "sun" (Act 2, Sc II); her eyes are such brightly shining stars that they make it seem like it's daytime; she is a "feast of light" (Act 5, Sc III).

Juliet's imagery which articulates her love is much more varied than Romeo's and less self-consciously "literary". Much of Romeo's imagery about Juliet being the "sun" would be familiar to Shakespeare's audience. However, Juliet varies her imagery to such an extent that it's difficult to anticipate how she might articulate her love. In Act 2, Sc II, she uses **abstract imagery** to explore whether Romeo is his "name" or not; she decides that he is not his name and that his "gracious self" is the "God of her idolatry". In other words, Romeo's physical body is the thing she worships. In her famous "gallop apace" speech (Act 3, Sc II), she develops her imagery about Romeo's body and her sexual feelings, talking about his body being a "mansion" she has not "possessed", and that she has been "sold" but not "enjoyed". She is just as extravagant (or extreme) in her emotions as Romeo but somehow the imagery is simpler and less ornate, and all the more powerful for it; she talks about her love being as "boundless as the sea" (Act 2, Sc II).

Both lovers use the **imagery of birds** to suggest and evoke their love: they refer to the fact that they are like birds of prey to each other (Act 2, Sc II), and discuss the birds outside their chamber in Act 3, Sc V.

They both also use **religious imagery** to evoke their love and devotion, talking about how they are "pilgrims" for each other; they are like pilgrims because they worship the holiness of each other's beings in the same way that a pilgrim worships God.

Other characters in the play also deploy much imagery connected with love. Mercutio appears disgusted with love but he nevertheless refers to it constantly; for him, Queen Mab, the fairy's midwife, leads people astray because they think they are in love when in fact they are really just feeling lust. For Mercutio, love is not to be trusted and is instead to be mocked; we see this very clearly in Act 2, Sc I when he mocks Romeo for his feelings for Rosaline, indicating that all he really wants to do is have sex with her.

We learn at the end of the play that Paris genuinely loves Juliet; he says he will cry at her grave every night, putting flowers there.

Other types of love are also explored through the imagery: the love a parent feels for a child – this is particularly striking when Capulet finds Juliet dead and calls her the "sweetest flower of the field"; the love a child feels for a parent; the love the Nurse and Juliet have for each other.

Nearly every page in the play has some image or other which is connected to love because it is the dominant theme of the play.

Tasks: what for you are the most powerful and memorable images connected with love in the play? Why is this the case?

Devise a flow chart/graphical organizer/mind map on the imagery discussed here.

Hate Imagery

Interwoven throughout the play in sharp contrast to the love imagery is the imagery which evokes hatred. The play works so well precisely because this is the case: if the play had only used imagery about love then it would be very boring indeed, but it is the contrasting imagery which suggests the intense hatred of the feud which gives the play such a dramatic edge. The play opens with imagery which suggests the hatred between the two families: the servants of the Capulets joke about raping the Montague women and then Tybalt arrives to really set off the first fight. The imagery here is both dramatic and poetic: the dramatic imagery of the biting of the thumbs and the drawn swords provides visual evidence of the hatred on stage, while the insulting language the two families trade with each other always reminds us of the strength of the feud. The imagery is based around insults: the nasty names the two families call each other. When the Prince stops the fight, he uses the **imagery of blood** to suggest the appalling destructiveness of the feud, talking about the fountains of blood which have poured out of the veins of the families as a result of the feud (Act 1, Sc I); he returns to talking about blood at the end of the play as well.

Both Tybalt and Lady Capulet use the **imagery of poison** to suggest the power of the feud and their hatred; Tybalt talks about his feelings for Romeo turning to the "bitterest gall" (terrible poison") in Act 1, Sc V, while Lady Capulet imagines giving Romeo such an "unaccustomed dram" (a shot of poison) that he will die after the death of Tybalt (Act 3, Sc V).

Ironically, it is probably the character who has no allegiance to either family but relations in both, Mercutio, who deploys the most striking imagery about the feud. All his mocking of Tybalt as the "Prince of Cats" is imagery connected with the feud because he is stirring up enmity about Capulets. He uses violent imagery to try and goad Tybalt into fighting him in Act 3, Sc 1: he talks about having a "word and a blow" with Tybalt. There is a pun on the word "blow" here with it meaning both a word, and an act of violence. Mercutio sees Romeo's confession of love to Tybalt as a "dishonourable, vile submission": this is highly emotive abstract imagery comparing Romeo's act of conciliation to a "submission" or someone who has surrendered his dignity in a "vile" or disgusting way. Finally, Mercutio's dying words "a plague on both your houses" is the most memorable phrase about the feud in the play: he wishes a ghastly death on both the Montagues and Capulets for what they have done to him.

Romeo's imagery connected with the feud evokes his violent feelings: he talks about "fire-eyed fury" informing his actions from that moment onwards and that Juliet's love has made him "effeminate"; turned him into a woman.

Friar Lawrence uses **abstract imagery** to represent the feud, referring to the feud as the "household's rancor"; the irrational bitterness between the families.

Tasks: what for you are the most powerful and memorable images connected with hatred in the play? Why is this the case?

Devise a flow chart/graphical organizer/mind map on the imagery discussed here.

Fate imagery

The Prologue contains perhaps the most striking image connected with fate in the play when it calls the lovers "star-crossed": in other words, it is written in the lovers' astrological charts that they will die. They are marked out both to love each other and to be doomed. Throughout the play, we find imagery connected with this idea: in Act 1, Sc IV, Romeo is overcome by a fear that "Some consequence, yet hanging in the stars" will lead to his untimely death as a result of him going to the party. In Act 3, Sc I, Romeo becomes aware after the death of Mercutio that "This day's black fate on more days doth depend" and that he is "fortune's fool". Later on, in Act 3, Sc V, just as Romeo is leaving her chamber, she thinks that she has a premonition of him being as one in a tomb. When Romeo learns of Juliet's supposed death (she isn't really dead); he says "Then I defy you stars!". In other words, he believes he can claim victory over fate by killing himself, while the irony is that he is actually fulfilling it. When he kills himself, he talks about shaking the "inauspicious yoke of stars" (unlucky weight or burden of stars) from his "world wearied flesh"; again there is more irony in that he thinks he is defying his fate when in actual fact he is fulfilling it. The image of the "yoke" is important because a yoke was what was tied around cattle in order to plough the fields; it suggests that the stars have set Romeo to plough a certain furrow on earth which is "inauspicious" or unlucky, but which he is now freeing himself from. Shakespeare's audiences would have loved this element of the play: watching a character killing himself in defiance of fate but actually living up to fate's decree.

And then in Act 5, Sc II when Friar Lawrence learns that his letter to Romeo has not got through, he talks about "unhappy fortune". While the imagery connected with fate is not so prevalent as the imagery which is based around love and hate, it is very important because it sets the overall fatalistic tone in the play; there is a real sense of foreboding in the play that the lovers are doomed from the very start.

Tasks: what for you are the most powerful and memorable images connected with fate in the play? Why is this the case?

Devise a flow chart/graphical organizer/mind map on the imagery discussed here.

Useful links: The BBC Bitesize website is good and clear on imagery in the play and can be found here.

This article, which is on themes and motif in R&J on Shakespeare online, refers to some of the traditional criticism connected with the play and its analysis of the imagery.

This page on imagery of light and fate by Rebecca Faecher contains some valid analysis, using some good references to Tillyard, who pioneered the examination of Shakespeare in context.

I enjoyed this Prezi on the theme of fate.

This RSC PDF booklet contains some useful line references in the play which will enable to look for your own thematic and imagistic quotations.

Thou and You

Pronouns = words which take the place of nouns, e.g. I, you, he/she/it, we, they

David and Ben Crystal say:

> In Old English, thou was singular and you was plural, but in the 13th century "you" started to be used as a polite form of the singular…changing from "thou" to "you" in a conversation always conveys a contrast in meaning – a change in attitude or relationship. Thou could be used as an insult if an upper class person calls another upper class man or woman thou.

Using the Crystals' points (which are in bold) I have highlighted some interesting uses of "thou and you" in *Romeo and Juliet*:

Both characters use "thou" because they are social/familial equals: Romeo and his friends, Mercutio and Benvolio, address each other as "thou" because they are social equals as do Romeo and Juliet, e.g.
ROMEO Let me stand here till thou remember it.
JULIET I shall forget, to have thee still stand there,
Remembering how I love thy company.

An upper class character uses "thou", a lower class person replies respectfully with "you": Lady Capulet in Act 1, Sc III addresses the Nurse as "thou" and "thee" etc. but both Juliet and the Nurse say "you" about and to her.

Both characters switch from "you" to "thou", as a sign of a deteriorating relationship: In Act 3, Sc V, Lady Capulet calls Juliet "thou" having addressed her as "you" in other scenes because of Juliet's refusal to marry Paris.

A character uses "thou" and then "you", marking a change of attitude: The Nurse addresses Juliet as "thou" in Ac 1, Sc III but then switches to "you" in Act 2, Sc IV when she knows Juliet is marrying Romeo: the Nurse's attitude towards Juliet has changed.

A character uses "you" and then "thou", marking a change of attitude: The Prince in Act 5, Sc III addresses Montague and Capulet as "thou" before he knows the truth about Romeo and Juliet's deaths and then addresses them as "you" when he condemns them for their feud: "See what a scourge is laid upon your hate".

IMPORTANT NOTE: Just about every scene in Shakespeare can be analyzed in an interesting way if you focus upon thou and you. It is worth looking through your chosen scene and working out when these pronouns are used and why they are used. You can say some very subtle things about character using this technique.

Useful links: you can learn more about the use of thee and thou on the Shakespeare's Words website here.

Task: draw a flow diagram or map which illustrates how people address each other using "thee" and "thou" in the play.

Beware the false friends!

False friend = a word/phrase which looks modern but actually had a different meaning in Shakespeare's time

The vocabulary lists that follow contain many "false friends"; these are words that look like modern words but actually have different meanings. One striking example is the adjective "gentle" which has a very obvious meaning now to be "soft, kind" etc., but in Shakespeare's day meant "noble" and was often associated as being a male characteristic, with knights being "gentle" because they were chivalrous and noble in the way they acted. But there are many, many other "false friends". That's why you must read this list carefully before reading the play. Try to learn the difficult false friends off by heart and they'll really help you understand Shakespeare.

Nouns

Nouns = persons, places, names, things, either concrete (things you can touch, see, feel) or abstract (e.g. concepts such as love, faith)

Noun phrase = a group of words, including the noun, that are centred around a noun, e.g. dark, smelly toilet

Preparatory task: what are some nouns which describe the place you're in now? What are some abstract nouns (concepts such as love, faith) which you feel strongly attached to or important in your life?

Nouns bring the world into being; they are naming words and absolutely vital in any language. Nouns are usually the first words humans ever say when they name their parents "Mama" etc. Like most authors, Shakespeare primarily uses nouns to create his "world". He uses concrete nouns – nouns which you can touch, feel and see – to provide his world with specific people and their personalities. His names like Mercutio and Benvolio give us a sense of his characters' natures. His use of words like "marchpane" (marzipan) and "trencher" (plate) make us feel we're at a party. Concrete nouns like "dug" (female breast) give us a sense of the physicality of the world; this is a world of flesh and blood, of breast-feeding etc.

His nouns which label and categorize women make us aware of the ways in which women were objectified and subjugated in his world: they are "maidens" (virgins), "dowdies" (ugly, plain women), "fresh buds" (young adolescents), "gossips", or "hildings", "harlots" (prostitutes), "minions" and "ancient damnation". You'll notice that many of the insults listed below refer to women. In stark contrast, men are usually associated with positive nouns and noun phrases: Paris is the "County" (a Count), a gentleman (a nobleman) and "a man of wax" (a person as perfect as a waxwork). But there were insults for men, usually nouns which question their social status. It was a great insult to be called "boy", which indicated that a man was immature and didn't own property, or "villain", which in Shakespeare's time meant a lower-class, uncouth peasant.

The play is also full of nouns which are references to classical mythology (see below); these give the play its educated, mythical quality. Look carefully at the list that follows and try and learn the vocabulary:

Nouns to do with violence: Mutiny = violence; Fray = fight; Shaft = arrow; Ambuscados = ambushes; Butt-shaft = arrow; Blade = sword; Fiddle-stick = bow or sword.

Nouns about women: Maidenheads = virginity; Dug = breast; Dowdy = plain looking woman; Hood = woman; Hildings = prostitutes.

Nouns about times of day or dates: E'en = evening; Lammas = Lammas Day is 1st August, the name comes from the Old English word for a loaf of bread, and the festival celebrates harvest. Lammas Eve is the day before Lammas.

Nouns to do with food, drink and parties: Crush = drink; trencher = plate; Marchpane = marzipan; Joint-stools = stools made by a carpenter; Masque = party; Visor = mask; Meat = food; Bladders = containers made out of animal's bladders used for storing liquids; Solemnity = ceremony or party.

Nouns about medicine: Dram = little drink; Vial = small bottle; Cordial = medicine for the heart; apothecary = chemist; Humour = mood.

Nouns about family and marriage: Suit = request, usually to marry; Nuptial = wedding; Kin = family; Contract = engagement; Bride = bridegroom, the term was then used to refer to both bride and groom; Rosemary = the herb of remembrance, worn at weddings and funerals.

Religious nouns: Heretics = people with religious beliefs that were considered evil by the church; Palmers = pilgrims to Jerusalem who brought back palm leaves to show where they'd been; Intercession = prayer, petition; Shrift = confession; Orisons = prayers.

Nouns which present people in a positive way: Man of wax = a perfect model of a man; Lineament = line (in a book); feature (on a face); Five wits = five senses: sight, hearing, smell, taste, touch; Wit = sense, intelligence; Chinks = lots of money.

Nouns which are references to other cultures, mythological references or superstitions: Tartar = the Tartars, from central Asia, were famous for shooting bows and arrows; Venus = Goddess of love; Titan's wheels = Hyperion, the God of the sun, was sometimes called Titan. He pulled the sun across the sky every day; Blind bow-boy = Cupid, the God of Love; Jove = Jupiter, chief of the God, who did not take lovers' promises seriously and laughed when they were broken; Phaeton = the son of Phoebus Apollo; he was allowed to drive his father's chariot for a day but went too fast and was killed by Jupiter; Mandrakes = plants which had roots that looked like men. People believed mandrakes screamed when they were pulled up and people who heard them went mad.

Nouns about body parts: Lineament = line (in a book); feature (on a face); Stone = testicle; Bosom = heart; Earth = body; Medlar = a small round fruit which was only eaten when it was almost rotten and overflowing with juice, and was nicknamed "open arse" and meant that; Poperin = a pear which was penis-shaped and was a slang phrase for penis; Prick = point/penis; Eyes' windows = eyelids; Maw = stomach, which is a metaphor for the vault; Pate = head.

Legal noun phrases about money and property: Forfeit = payment; Fee simple = absolute possession (legal term); Pilcher = case; Demesnes = property; Label = the wax seal attached to a document to make it legal; Ducat = small, valuable gold coin.

Nouns which are insults: Princox = rude young man; Saucy boy = cheeky young fool; Counter-feit = cheat; Scurvy knave = rotten man; Goose = fool; Bauble = coxcomb, which is the decorated stick of a clown/jester; Bawd = a female keeper of a brothel (the male equivalent is a pimp) or a hare; Villain = peasant, pleb, riff-raff (a terrible insult to a posh person like Romeo); Minion = naughty girl; Hilding = worthless girl; Chop-logic = nonsensical way of speaking; Whining mammet = crying doll; Dishclout = dishcloth; Ancient damnation = damned old woman; Cot-quean = a man who does women's work, i.e. housework; Harlotry = worthless woman; Gleek = a nasty gesture; Mouse-hunt = woman chaser; Caitiff = miserable person.

Abstract nouns and phrases: airy word = trivial comment; Bent = intention; Ropery = joking about; Countervail = equal; Conceit = imagination; Jaunt = long trip; Sojourn = stay.

Negative, emotive nouns: Gall = poison (this word is used metaphorically by Tybalt in Act 1, Sc V); Extremity = a bad thing, something severe; Gyves = chains; Canker = cancer, sickness; Pox = plague; Brine = salt water, tears; Spleen = temper.

Nouns about animals: Tassel-gentle = the most noble of the falcons; Nyas = a young hawk; Nimble-pinioned doves = quick flying doves, who in classical mythology, drew the chariot of Venus, the goddess of love; Cockatrice = a fantasy snake who killed people if it looked at them; Steeds = horses who, when Juliet refers to them in Act 3 as she waits for Romeo to come to her bed, draw the chariot of the sun-god, Phoebus Apollo.

Nouns about clothes and fashion: The pink = perfect example and/or pattern made with holes in leather; Slop = wide trousers; Cheverel = soft, stretchy leather; Clout = sheet/cloth; Doublet = sleeveless jacket; Riband = ribbon; Mantle = cloak; Livery = uniform; Attires = clothes.

Concrete nouns: Osier cage = willow basket; Cords = rope ladder; Reflex = reflection; Conduit = water-pipe; Charnel-house = the place for bones dug up in the course of digging new graves in the churchyard; Inundation = flooding; Curfew bell = the bell marking the beginning and end of the day; Crow = crowbar; Ensign = flag.

Nouns about music: Catling = the string of a small lute; Soundpost = wooden peg fixed below the bridge of a violin; Prick-song = printed music.

Verbs and verb phrases

Verb = doing word
Verb or verbal phrase = a group of words, including the verb, which are focused around a verb, e.g. he was running quickly

Preparatory task: What are some verbs which describe the actions you have been doing today, e.g. walking, talking etc.? Put them into different categories, using the categories below for guidance.

Verbs are doing words. Shakespeare, like all of us, uses them in many different ways. One striking way he uses verbs is to evoke the world of the "feud", the fight. The verb "to draw" is particularly important in this regard; it can mean to "withdraw" from an event, such as a fight, or it can mean to "draw" a sword. Shakespeare really enjoys playing with the double-meaning of this word, actively trying to confuse us as to what it means. We're meant to appreciate this confusion and think hard about what is actually going on.

Shakespeare plays with many words; he frequently uses "puns", playing on the double-meaning of words. This still happens in our culture, particularly in comedy when comedians play on the double-meaning of words which often have sexual connotations, e.g. "pussy" etc. In Shakespeare's time people constantly played with words, frequently "jousting" with words in the way that Romeo and Mercutio do in Act 2, Sc IV. Understanding Shakespeare's puns helps you appreciate his plays more.

Verbs are also used to create serious, tragic moods and atmospheres; verbs connected with ending things or dying are particularly important in the play. The verb "to expire" (to stop, to die, to end) has real resonance in the play because we know from the outset that the lovers will die.

Look carefully at the list that follows and try and learn the vocabulary:

Verbs to do with seeing/perceiving or working things out: To wot = to know; To devise = to imagine; To sum up sum = to add up the total; To descry = to see, perceive; Winking at = ignoring; To misgive = to warn, to worry about

Verbs about fighting/ being bad/violent: Draw/drew = has different meanings: keep, hold back; draw their swords; Draws him = draws his sword on him; To deal double = cheat; To beguile = cheat; To dry-beat = hit someone without drawing blood

Verbs to do with being certain: I trow = I am sure; I warrant = I'm sure; To befit = to suit, to be fitting; To measure = to judge; To forswear = deny

Verbs about ending and changing things: To expire = put an end to, to die; To doff = shed, get rid of; I am sped = I am killed; To prorogue = put off, postponed; To forbear = stop; To surcease = stop

Verbs about speaking: To make dainty = makes a fuss; To breathe = speak; Blaze = announce; To chide = tell off; To beshrew = curse

Verbs about wanting, having desires: To conjure = make appear like magic; To gape = to want; Fain would I = I would like to; I would = I wish

Verb phrases about specific customs or cultural assumptions: To walk a bout = dance; To lay knife abroad = in Shakespeare's time people brought their own knives to dinner and laid them on the table to show they wanted food; Purchase out = buy pardon for; Exhales = breathes out. People in Shakespeare's time believed that the sun sucked up gases from the earth and sets fire to them, and so breathed out or "exhaled" shooting stars; Will I rouse ye = I will get you up. In Shakespeare's time the wedding day started when the bridegroom, with musicians playing beside him, fetched his bride from her bed and took her to church; to Deck up = dress up

Other verbs: Abate = lessen/weaken; To amerce = punish; To counterfeit'st = copy; To tarry = wait for

The Crystals points out the most common verbs, both in Shakespeare and modern English, are: "to be", "to have", "to do" and the set of auxiliary verbs (helping verbs) known as the modals, such as: "can", "may", "would", and "shall". The chief differences between then and now are shown below.

The verb to be: Art = are; Beest, be'st = be; Been = are; Wast = were; Wert = were

The verb to have: Ha' = have; Hast = have; Hath = have; Hadst = had

The verb to do: Dost = do; Doth = does; Didst = did; Didest = did

Modals (verbs which express possible actions): Canst = can; mayst = may; shouldst = should; wilt = will; woo = would; wot = will (it can also mean 'know') wouldst = would (can also mean wish)

Useful link: find out more on the Shakespeare's Words website.

Adjectives

Adjective = words which describe a noun

Preparatory task: What are the adjectives that best describe yourself in terms of your appearance, your intelligence, your friends, your moods etc.?

Adjectives are words that describe nouns. Shakespeare frequently uses them to create specific emotional atmospheres. For example, in Act 1, Sc V, Juliet describes her meeting with Romeo as "prodigious", an adjective which means "terrible, or frightening". The adjective conveys Juliet's extremes anxiety about what might happen now that she's discovered Romeo is a Montague. This adjective sets the mood for the end of the party scene, with the audience being reminded that something awful is going to happen. In such a way, you could argue that the adjective actually creates suspense in the way it evokes a threatening atmosphere. In sharp contrast to adjectives like "prodigious" is an adjective like "wanton" which has multiple meanings in the play and nearly always is used to create a positive, passionate atmosphere; the adjective means at different times "lusty" "passionate" "wild" and "playful".
 Emotive adjectives about bad things happening: Unaccustomed = unexpected; Star-crossed = ill-fated; Misadventured = unfortunate; Prodigious = terrible, frightening, suggesting something terrible is going to happen; Baleful = harmful; Inauspicious = unlucky, ill-fated; Ill-divining = predicting disaster; Heavy = sad; Untimely = early;
 Emotive adjectives: Fair = beautiful; Lusty = energetic;
 Descriptive adjectives about appearance: Dun = dark brown; Rude = rough; Fleckled = dappled with red blotches like a drunk's face; Ghostly = holy, spiritual; Green-sickness = very pale, anaemic; Hoar = old but also a pun on "whore" (prostitute); Vestal = virgin; Stout = brave; Cunning = skillful
 Descriptive adjectives about emotional states or personalities: Tempering = making soft; Antic = stupid, absurd; Wanton = uncontrolled, passionate and/or playful; Civil = respectable; Riddling = confusing

Prepositions

Prepositions = placing words which tell you the place of something in time or space
 Ere = before

Adverbs

*Adverbs = words that describe a verb, giving more detail about it.
Adverbial phrase = words which are focused around an adverb, e.g. as soon as*

Adverbs are words which describe verbs; they are must easily recognized as "ly" words such as "skilfully" "truthfully" etc. However, adverbs are much more common words than these "ly" words; adverbs are actually some of the most frequent word classes to be found in language. Adverbs and adverbial phrases connected with time and place are common because they help situate an event in a particular place and time: words like "immediately", "at once", "late", "quickly" are all adverbs. Adverbial phrases connected with time are very important in *Romeo and Juliet* because they create a sense of urgency. As we have seen the play takes place in a very short space of time with the main characters rushing to do things like marry, kill each other, take potions and commit suicide without much forethought. Adverbs such as "anon" and "apace" help create this sense of urgency.

Adverbs of time and place: Anon = at once; Tardy = late; Apace = quickly; Aloof = at a distance
Adverbs of quantity: Scant = scarcely; Mickle = much
Expressive adverbs: Marry = by the Virgin Mary
Questioning adverbs: Wherefore = why; Perchance = perhaps

Regrets

David and Ben Crystal point out that there are several distinctive ways of expressing regret, remorse, guilt, sorrow or lament in Shakespeare. These are used a great deal in *Romeo and Juliet*:

Alack, alack; Alack the day; Alack for woe; Alas; Alas the day; Ay me 'lack; out alas; well-a-day; well-a-near; weraday; woe

Useful link: find out more on the Shakespeare's Words website.

Hence, thence and whence

As the Crystals point out these adverbs are rarely used now but much used by Shakespeare:

Hence = from here
Thence = from there, from that place
Whence = from which/what place, from where
Whencesoever = from whatever place, from somewhere or other

Useful link: find out more on the Shakespeare's Words website.

Hither, thither, whither

Hither = here, to this place
Thither = there, to that place, to that end
Whither = to which place, to whatever place, to what result, for what purpose

Useful link: find out more on the Shakespeare's Words website.

Stage directions

Aside = to one side, away from the others
Exeunt = more than one character leaves the stage
Within = behind the stage façade

Useful link: find out more on the Shakespeare's Words website.

Tasks on language

Illustrate and annotate the language discussed in this section with pictures of relevant scenes e.g. draw people saying insults to each other; draw pictures of the women discussed, draw the verbs etc. using speech bubbles or annotation. The quality of the picture is not important as long as things are clearly labelled.

How and why does Shakespeare deploy imagery in the play? You could if you like focus upon one specific type of imagery such as love, hate, fate etc., or offer a more general overview of the play.

Using an e-text version of the play do a search and find (usually CTRL + F) the words listed above and copy out the lines they come from; then try to **explain what the whole lines mean**. Why do you think Shakespeare has chosen these words?

Pick out the words which are **"false friends"** and explain how the meanings of these words have changed. Consider why these words have changed: you could use the Shakespeare's Words website to help you with this.

Re-categorize these words, putting them into **different categories** of your own choosing. Do this in the form of mind-maps, charts or graphical organizers.

Invent some sentences/lines from the play that might happen in the play using the words listed above, using a minimum of ten words. Or write a

version of the play using as many of the words listed above as you can.

Do some **further research** about the words listed above using the Crystals' Shakespeare's Words website and glossary.

Write your own **glossary** as you read the play.

Test a partner on their **knowledge** of these words after they've learnt the words off by heart.

Find out more about all the **puns** Shakespeare uses in the play and write about the way in which he plays with words; think about how and why he does this.

Write an **essay** entitled: "How does Shakespeare use nouns, verbs, adjectives and adverbs to create a vivid and engaging play?"

Rhythm & rhyme

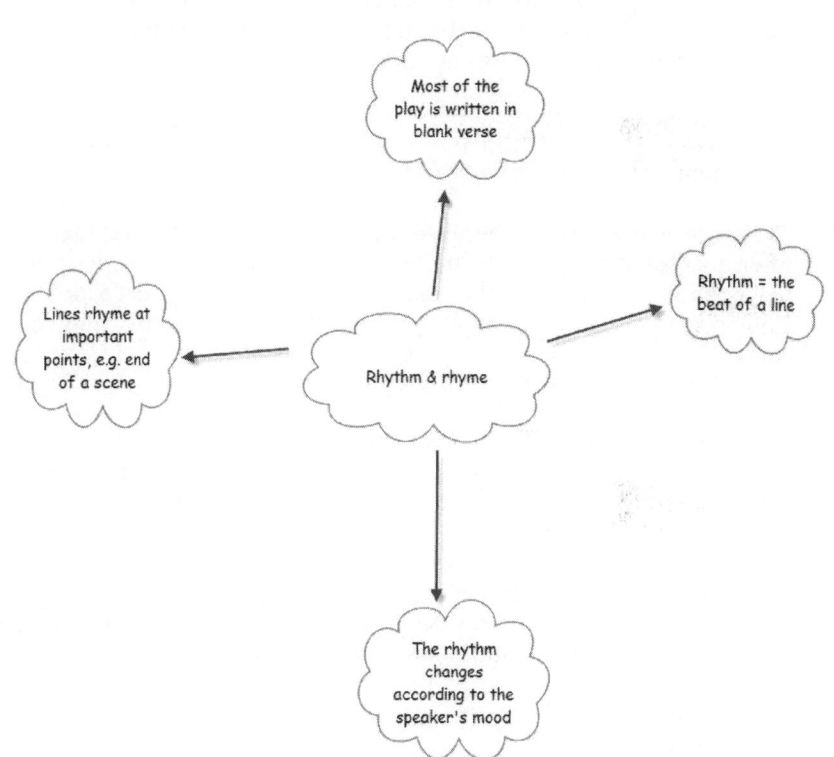

- Most of the play is written in blank verse
- Rhythm = the beat of a line
- Lines rhyme at important points, e.g. end of a scene
- The rhythm changes according to the speaker's mood

Figure 11 Rhythm & rhyme in the play: you can find a larger

version on the Romeo and Juliet Reloaded website here

Shakespeare's play is based on Brooke's poem, and there are many times in it that it moves from "blank verse" into rhyme. Blank verse is poetry which does not rhyme but has a regular, clear beat; many of Shakespeare's plays are written in blank verse in a metre called "iambic pentameter". The prefix "pent" means "five" and an "iamb" is a unit of rhythm which has two syllables with the heavy stress going on the second syllable: di-DUM. Effectively this means that "iambic pentameter" has five main stresses in a line with the heavy beat of the verse falling on the second syllable: di-DUM (1st iamb), di-DUM (second iamb), di-DUM (third iamb), di-DUM (fourth iamb), di-DUM (fifth iamb). The iambic pentameter creates a rolling, "rising" rhythm which generally causes the listener to think he or she is listening to the rhythms of "normal" speech. Let's look at Romeo's speech when he first sees Juliet, he says:

> It SEEMS she HANGS upON the CHEEK of NIGHT

This is a perfectly iambic line with the syllables in capitals being the ones that are more heavily stressed. Shakespeare frequently varies the rhythm of the iambic pentameter by changing the places where the stresses of the line go. He uses different "metrical feet" to do this. The most commonly used units of rhythm he uses are rising rhythms which are:

> Iambs = di-DUM
> Anapaests = di-di-DUM (two soft stresses followed by a heavy beat)

These are rising rhythms because they rise to the heavy beat; there is often a sense of hope in the line, an optimism and energy which you can feel in both the rhythm of the words and their meaning. Let's look at Romeo's next line which follows on from the one previously quoted:

> Like a RICH JEWel in an ETHiope's EAR;

Here we can see Romeo deploying an anapaestic rhythmic to convey his overwhelming feeling of love for Juliet; the rhythm is faster than the previous line because we have two light beats in the first metrical feet (an anapaest) "like a RICH". There are two other anapaests in the line: "in an ETHiope's EAR"; this rhythmical pattern creates a rising sense of hope and passion. Notice too though that Shakespeare uses another metrical foot, a "trochee", when Romeo says "JEWel". Trochees create a "falling" rhythm. There are two main types of "falling" rhythms:

> Trochees = DUM-di
> Dactyls = DUM-di-di

In the line quoted we can see that the falling rhythm of the word "JEWel" creates a contrast to the rising anapestic rhythm giving a sensational of both "rising" and "falling"; perhaps this mirrors Romeo's own extreme emotions because he is both feeling great passion and hope, but also possibly concern that this beautiful woman will not return his passion. When analyzing the rhythm of a line it is very important to engage with the meaning of the line and think about how the rhythm of the line emphasizes the overall mood, atmosphere and meaning of the line.

Shakespeare was a master-craftsman and loved to show off how skilled he was at using various rhythms: at the time he was writing there were many other playwrights and poets who were using the same techniques and would have formed an appreciative audience for him.

One particularly striking aspect of *Romeo and Juliet* is the way that it shifts from blank verse to rhymed poetry: Shakespeare is so skilful at this that you may not notice it; his rhymes work because they are not "forced", they feel completely natural. Some notable places where the play uses rhyme are:

> The Prologues to Acts 1 and 2; rhyme is used to bring clarity and excitement to the play; the rhymes "ring out" the key themes and images of the play.
> When Benvolio and Romeo are talking about love in Act 1, Sc I: Benvolio proposes through a six-line rhymed (sestet) poem that Romeo should look at other beautiful women apart from Rosaline;
> When Romeo first sees Juliet at Capulet's party and says ten lines of what is to become a sonnet (a fourteen-lined rhymed love poem) when Juliet joins in with his rhymes.

Shakespeare will frequently end his scenes with a rhyming couplet (two lines that rhyme which are next to each other). The most striking of these is the last lines of the play, where the Prince says:

> For never was a story of more woe
> Than this of Juliet and her Romeo.

Useful links: This Globe Education article on rhyme in Romeo and Juliet is very useful.

My website devoted to *Romeo and Juliet* has a section which contains video lessons on the rhythm and rhyme here.

This SlideShare covers the basics about rhythm and rhyme.

This Theatrefolk website explains the basics and has a good series of questions to answer on this issue.

Exercise

Fill in the blanks here in order to learn more about rhythm and rhyme in Shakespeare's play:

> Shakespeare wrote most of his plays in ----- VERSE: each line has -

--- SYLLABLES and ----main BEATS.
Much of his verse is -----, it consists of a regular pattern where the stress on a word comes SECOND: di-DUM.
The verse is written in ---------- because there are FIVE main beats (PENT = ----).
Good actors develop a "FEEL" for the verse, emphasizing its --------- qualities.
"But SOFT, what LIGHT through YONder WINdow BREAKS?"
It IS my LADy, O it IS my LOVE".
Notice how the heavy stresses come --------- in an iamb.
Notice how the words GENERATE a music, a melody...
Some of Shakespeare's verse is not --------, i.e. not in "iambic pentameter".
The ONLY way to work out the rhythm is to ---------- it aloud a FEW times and LISTEN to the beats...
"O ROMeo, ROMeo, WHEREfore ART thou ROMeo?" Juliet is speaking in dactyls here at the beginning of the line because there is a heavy stress followed by two soft beats, e.g. "ROMeo". This creates a falling rhythm which suggests that she is very upset and concerned.
The line creates a "-----" rhythm, particularly on "ROMeo" where there is a STRESS on the first syllable and then TWO "soft" stresses, creating a "FALLING" sensation. The effect of the rhythm is to create an ------------ and PASSIONATE atmosphere...
The crucial thing to think about is the ---------- the rhythm of a line creates.
You can only work this out by listening to actors perform the line, and reading it yourself...
Anapaests (di-di-DUM) are RISING beats too, creating often a -------, "proud" EFFECT.
"I am NO piLOT, yet wert THOU as FAR/As that VAST shore WASHED with the FARTHEST sea/ I should ADventURE for such MERchandISE".
Trochees (DUM-di) create a "------" effect, and often sound --------- and disjointed. E.g. "DOST thou LOVE me (TWO TROCHEES)? I KNOW thou WILT say 'Ay'/ And I will TAKE thy WORD?"
Dactyls (DUM-di-di) create a "FALLING" effect too, and can create the --------- effects of despair, worry, anxiety.
"TOO like the LIGHTening, WHICH doth CEASE to BE/ERE one can SAY, 'It LIGHTens'.
Look for ------- (run-on) lines; this often creates the sensation of "pace", "speed", "thinking things through"...
"But trust me gentleman, I'll prove more true/Than those that have more cunning to be strange."
Pauses or the ends of sentences in the middle of lines create ---------pauses that generate dramatic tension...
E.g. JULIET: "Well do not swear. Although I joy in thee,/I have no joy of these contract tonight."
E.g. ROMEO: "Wouldst thou withdraw it? For what purpose, love?"

Both Romeo and Juliet are presented as poetic lovers by Shakespeare. This means that they speak in rhythmic verse. Most of the time, they speak in ----- pentameter, which means their lines have --- main stresses and five soft beats. However, when they become upset or very emotional, Shakespeare ----- the rhythm, and they speak in a more irregular ----.

"O ROMeo, ROMeo, WHEREfore ART thou ROMeo?" Juliet is speaking in dactyls here at the beginning of the line because there is a heavy stress followed by two soft beats, e.g. "ROMeo". This creates a falling rhythm which suggests that she is very ----- and --- -.

When Romeo tries to suggest the power of his love, Shakespeare presents him as speaking in anapaests. He says: NOW COMPLETE THIS SECTION YOURSELF

Extension task: Find your own examples of Shakespeare using rhythm to create an emotional effect. Remember rhythm draws attention to vocabulary.

Answers in this order: blank; ten; five; iambic; pentameter; five; rhythmical; second; regular; read; falling; loving; effect; rising; falling; irregular; emotional; enjambment; striking; iambic; five; changes; rhythm; passionate; concerned.

Characterisations

When discussing the characters in *Romeo and Juliet* it is important to remember that they are not real people; they are literary creations, inventions of Shakspeare's imagination. As a result, a literary critic examines the ways in which Shakespeare presents a particular character; he or she examines his "characterisations", that is the way Shakespeare "constructs" his character out of language and dramatic action. A literary critic thinks about why and how characters are engaging; he or she examines Shakespeare's techniques – his ability to construct an exciting story out of his characters – and why we found his techniques engaging.

Task: who are the **most memorable fictional characters** you have read about or seen in films/theatre? Why are they memorable? Draw a spider-diagram of them.

Being a man & a woman

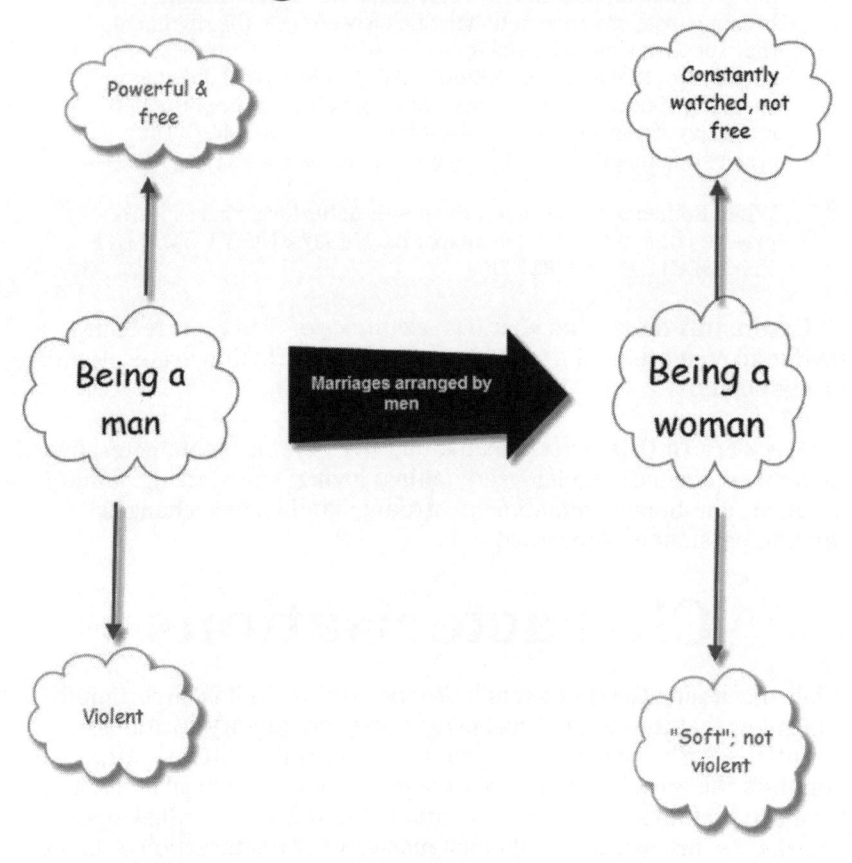

```
    Powerful &                          Constantly
      free                           watched, not free
        ↑                                    ↑
        |                                    |
    ┌─────────┐    Marriages arranged    ┌─────────┐
    │ Being a │ ═══════ by men ═══════▶ │ Being a │
    │   man   │                          │  woman  │
    └─────────┘                          └─────────┘
        |                                    |
        ↓                                    ↓
     Violent                            "Soft"; not
                                          violent
```

Figure 12 Being a man & woman in the play: you can find a larger version of this diagram on the Romeo and Juliet Reloaded website here

One major topic to think about when analyzing Shakespeare's characters in the play is that of "gender". It is people's gender that often decides what they do and how they behave. Look at the diagram above which illustrates how men and women are expected to behave in the world of the play. Then **devise your own chart** for the modern day, exploring perhaps in more depth how men and women are expected to behave now and the power they have in society. Then consider the similarities and differences in the treatment of men and women in Shakespeare's time and now.

The similarities and differences between the characters

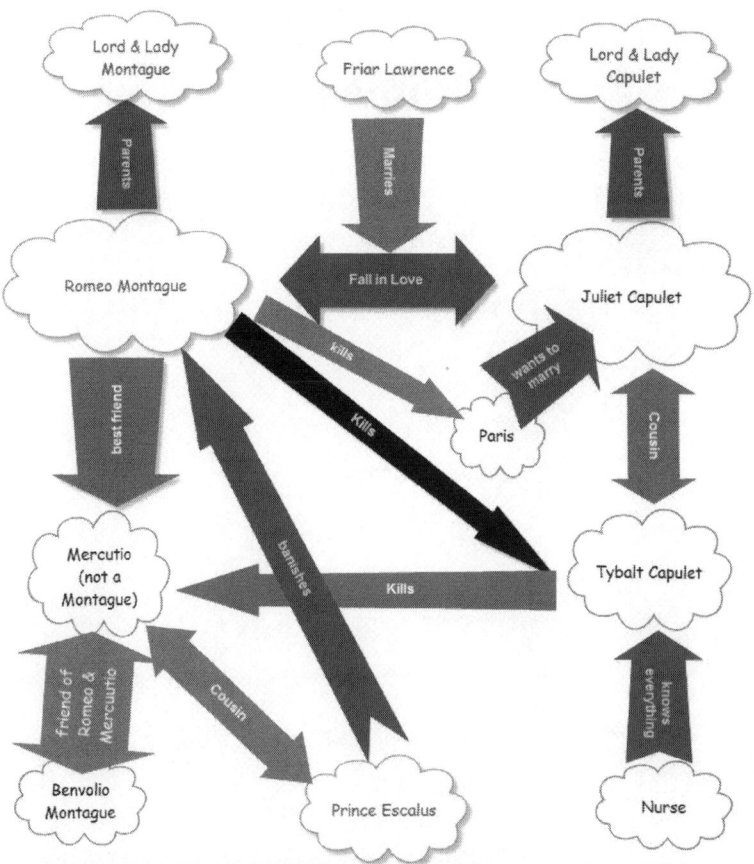

Figure 13 Character map: you can find a larger version of this diagram on <u>the Romeo and Juliet Reloaded website here</u>

Above is a diagram which shows some of the major relationships in the play. You will be able to see that some characters are similar in their roles, even though they are on the "opposite" side to each other. For example, Lord and Lady Montague are on the opposite side to Lord and Lady Capulet but they are **both parents**; Romeo and Tybalt are on opposite sides but they are **both killers**. These similarities and differences are very important in the play and need thinking about: you should consider the ways in which characters are similar and different. Shakespeare makes his play interesting by having similarities and differences which engage our interest. For example, it is very interesting to see that Romeo and Tybalt are both killers, even though they are so different.

Exercise: when you've finished reading the play, devise your own diagram which shows the similarities and differences between the characters. Then consider the effect that these similarities and differences have upon the audience. **Definition:** "effect" means what an idea/character/phrase makes you think, feel and see.

Romeo

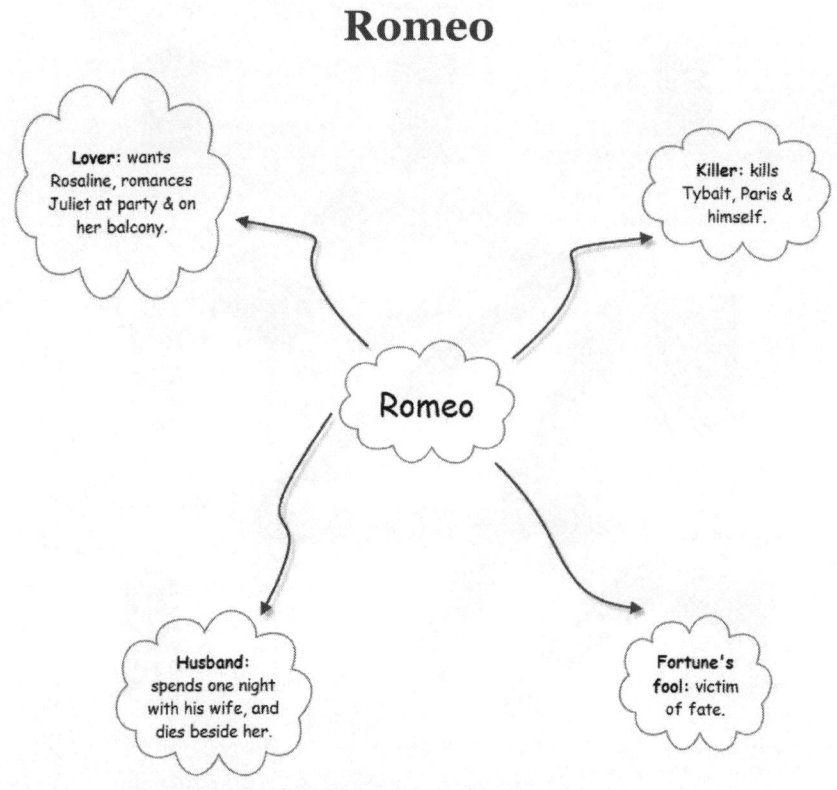

- **Lover:** wants Rosaline, romances Juliet at party & on her balcony.
- **Killer:** kills Tybalt, Paris & himself.
- **Husband:** spends one night with his wife, and dies beside her.
- **Fortune's fool:** victim of fate.

Figure 14 Romeo's character: you can find a larger version of this diagram on the Romeo and Juliet Reloaded website here

Much of the early part of the play, particularly from Acts 1-3, follows Romeo's progress as a lover. He appears after the fight in Act 1, Sc I, and is miserable because the object of his love, Rosaline, has rejected him. Throughout the play, Romeo often makes use of "opposites" in his imagery. He uses what Weis calls "contrapuntual conceits" (*William Shakespeare*, René Weis, 2014 p. 8), which means they are literary devices or techniques (conceits) which work by being in opposition with each other (contrapuntual). This makes Romeo very self-consciously literary i.e. he behaves like a lover you would expect to find in a book or a poem of the time. Let's look at what he says about Rosaline to Benvolio in Act 1, Sc I:

> Mis-shapen chaos of well-seeming forms!
> Feather of lead, bright smoke, cold fire, sick health!
> Still-waking sleep, that is not what it is!
> This love feel I, that feel no love in this.

He means here that the "well-seeming form" or beautiful body of Rosaline has caused him "mis-shapen chaos", a confusion or chaos of emotions that are "mis-shapen" or not fitting for a person of Romeo's high standing. Romeo then uses a series of oxymoron (opposites which are put next to each other) to describe his feelings for Rosaline: she is to him "bright smoke, cold fire, sick health". In other words, he loves her, she brings him health, fire, brightness, but for him she is also cold, sick and smoky. Many critics have pointed out how "mannered" and unconvincing Romeo's language is before he meets Juliet. Weis writes: "Up to the moment where he sees Juliet, Romeo's language of love consists of strings of self-conscious oxymoron, lifeless clichés incapable of expressing true emotion" (William Shakespeare, René Weis, 2012 p.9). While Romeo does show evidence of this, there are times when Romeo's language is much more revealing. He says to Benvolio:

> She will not stay the siege of loving terms,
> Nor bide the encounter of assailing eyes,
> Nor ope her lap to saint-seducing gold:
> O, she is rich in beauty, only poor,
> That when she dies with beauty dies her store.

One interpretation of these lines could be that Romeo has been stalking Rosaline with his "siege of loving terms" and "assailing eyes" and also seeing her as no better than a prostitute by offering her gold in return for opening her lap, i.e. having sex with him. Sex does seem uppermost in his mind; this is emphasized by the rhyming couplet of "poor" and "store" because he believes her richness in beauty will prove "poor" when she fails to produce any children; her "store" or beautiful treasure will die with her. Weis says that compared to Juliet, Romeo is almost a "cipher, at least as far as family and past life are concerned. We know nothing about him other than his infatuation with Rosaline" (p. 7). Weis is possibly arguing that Romeo is not as a richly imagined character as Juliet, who has much more of a past history and a vivid personality. Again, it is possible to disagree with this view: we learn a great deal about Romeo at the beginning of the play; Romeo has very concerned parents who clearly dote upon him, allowing him to do whatever he wants, and are sensitive. They ask Benvolio to talk to Romeo because they feel they are not succeeding in finding out why Romeo is so miserable.

Throughout the play, Romeo is aware that he is possibly the "plaything" of forces out of his control, he is "fortune's fool" (Act 3, Sc I). In Act 1, Sc IV, just before he, Mercutio and Benvolio gate-crash Capulet's feast, he says:

> I fear, too early: for my mind misgives
> Some consequence yet hanging in the stars
> Shall bitterly begin his fearful date
> With this night's revels and expire the term
> Of a despised life closed in my breast
> By some vile forfeit of untimely death.

In other words, he is aware that "some consequence yet hanging in the stars" – some intention written into his astrological chart – will begin to "kick in" from the point of the night's "revels" and lead to his "untimely death". However, these worries are forgotten when he is at Capulet's party and sees Juliet. Many critics have pointed out how his poetry is transformed when he sees Juliet; it becomes much more original, livelier and passionate.

> ROMEO O, she doth teach the torches to burn bright!
> It seems she hangs upon the cheek of night
> Like a rich jewel in an Ethiope's ear;
> Beauty too rich for use, for earth too dear!
> So shows a snowy dove trooping with crows,
> As yonder lady o'er her fellows shows.
> The measure done, I'll watch her place of stand,
> And, touching hers, make blessed my rude hand.
> Did my heart love till now? forswear it, sight!
> For I ne'er saw true beauty till this night.

There is a common link with the poetry he proclaimed in the name of Rosaline though because the rhyming poem he says in homage to Juliet is full of "opposites"; he in love with the rhetorical device of "antithesis", putting opposites next to each other. The jewel in the black man's ear is an oppositional image, contrasting the whiteness of the jewel with the blackness of the Ethiopean's ear. Likewise, the snowy dove contrasts with the blackness of the crows. Romeo consistently associates Juliet with a bright, heavenly light throughout the play. Unlike Juliet, Romeo's primary focus is not his lover's body but what might be called her "inner light": he sees her as a Goddess who has the power to make him "sin" and be forgiven at the same time. In the party scene, the lovers have this exchange:

> ROMEO ...Thus from my lips by thine my sin is purged.
> JULIET Then have my lips thee sin that they have took.
> ROMEO Sin from my lips? O trespass sweetly urged!
> Give me my sin again. (Kisses her)
> JULIET   You kiss by the book.

Here we see Romeo feeling that Juliet "purges" or takes away his "sin" of being in love with her by kissing him; Juliet then asks him to take the sin back, and he asks for the "sin" again to which Juliet tells him that he is a good kisser and he kisses like a hero in a romantic book. This exchange shows the power of the lovers to think alike: they play with the religious imagery of "sinning" and they also rhyme their words together, with "purged" and "urged", and "took" and "book" rhyming. As Weis points out "rhyme plays a crucial role in the rhetorical texture of a play which attributes extraordinary power of control to language" (p. 20). Romeo is a very literary lover, who moves from clichéd (over-used) language about love to talking about love in an extraordinarily subtle and original fashion. Weis argues that Romeo "stays in the realm of idealizing love" (p. 13) more than Juliet, who, as we shall see, is more of a realist. Juliet for Romeo is always perfection, more Goddess than human being. Nevertheless, in the balcony scene after he has called her his sun, and suggested that if her eyes were in the night sky they'd make it seem like it was daylight, sex does appear to enter his mind when he says:

O, wilt thou leave me so unsatisfied?

The Zeffirelli film makes it very clear that this is what Romeo is thinking because Juliet looks at him in such a shocked fashion when he says this. And yet, when Juliet does question him, he explains that he wants to "exchange faithful vows" with her; in other words, he wants to marry her. From this moment onwards, the marriage is never in any doubt. Indeed, the whole of Act 2 is suffused with a sense of Romeo's happiness: he shown to be lit with love in the balcony scene, during the scene when he explains to Friar Lawrence that he is in love with Juliet and wishes to marry her; during the comical episode when he trades sexual jokes with Mercutio in the market square; when he speaks to the Nurse as he makes the arrangements for the marriage; and just before he marries Juliet at the end of Act 2. Perhaps more than Juliet, his loving attitude of mind sets the tone for Act 2, which is by far the happiest and most comical act of the play.

The mood changes sharply at the beginning of Act 3, when Romeo is confronted by Tybalt who calls him a "villain" – a much harsher term of condemnation in Shakespeare's day than it is now because it was a "snobby" term which suggests someone is a peasant and from a lower class. In my modern translation, I use the word "pleb" –a common, stupid person -- which possibly conveys the nastiness of Tybalt's tone: the word "pleb" still has the power to insult, you only have to read about the row over the way a politician supposedly called the police "plebs" to realise how insulting it still is. Romeo's reply is suffused with love:

I do protest, I never injured thee,
But love thee better than thou canst devise,
Till thou shalt know the reason of my love:

We see here Romeo truly breaking the rules; stepping completely outside the code of the society he lives in. He says that he loves Tybalt more than Tybalt could possibly know. His love for Juliet has made him, albeit temporarily, totally re-evaluate his attitudes. But to talk of loving a Capulet, especially Tybalt, is totally "taboo" (forbidden) in Veronese society. Mercutio can't understand it at all and believes that Romeo is being cowardly, when actually we know the opposite is the case. He is being brave in that he is challenging the existing social order in Verona: he is saying that the feud, which shapes the lives of so many people, does not exist for him and, more than that, he actively wishes to socialize with and love the Capulets. He is also challenging the existing gender roles in the society: it was not a fitting thing for a man to refuse a challenge to a duel.

> Alive, in triumph! and Mercutio slain!
> Away to heaven, respective lenity,
>
> And fire-eyed fury be my conduct now!

However, Mercutio's death leads to Romeo regretting this approach. The feud returns into his mind with vengeance. He feels that his love for Juliet has made him "effeminate" – too much like a woman and not enough like a true man who would be violent towards Tybalt. From this time onwards, "fire-eyed fury" informs his "conduct", his way of being: he kills Tybalt, tries to kill himself when he is with Friar Lawrence, he kills Paris and then finally poisons himself to death. The death of Mercutio triggers a different side to his personality. When he learns from the Nurse how he has upset Juliet by killing her cousin, he tries to kill himself. He says:

> In what vile part of this anatomy
> Doth my name lodge? tell me, that I may sack
> The hateful mansion.

Above all, he comes to hate his "name" – his Montague name – because it is the part of him that has separated him from Juliet. He feels at this point that his Montague identity is what defines him and therefore is stopping him from being with Juliet; as a result, he tries to "sack/The hateful mansion" or destroy the hated house of his body. Here we see him possibly remembering Juliet's request in Act 2, Sc II for him to "doff", or get rid of, his name. He accepts this request readily but here we see that he feels that getting rid of his name is impossible. Thus we can see that Shakespeare characterises Romeo as someone who really struggles to come to terms with who he is: is he Juliet's lover and husband, or is ultimately a Montague and therefore her enemy, and therefore an enemy to himself? Or is he "fortune's fool", the idiot or clown of fate? He explores all these identities and ultimately comes to the conclusion that the only way he gain control of his destiny and his identity is by killing himself. He says when he learns of Juliet's death in Act 5, Sc I:

> Is it even so? then I defy you, stars!

The irony here is that he is actually fulfilling the destiny mapped out for him in the Prologue by killing himself: he is not defying his destiny at all. Just before he poisons himself to death beside the unconscious Juliet, he says:

> O, here
> Will I set up my everlasting rest,
> And shake the yoke of inauspicious stars
> From this world-wearied flesh.

Again, we have the idea that he is leaving his "bad fate" behind by killing himself. He is "shaking the yoke of inauspicious stars" from his "world-wearied flesh" by committing suicide. This is tragically ironic once again because he is, in fact, fulfilling his destiny by dying.

Perhaps a hard concept for us to understand is that the Elizabethans loved to see their central protagonists, their heroes, die.

Questions

How does Romeo change in the play? **Map out** all the things that happen to Romeo – or the things he does -- in a flow or spider diagram.

Extension: What do you think of Romeo as a character? How does he come across to you? Is he a fully-rounded character for you, or does he remain a "literary construct"?

Juliet

As Weis and many other literary critics have pointed out, Juliet seems a more fully rounded character than Romeo in that we learn a great deal about her past and her family – and her personality seems more real. Her lines are much less consciously "literary" than Romeo's: this means the lines Shakespeare gives her are not what you'd normally expect a female lover to say in a play of this type. In many ways, she is not a stereotypical female lover: she is not particularly "girly": Shakespeare never tells us what she looks like, she is not defined by her looks in the sense that we never learn what kind of face, body or hair she has. Instead, we just know from Romeo that she emits an unspeakably powerful light; her beauty is "too rich for use". In Acts 1 and 2, we learn that she does not enjoy the freedom to roam about the town whichRomeo does: she is confined to the Capulet mansion unless she is allowed to go to confession. Her father is already in negotiations about marrying her off to the Count Paris, but at the beginning of the play wants to wait a couple of years until she is fifteen or sixteen before she marries. He also wants her to decide who she marries – or so he says. Feminist critics have noted that Juliet is presented as the victim of a "patriarchal society"; that is she, like many women in Shakespeare's time, has no real power and is expected to do exactly what her father tells us to do. This is a society where men have all the power; what we call a "patriarchal society". Some other critics such as Weis and Julia Kristeva think Juliet is actually a veiled portrait of Shakespeare's own daughter, Susanna (William Shakespeare, René Weis, 2012 p.37).

Although Juliet may be very confined physically, she appears to be free mentally, thinking the unthinkable throughout the play. Let's look at her famous lines on the balcony when she believes no one is listening:

> O Romeo, Romeo! wherefore art thou Romeo?
> Deny thy father and refuse thy name;
> Or, if thou wilt not, be but sworn my love,
> And I'll no longer be a Capulet.

She asks why (wherefore) Romeo is called Romeo: she challenges him in her head to reject his family, to "deny his father" and reject his own name, or if he agrees to marry her, she'll no longer be a Capulet. She then goes on to ask what actually a name means. Critics like Catherine Belsey have pointed out that (Belsey, 2001) Juliet is aware that names are "arbitrary signifiers" which mean nothing in themselves i.e. words that have no real meaning; they are only significant if you accept all the cultural baggage that comes with them. She raises here a major theme of the play: the power of names and language to define people and situations.

Juliet is innocent but not naïve: she is aware that Romeo could misconstrue her immediate passion for him. She says if he thinks she is too quickly won over by him:

> I'll frown and be perverse an say thee nay,
> So thou wilt woo; but else, not for the world.
> In truth, fair Montague, I am too fond,
> And therefore thou mayst think my 'havior light:
> But trust me, gentleman, I'll prove more true
> Than those that have more cunning to be strange.

This is a very human touch: she is aware that Romeo could think of her as a woman of "easy virtue" who has given herself over to Romeo without playing hard to get and going through the customary rituals of courting. But she says that in the end she will "prove more true/Than those that have more cunning to be strange". Juliet expresses her love more simply but possibly more powerfully than Romeo; her metaphors are not so self-consciously clever but they have a directness and passion which is unmistakable:

> My bounty is as boundless as the sea,
> My love as deep; the more I give to thee,
> The more I have, for both are infinite.

Both Romeo and Juliet are critical at times of the older generation but

Juliet's criticisms are more genuine somehow. Romeo's criticism of Friar Lawrence in Act 3, Sc III is desperate and unconvincing because he says the Friar's philosophy can be of no use to him now that Juliet is banished, but then a little later he changes his mind and feels that the Friar has comforted him a great deal with his words. Juliet however is critical of the older generation as a whole because older people don't understand the passions of youth. As she is waiting for the Nurse to return from seeing Romeo in Act 2, Sc V, she complains about the Nurse's lateness:

> JULIET Had she affections and warm youthful blood,
> She would be as swift in motion as a ball;
> My words would bandy her to my sweet love,
> And his to me: But old folks, many feign as they were dead;
> Unwieldy, slow, heavy and pale as lead.

Here Juliet fundamentally criticizes the nature of old people: they are "unwieldy, slow, heavy and pale as lead". In other words, they are "unwieldy" which could mean clumsy in the way they deal with matters, they are "slow" to understand things, to understand young people, they are "heavy" in that they are overly serious about things, and they are without passions, being "pale as lead". They might as well be dead. This is strong, rebellious stuff.

Juliet also breaks with the traditional stereotype of the female lover because she is very physically passionate. In a famous speech at the beginning of Act 3, Sc II, she talks breathlessly about her desire to make love to Romeo:

> O, I have bought the mansion of a love,
> But not possess'd it, and, though I am sold,
> Not yet enjoy'd: so tedious is this day
> As is the night before some festival
> To an impatient child that hath new robes
> And may not wear them.

She talks here about Romeo being the "mansion of a love": she emphasizes here his physicality. This is something she does a number of times in the play. During the balcony scene, she talks about how his body is the "God of my idolatry": in other words, she worships his body like a God and wants him to swear that he loves her by that rather than the "inconstant moon". In the above speech, she also refers to herself as being "sold" to Romeo but "not yet enjoyed". The fact that she refers to herself "buying" the "mansion" shows that she is aware of her own "agency" in being a lover: the fact that she has the power and right to enjoy Romeo physically. But she is also aware that she is going to be enjoyed by Romeo as well: she is both the subject and the object of a love. Thus, we could say that Juliet exemplifies how many women think of themselves as lovers: they are perhaps more aware than men that they are "sexual objects" to be enjoyed and also agents of desire. Her speech is remarkable for its candour and honesty in this regard and still challenges us to think differently about sex.

Juliet has clearly enjoyed her wedding night in Act 3, Sc V because she is dreamily convinced that it is the nightingale singing and not the lark outside and so is still night. We realize that she is desperate for Romeo to stay. When she wakes up properly and realizes that it is the lark singing, she shoos Romeo out of the bed:

> It is, it is: hie hence, be gone, away!
> It is the lark that sings so out of tune,
> Straining harsh discords and unpleasing sharps.
> Some say the lark makes sweet division;
> This doth not so, for she divideth us:
> Some say the lark and loathed toad change eyes,
> O, now I would they had changed voices too!

For Juliet, the lark's song is "out of tune" and full of "harsh discords and unpleasing sharps", despite the fact that the lark traditionally sings beautifully. But it is "out of tune" because it tells the lovers that it is morning and therefore means Romeo must leave. Here again, we see Juliet taking a familiar image – that of the lark singing – and making it her own, making it more engaging than other people might. Juliet is a creature of the night who loves having sex with Romeo, but hates the divisions and discords of the day. She wants to be part of a world where the rules of daylight don't apply.

In some ways, Juliet is a rebel. Juliet stands up to her father, Capulet, and says that she will not marry Paris, despite his evident anger and power.

> Not proud, you have; but thankful, that you have:
> Proud can I never be of what I hate;
> But thankful even for hate, that is meant love.

Here we see Juliet using the "chop-logic" that Capulet complains about: she speaks in a riddle to her father, twisting his words so that she manages to express in a unique way her rejection of Paris. Her rejection of Paris is not met sympathetically; no one will support her, not her parents or the Nurse. For Juliet, it is the Nurse's rejection of Romeo which is the most painful:

> Ancient damnation! O most wicked fiend!
> Is it more sin to wish me thus forsworn,
> Or to dispraise my lord with that same tongue
> Which she hath praised him with above compare
> So many thousand times?

Once again, as we saw in a more comic form in Act 2, Juliet attacks the age of the Nurse: she is "ancient" and damned. In Juliet's eyes she is a "wicked fiend", a terrible devil who has been doubly hypocritical: she has asked Juliet to commit bigamy – to be "forsworn" or marry two men – and she has also criticized Romeo who she has praised above all men many thousands of times. These words are said in the heat of the moment of her treatment at the hands of Capulet and really convey Juliet's bitter sense of betrayal. In this sense, Juliet is a more convincing psychological portrait of a young, highly intelligent girl than Romeo is of a young man. Romeo seems at times too much of a literary device rather than a plausible young, passionate man.

Similarly, Juliet's feelings when taking Friar Lawrence's potion are psychologically convincing. Her soliloquy before she takes the potion is amongst the best in the play because we see her changing her mind so often. At first, she's worried that Friar Lawrence may have given her poison, then she worries about whether Romeo will find her in time; and then she becomes almost hysterical at the thought of waking up in the tomb surrounded by the dead bones of her family, with Tybalt's mangled body next to her. She says at the very end of the speech:

> O, look! methinks I see my cousin's ghost
> Seeking out Romeo, that did spit his body
> Upon a rapier's point: stay, Tybalt, stay!
> Romeo, I come! this do I drink to thee.

In the above speech she thinks she sees her "cousin's ghost" – Tybalt – looking for revenge. She implores Tybalt's ghost to stop his hunt for Romeo and then says she is coming to Romeo by taking the potion. Her speech illustrates another element to her character: her bravery. She takes the potion despite being terrified that something terrible may happen.

This speech is, in effect, her "death speech" because she says few lines when she wakes up. She says that her dagger is "happy" because it is taking her back to Romeo.

> Yea, noise? then I'll be brief. O happy dagger!
> This is thy sheath; there rust, and let me die.

She says here that her body is the dagger's "sheath": its protective cover. Her stabbing of herself is deeply symbolic: she feels that she is protecting and preserving her love forever by killing herself. In some of Shakespeare's plays such as Hamlet, the morality of suicide is discussed but this is not the case in *Romeo and Juliet* where the suicides of the lovers are presented as positive, preserving the love of the lovers forever and ending the feud.

Questions

Map out all the things that happen to Juliet – or the things that she does -- in a flow or spider diagram.

Devise a chart which compares and contrasts Romeo and Juliet in terms of their characters: their genders, what happens to them, their parents/backgrounds, their personalities etc.

Extension questions: Why do some critics think Juliet is presented as the victim of a patriarchal society?

How might you argue that Juliet is a more convincing and fully rounded character than Romeo?

Where and when is Juliet presented as brave?

Why might you argue that Juliet breaks the traditional stereotype of the female heroine/lover who is typically found in many stories? Think how different she is from a character such as Cinderella etc.

Capulet

Capulet, the father of Juliet, is a vivid portrait of a domineering parent who has conflicting views and changeable moods. Like Juliet, he is a psychologically convincing portrait of a man under a great deal of stress – much of which is of his own making. We see him at the very beginning of the play, before we are introduced to Juliet, apparently defending her right to choose who she might marry and rebuffing Paris's attempts to marry Juliet at thirteen. He says:

> And too soon marr'd are those so early made.
> The earth hath swallow'd all my hopes but she,
> She is the hopeful lady of my earth:

In the Zeffirelli film (Zeffirelli, 1968) the camera cuts to Capulet's wife as he says this, making it clear that this talk of women being "marred" or ruined if they marry young is a reference to Capulet's own wife. We get the sense that Capulet has invested the whole of his future in Juliet: "she is the hopeful lady of my earth" he says. In other words, she is the woman that he puts his faith and hope into, rather than his wife. Later on in this act, we see Capulet commanding the servants to be prepared for the feast in a very terse and "stressed-out" fashion while putting on the appearance to his posh guests that he is in a very good and convivial mood. He is a man who is the "public" face of his family; an important man in Verona who has a "public persona" of respectability and propriety. People clearly look up to him. He is a bit of a joker too: he jokes at the beginning of the feast that any lady who doesn't dance has ugly corns on her feet. We also learn from him that he was once a flirt, chatting up women as a young man at feasts like the one he holds for Juliet to meet Paris. He is very distressed regarding Tybalt's desire to kill Romeo at the feast and tells us that he knows Romeo to be a "well-governed youth", a well-behaved young man, who he doesn't want harmed. When Tybalt appears not to listen to him, he loses his temper, shouting:

> Go to, go to;
> You are a saucy boy: is't so, indeed?
> This trick may chance to scathe you, I know what:
> You must contrary me! marry, 'tis time.
> Well said, my hearts! You are a princox; go:

His annoyance at Tybalt is vividly conveyed here: he calls Tybalt a "saucy boy". This is a real insult; he calls him both a "boy" – as opposed to a gentleman – and "saucy", someone who is cheeky and irritating. He hates the idea that his nephew might "contrary" or contradict him: this is totally unacceptable for Capulet who is used to be obeyed. Finally, he calls him a "princox", an even stronger insult than "saucy boy"; it means a total idiot.

Capulet is presented by Shakespeare as a changeable person, particularly in regard to Juliet's marriage. He decides the day after he rejected the idea that it is suitable for Juliet to marry Paris: quite why we never know other than he thinks it would a good distraction from what he thinks is her grief about the death of Tybalt. When she refuses to marry Paris, he loses his temper in a far more uncontrolled fashion than he did with Tybalt:

> Hang thee, young baggage! disobedient wretch!
> I tell thee what: get thee to church o' Thursday,
> Or never after look me in the face:
> Speak not, reply not, do not answer me;
> My fingers itch.

He virtually calls for her death here: he says that she should hang herself, he calls her "young baggage", an utterly useless thing or lump. He judges her as "disobedient" and says that he will disown her if she doesn't marry Paris. Furthermore, he says she has no right to answer because his "fingers itch". It's clear from the dialogue of Lady Capulet and the Nurse that he hits Juliet during this scene.

However, he quickly forgets his anger with her when she agrees to marry Paris and is grief-stricken when he believes her to be dead. He says:

> Death lies on her like an untimely frost
> Upon the sweetest flower of all the field.

Capulet calls his daughter the "sweetest flower of all the field"; the most beautiful, the nicest woman in the world, who has been killed by an "untimely frost". He notes her beauty and appears to have entirely forgotten the character traits of his daughter that he once hated so much: her disobedience, her "chop-logic", and her willfulness.

Questions

Map out all the things that happen to Capulet – or the things that he does -- in a flow or spider diagram.

How and why does Shakespeare present Capulet as such a changeable character?

Extension: In what way does Capulet represent familial patriarchal power?

The Nurse

The Nurse is a lively, comic presence at the beginning of the play but becomes a darker, more sinister figure towards the end. We first find her making jokes about the antics of Juliet as a little child. She was Juliet's wet nurse; this meant that she breast-fed Juliet. It appears that Juliet really liked this and the Nurse jokes that she had to put "wormwood" (a bitter paste) on her breasts to stop the little Juliet sucking on them. She also jokes about incident when Juliet fell on her front when she was little:

> 'Yea,' quoth my husband,'fall'st upon thy face?
> Thou wilt fall backward when thou comest to age;
> Wilt thou not, Jule?' it stinted and said 'Ay.'

The Nurse's husband had joked that Juliet will fall on her back -- i.e. have sex -- when she is older and the little Juliet had replied yes. This causes the Nurse much merriment; it reveals that the Nurse is a "bawdy" figure. She is a lower-class person who revels in rude jokes. However, it's important to note that the Nurse does not like these rude jokes to go too far or to be at her expense. When Mercutio makes fun of her in the market-square, calling her a hairy whore, she is very annoyed and tells off Romeo for having a friend, a "flirt-gill", like this.

Apart from Friar Lawrence, the Nurse is the only person who knows the truth about Romeo and Juliet's marriage. She has a very close relationship with Juliet at the beginning of the play; it is clear that Juliet is much more comfortable being around the Nurse than her mother. Effectively, the Nurse is Juliet's real mother. However, the relationship is not without its tensions: Juliet complains that the Nurse is slow, old and passionless when the Nurse takes her time returning home after learning from Romeo about the marriage arrangements. After Romeo kills Tybalt, Juliet also gets angry with the Nurse when the Nurse condemns Romeo, saying:

> There's no trust,
> No faith, no honesty in men; all perjured,
> All forsworn, all naught, all dissemblers.

The Nurse's words here are revealing because they show how quickly she can change her opinion: she had been only a few hours before saying how wonderful Romeo was. Now she's saying that there is nothing "honest" about men at all. Juliet shouts that the Nurse's tongue should be "blistered" for saying this, even though she herself has criticized Romeo for killing Tybalt.

The Nurse is not presented as a particularly clever person: much of her speech is rambling and sometimes incoherent.

Shakespeare's portrait of her changes as the play progresses. She shifts from being a comic, friendly figure to being more sinister after Juliet has been ordered to marry Paris. She says in Act 3, Sc V:

> Faith, here it is.
> Romeo is banish'd; and all the world to nothing,
> That he dares ne'er come back to challenge you;
> Or, if he do, it needs must be by stealth.
> Then, since the case so stands as now it doth,
> I think it best you married with the county.
> O, he's a lovely gentleman!
> Romeo's a dishclout to him: an eagle, madam,
> Hath not so green, so quick, so fair an eye
> As Paris hath.

This is an astonishing statement in which the Nurse says that Juliet should marry Paris and that Romeo is a "dish-cloth" compared with the "lovely gentleman" of Paris, who is youthful, "green", clever "quick", and good-looking "fair an eye". This advice perhaps shows how the Nurse is someone who ultimately always does the expedient (the easiest) thing; she doesn't seem to have any real moral compass and is happy to go along with whatever is the easiest thing to do. Juliet accuses her after this speech of extreme hypocrisy and realizes that she can never trust her again.

Questions

Map out all the things that happen to the Nurse – or the things that she does -- in a flow or spider diagram.

In what ways does Shakespeare present the Nurse as a comic figure?

Extension: How does Shakespeare present the Nurse as a very inconsistent figure?

Mercutio

Mercutio is one of Romeo's best friends and is notable for being a joker who makes a number of very rude jokes in the play. He mercilessly mocks Romeo about his relationship with Rosaline. We first encounter him when Romeo, Benvolio and he are making their way to Capulet's feast. Mercutio gives a long speech about Queen Mab, who is a mythical figure of mischief, the fairies' midwife, who makes people do things that they shouldn't, particularly sexually. Mercutio becomes carried away with his description of Queen Mab's anarchic antics when he says:

> This is the hag, when maids lie on their backs,
> That presses them and learns them first to bear,
> Making them women of good carriage:

Here we see Mercutio's obsession with sex. He thinks that Queen Mab makes maids "lie on their backs" and "presses them" or persuades them to have sex even when it is against their own interests because they have to learn "to bear" or give birth to children as a result of having sex, which makes them "women of good carriage", or women who are carrying an extra person in their stomachs. In Baz Luhrmann's film, Mercutio is a "transvestite" – he wears women's clothes to Capulet's party -- and there is a suggestion that Mercutio is infatuated with Romeo and is a "misogynist": in other words he doesn't like women. This, in part, explains why Mercutio becomes very insulting when he thinks that Romeo has given him the "slip" – or escaped – to be with Rosaline. After the feast, Mercutio shouts out in the street that he will conjure Rosaline for Romeo and therefore produce an erection in Romeo. Benvolio tells him he is being too rude but he continues:

> Romeo, that she were, O, that she were
> An open arse, thou a poperin pear!

This is perhaps the rudest Shakespeare ever gets because Mercutio is suggesting her that Romeo fantasizes about having anal sex with Rosaline: anal sex in Shakespeare's day was the only sure way of having sex without any chance of pregnancy.

As well as being a joker, Mercutio is highly aggressive. He talks about Tybalt, who he refers to as the "Prince of Cats", in a derogatory way a number of times in the play and is desperately disappointed when Romeo refuses to fight Tybalt after Romeo has told the astonished Tybalt that he loves him more than he could possibly "devise" or know. Mercutio says:

> O calm, dishonourable, vile submission!

His disgust is fully expressed here and is revealing of his character. He feels that Romeo has given in; he has "submitted". He believes that

Romeo has dishonoured his family by not fighting and he hates the way Romeo has done all of this so calmly. As a result, Mercutio takes up what he sees as Romeo's fight. This is ironic because Mercutio is not of the Montague family and therefore not technically part of the feud. Possibly Mercutio is obsessed with being a "man" in that he – along with many other people in the play – feel that being a man means you have to fight if you're insulted or challenged.

When Mercutio dies, he gives this famous speech:

> No, 'tis not so deep as a well, nor so wide as a church-door; but 'tis enough,'twill serve: ask for me to-morrow, and you shall find me a grave man. I am peppered, I warrant, for this world. A plague o' both your houses! 'Zounds, a dog, a rat, a mouse, a cat, to scratch a man to death! A braggart, a rogue, a villain, that fights by the book of arithmetic! Why the devil came you between us? I was hurt under your arm.

We can see here the quintessence of Mercutio's personality: he is still joking as he is dying. He makes a pun on the word "grave" which means both "serious" and "someone lying in his grave". In many productions of the play, we have the other characters laughing as he says these lines because they don't believe he is hurt. However, Mercutio follows this joke with a curse on the two families: he clearly blames the feud for his death. He also blames Romeo for coming between him and Tybalt, saying he was hurt underneath Romeo's arm. This speech and his death drives the distraught Romeo to kill Tybalt. Thus, you could argue that it is Mercutio, not fate, love, the feud or any other character who is most to blame for the ultimate tragedy.

Questions

Map out all the things that happen to Mercutio – or the things he does -- in a flow or spider diagram.

Draw or devise a chart which compares and contrasts Tybalt and Mercutio as characters.

In what ways is Mercutio a humorous figure in the play?

How is Mercutio presented as an aggressive person?

Extension: To what extent is Mercutio to blame for the tragedy?

Friar Lawrence

Friar Lawrence is Romeo's closest confidante: he is the person Romeo tells everything to. When he first appears he has been helping Romeo deal with his problems with Rosaline and is shocked when Romeo suddenly arrives early on Monday morning to tell him that he is in love with Juliet. Friar Lawrence is initially skeptical that the passion is serious because he believes that men make judgements with their eyes rather than with their hearts, but he is quickly persuaded by Romeo's evident passion. He decides to marry the couple because:

> But come, young waverer, come, go with me,
> In one respect I'll thy assistant be;
> For this alliance may so happy prove,
> To turn your households' rancour to pure love.

In other words, he believes that the marriage will end the feud; this is emphasized by the half rhyme of "prove" and "love". He proved to be correct that the marriage will end the feud, but his wish is fulfilled in the most tragic fashion possible. Throughout the play the Friar represents both a religious and rational approach to life. He is a philosopher and a scientist, knowing about potions as well as the right way to live life. He warns the couple before they marry:

> These violent delights have violent ends
> And in their triumph die, like fire and powder,
> Which as they kiss consume: the sweetest honey
> Is loathsome in his own deliciousness
> And in the taste confounds the appetite:

His attitude contrasts with the approach of the young people in the play – the lovers, Mercutio and Tybalt – who are all consumed with violent passions of one sort or another. During the second half of the play, the Friar has to use all his ingenuity to deal with these violent passions. Here we see him stopping Romeo killing himself because he has been banished from Verona and therefore can't see Juliet:

> Hold thy desperate hand:
> Art thou a man? Thy form cries out thou art:
> Thy tears are womanish; thy wild acts denote
> The unreasonable fury of a beast:
> Unseemly woman in a seeming man!

He accuses Romeo of acting like a "woman" – i.e. someone who lets their passions get the better of them – and of being like an animal – a thing which has no rational control of the emotions. Both of these to modern minds are stereotypes but probably were widely held views amongst educated men in Shakespeare's time. The Friar's battle is against the passions, but it is also against fate. His clever plan for Juliet to take the potion which will make it look like she is dead backfires because of fate: his letter doesn't get through. As the Friar says, this is "unhappy fortune". Perhaps the most troubling part of his presentation is when he goes to the tomb at the end of the play and says this to Juliet:

> Come, I'll dispose of thee
> Among a sisterhood of holy nuns:
> Stay not to question, for the watch is coming;

The Friar is frightened of being discovered by the watch – the equivalent of the police – and runs away, having told Juliet that he will "dispose" – or get rid – of her by putting her in a nunnery. When he is called to account by the Prince, he says that if he is found guilty of wrong-doing he should be executed: he is a woebegone, defeated figure at the end of the play. Nevertheless, his wish that the feud should end comes true.

Questions

Map out all the things that happen to the Friar – or the things he does -- in a flow or spider diagram.
   Extension: In what way is the Friar presented as both a rational and a religious man?
   What is troubling about the presentation of the Friar?

Tybalt

Tybalt has relatively few lines in the play but he plays a pivotal role. First and most important, he is the chief "antagonist" in the play. In the first scene, it is he who really triggers the fight that leads to the Prince threatening to execute anyone who starts fighting again. Here we see the words that trigger the first fight in Act 1, Sc I:

> What, drawn, and talk of peace! I hate the word,
> As I hate hell, all Montagues, and thee: Have at thee, coward!

These lines embody Tybalt's attitude: the feud appears to completely occupy his mind. He hates "all Montagues" and views them as cowards.
   Second, he vows to get revenge on Romeo for appearing at Capulet's feast. Weis notes that Tybalt appears to want revenge on Romeo after being humiliated by uncle, Capulet, at the party. He says that he will appear "seeming sweet" but in reality his feelings will turn into the "bitterest gall", the worst kind of poison. Tybalt obeys his uncle but his obedience has a terrible consequence: the death of Mercutio. He writes a letter to Romeo, presumably challenging him to a duel. A few hours after Romeo is married, he meets him in the market-square and says:

> Romeo, the hate I bear thee can afford
> No better term than this,--thou art a villain.

These are extremely strong words: he publicly proclaims Romeo to be despicable, a far worse insult than the biting of thumbs, which is the insult which starts the first fight in Act 1, Sc I. His death is much talked about and leads to Romeo being banished. It also inadvertently leads to Paris being killed because Paris believes in Act 5, Sc III that Romeo has come to the tomb to desecrate Tybalt's body and therefore fights him, which causes Paris's death. Lady Capulet is particularly upset about his death: some directors have intimated that her distress has been caused by the fact that she either fancied Tybalt or had an affair with him. While he has few lines, his influence is pervasive throughout the whole of the play.

Questions

Map out all the things that happen to Tybalt – or the things he does -- in a flow or spider diagram.

Why is Tybalt such an important figure in the play?

How does Shakespeare use Tybalt to create suspense in the play?

Benvolio

Benvolio is an interesting character who is one of Romeo's best friends. He is entirely Shakespeare's invention because he doesn't appear in Brooke's original poem, the text the play was based upon. His name means "well-meaning". We see him living up to his name on a number of occasions. Most strikingly, he tries to help Romeo's parents by finding out why Romeo is so sad and locks himself up in his room all day. He discovers through questioning his friend that Romeo is in love. Presumably he must tell Mercutio this information because Mercutio makes fun of Romeo's attachment to Rosaline. Benvolio appears on the surface to try to keep the peace in the feud. In Act 1, Sc I, just before the fight begins Benvolio says to Tybalt:

> I do but keep the peace: put up thy sword,
> Or manage it to part these men with me.

Tybalt mocks him here saying that he is "drawn" – i.e. he has got his sword out – and yet he is talking of peace. Thus we can see that Benvolio is not all he seems to be. He claims to be keeping the peace but we are never quite sure whether he is; he appears to be a "goody-two-shoes" but always seems to be around when there's trouble. In Act 3, Sc III, he says to Mercutio and Tybalt that they should retire to a private place but he doesn't significantly try and stop their quarrel. Mercutio accuses him of being someone who loves quarrelling. He is no doubt joking here, but there may be a grain of truth in Mercutio's hyperbole (his exaggerations); maybe Benvolio isn't as well-meaning as he seems. Certainly, when the Prince asks him to explain who caused the fight between Romeo and Mercutio, Benvolio doesn't give a straight answer:

> Tybalt, here slain, whom Romeo's hand did slay;
> Romeo that spoke him fair, bade him bethink
> How nice the quarrel was, and urged withal
> Your high displeasure:

Here we see Benvolio emphatically blaming Tybalt for the tragedy when we know that it was Mercutio who caused the first fight and it was Romeo who instituted the second. Benvolio is first and foremost a "Montague" rather than a "well-meaning" man I think.

Questions

Map out all the things that happen to Benvolio – or the things he does -- in a flow or spider diagram.

In what way to Benvolio live up to his name, and in what ways does he not?

Prince Escalus

The Prince is presented an exasperated ruler who does not know how to deal with the fight between the families. Like Tybalt and Paris, he has relatively few lines but he plays a vital role in the plot because it is his threat to execute anyone who starts a fight which has such dire consequences for Romeo. In Act 1, Sc I, he spits out furiously:

> Rebellious subjects, enemies to peace,
> Profaners of this neighbour-stained steel,--
> Will they not hear? What, ho! you men, you beasts,

Here we see how he believes all of his people are "rebellious": they won't do what he says. They are also "profaners" – they are breaking the law of God by killing each other. He feels that they do not hear his words and that they are little better than "beasts". The Prince though can't carry out his promise to execute the next trouble maker when he hears from Benvolio how Tybalt was killed by Romeo, who killed Tybalt after Tybalt killed Mercutio. As a result, he alienates the Capulet family because he banishes Romeo rather than executing him:

> And for that offence
> Immediately we do exile him hence:

The Capulets are annoyed, particularly Lady Capulet, because they believe that Romeo should be executed. Consequently, Lady Capulet hatches a plan, which is never carried out, to have Romeo poisoned in

Mantua. Meanwhile, the Montagues are stricken by Romeo's banishment, with Lady Montague dying of grief because of it. It appears that the Prince is in an impossible position: he can please no one. This said he does seem to have a degree of moral authority: the families do stop fighting when he intervenes, and his speech at the end of the play is taken seriously:

> I have an interest in your hate's proceeding,
> My blood for your rude brawls doth lie a-bleeding;
> But I'll amerce you with so strong a fine
> That you shall all repent the loss of mine:

We learn here that his family has been affected by the feud and he threatens to punish them so severely that they will feel his loss. What his loss is we never learn. At the very end of the play, he shouts at the two grief-stricken families:

> Capulet! Montague!
> See, what a scourge is laid upon your hate,
> That heaven finds means to kill your joys with love.
> And I for winking at your discords too
> Have lost a brace of kinsmen: all are punish'd.

This is the Prince's final judgement: everyone has been punished by the tragic deaths of lovers and other family members. The Prince says that he "winked" at their "discords", in other words ignored the feud for far too long and didn't deal with it properly. He clearly is racked by guilt at his powerlessness.

The critic Dymna C. Callaghan points out that the Prince plays a pivotal role in the plot because he represents the power of the state gaining control over the power of the two families. By the end of the play, the two families have reconciled to the Prince's way of thinking about things: they have agreed that people from the two families can marry who they want and they shouldn't be banned from marrying people from the "other side". It is agreed that "love-matches" should be allowed because otherwise tragedies like Romeo and Juliet's will occur. Callaghan writes: "Romeo and Juliet consolidates the power of the absolutist prince as he...can take marriage alliances out of the hands of kin and promote what is to become a bourgeois family form" (Callaghan, 2001, p. 107). In such a way, Callaghan reveals the Prince to represent the triumph of one social order over another: he is the "absolutist" (all-powerful) prince who can set the agenda as to who marries who in the name of social harmony.

So we can see that the Prince plays a number of different roles in the play: he's the "policeman", trying to enforce law and order, he's the judge, saying who is guilty and who is not, and he's the jury: he passes sentence.

Questions

Map out all the things that happen to the Prince – or the things he does -- in a flow or spider diagram.

How does the Prince try to stop the feud?

To what extent is the Prince presented as being to blame for the tragedy?

How could you argue that the Prince's power is asserted over the families at the end of the play?

Paris

Paris doesn't have many lines in the play but he has an important role in the plot: it is his insistence upon marrying Juliet that leads to her taking the potion which makes it look like she is dead. We gain little sense of his personality until the very end of the play when we learn that he will bring flowers to Juliet's grave every night and cry for her (Act 5, Sc III). At the beginning of the play, in Act 1, Sc II, he is very anxious to marry the 13-year-old Juliet but Capulet tells him to wait two years and to woo her, which he agrees to do. He is clearly on friendly terms with Capulet and we learn from both Lady Capulet and the Nurse that he is a man of "wax": a perfect gentleman in all respects, he has high status, he is clever, good-looking and has perfect manners. Shakespeare leaves him out of the party scene where Juliet meets Romeo but we assume that he must have been there: some directors have had Juliet dancing with him and appearing to be reasonably happy in his company. Possibly an important point is that he is not a "bogeyman"; he is not the "antagonist" in the play, but inadvertently becomes the cause of the central dilemma of the second half of the play: should Juliet marry him or not? Rather like Tybalt, Paris is a character who is more talked about than seen, and like Tybalt plays a pivotal narrative role in creating suspense because the fact that Capulet forces Juliet to marry him makes us wonder what on earth Juliet is going to do.

Questions

Map out all the things that happen to Paris – or the things he does -- in a flow or spider diagram.

What do we learn about Paris in the play?

Why does he play such a pivotal narrative role?

Web links for characters

The Sparknotes.com website has a detailed analysis of the characters: I find the site a bit problematic because it treats Shakespeare's literary creations as "real people".

The Cliffnotes character profiles are much briefer and more aware that the characters are "presentations".

The BBC Bitesize profiles of Romeo and Juliet are brief but offer some good exercises for revision.

The Absolute Shakespeare profiles are brief but useful.

The Collaborative Learning Project has a good PDF which offers a fun "card" activity that enables you to get to know the characters better. Well worth checking out – especially if you're a teacher.

You can find some Year 4 descriptions of the characters in the play here and see how the play has been taught in primary schools.

This internet set of flashcards for Romeo and Juliet is very good at testing your knowledge.

There's a character quiz here which is brief but useful.

Part II: Activities on the play

An explanation of the activities

The **thematic questions** on the play are designed to help you make connections between your own life and the play: thinking about them will help you remember the play and assist with you when you have to write a personal response in an essay. They are placed before the relevant part of the play because thinking about these themes as you are reading will help you relate to the play more. The **fill-in-the-blanks** check basic understanding while the **questions** and **analysis** are there to help you think more deeply about the play. **Creative response questions** are there to help you stretch your imagination and think like an artist, which obviously Shakespeare was. Tasks that ask you to act out sections of the text or role play particular situations are designed to get you thinking about the play as **performance**. The **analytical response** questions are usually questions that you'll typically find in an exam or set for coursework. I recommend that you do at least **two activities** from each section, varying the activities as you go along so that you gain a variety of skills. All titles are hyper-linked in the Kindle version to the Shakespeare's Words website's annotated version of the relevant scene.

Prologue

Important vocabulary: mutiny = violence
Star-crossed = ill-fated
Misadventured = unfortunate (Roma Gill, William Shakespeare, 1982, p. 1)

Thematic questions: Do you like watching films/reading books where you know the story already? If so, why? What are your attitudes towards fate? Do you think that your life is mapped out for you and there's nothing you can do about it?

Read the Prologue and then answer these questions.

Fill-in-the-blanks (answers below): The Prologue tells us that the play is set in ---- and is about two --- families who give birth to two lovers. Romeo and Juliet will --- because it is their fate – it is written in the ---.
Questions: What does the Prologue say?
Why do you think Shakespeare tells us the basic story-line in the

Prologue?

Analysis: Baz Luhrmann's film version of the play has a modern news reader saying the prologue, together with key images in the play. This is a very clever, modern interpretation of this section because the Chorus, who says the prologue, is like a news reader in that he represents a group of people, the public, and says their views, in the same way many news readers aim to represent "ordinary" people's interests. The Prologue is a sonnet, a 14 line poem, which has three sections: an octet (8 lines), a sestet (6 lines), a rhyming couplet (2 lines which rhyme and end the sonnet. Shakespeare wrote many sonnets, which are usually love poems. This is not a love poem, but is about love. The sonnet form gives the opening "gravitas" – this means it creates a serious atmosphere. This is important because what follows immediately is a conversation which is full of black humour: Shakespeare loved creating contrasts in his plays because the contrasting mood keep the audience entertained, surprised and makes them wonder: what is going to happen next. The Prologue creates what is known as "dramatic irony" throughout the whole play: this is when the audience knows things that the audience does not. We know from the beginning of the play that Romeo and Juliet are doomed to die; when we see them fall in love, we know they will die. What sort of thoughts and feelings does this create in us? This is a big question and can't be answered in a few sentences: you need to look at all the times when Romeo and Juliet talk to each other and think about the effect that knowing they will die has on you.

Creative response: Write a short passage or poem which describes all the things that you think might happen in your life or the life of someone you know, even things that haven't happened yet. Write a happy and sad version. After writing it, reflect upon how this made you feel; was it a difficult thing to do? Was it upsetting? Why was it upsetting? Re-read the Prologue: can you think now about the feelings and thoughts that the Prologue creates in you now?

Act it out: In groups of three or four, learn the Prologue off by heart and act it out with real passion, using echoes, sound effects, music if you want to.

Analytical response: When you have finished reading the play, write an essay entitled: "Why does the Prologue create a great deal of suspense in 'Romeo and Juliet'?"

Fill-in-the blanks answers: feuding, die, stars.

Act 1, SCENE I. Verona. A public place.

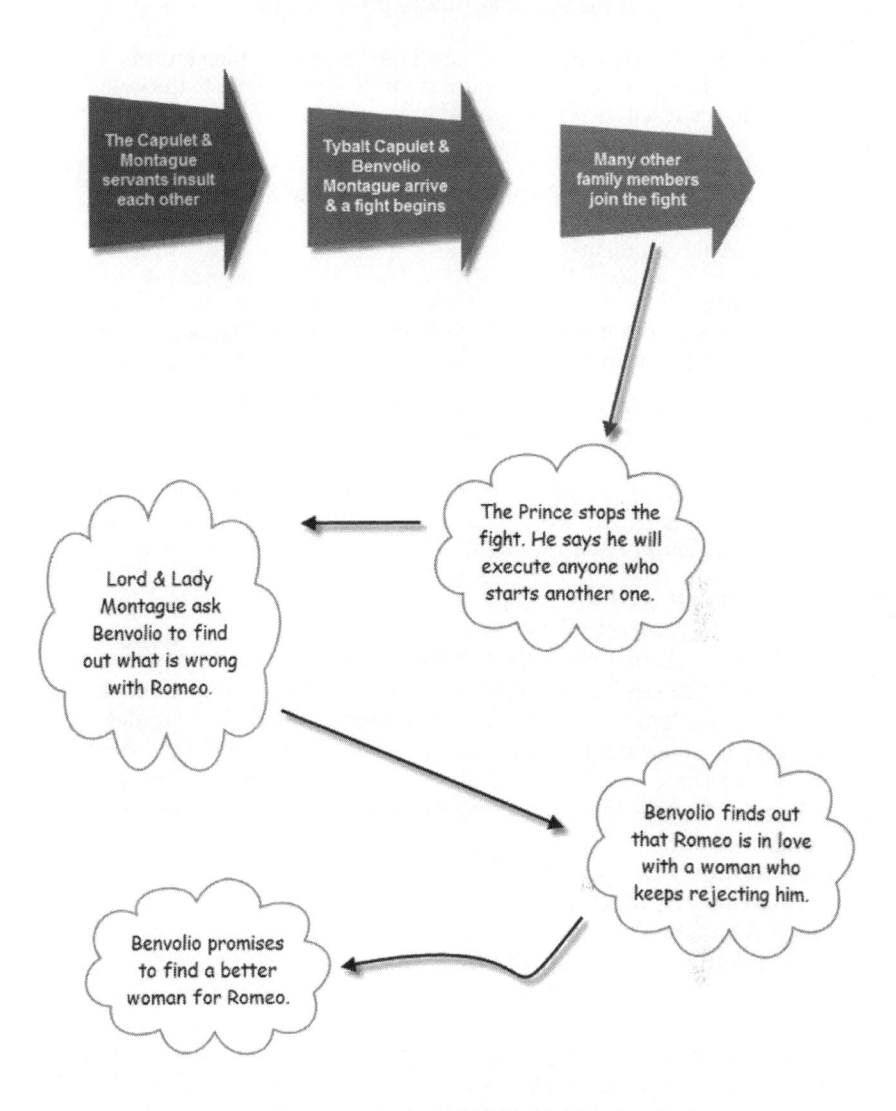

- The Capulet & Montague servants insult each other
- Tybalt Capulet & Benvolio Montague arrive & a fight begins
- Many other family members join the fight
- The Prince stops the fight. He says he will execute anyone who starts another one.
- Lord & Lady Montague ask Benvolio to find out what is wrong with Romeo.
- Benvolio finds out that Romeo is in love with a woman who keeps rejecting him.
- Benvolio promises to find a better woman for Romeo.

Figure 15 Act 1, Sc I flow chart: you can find a larger version of this diagram on the Romeo and Juliet Reloaded website here

Activities 1.1

Important vocabulary: "carry coals" was a slang phrase from the time which meant to be insulted; "collier" was a man carrying coal; "choler" means anger; "collar" meant the hangman's noose. "Coals", "collier", "choler" and "collar" all sound the same. Look at the way Shakespeare plays with these words in the coming scene.
Draw/drew = has different meanings: keep, hold back; draw their swords.
Take the wall = In Shakespeare's time it was safest to walk close to the wall because people chucked their rubbish and toilet contents into the middle of the street.
Maidenheads = virginity.
Bite my thumb = make a rude gesture like putting up two fingers.
Moved = angry
Airy word = trivial comment
Fray = fight
Humour = mood
Cupid's arrow = Cupid was the god of love in classical mythology and is usually drawn as a blind boy, with wings, who shoots an arrow; whoever is hit falls madly in love.
Dian/Diana = Goddess of chastity/virginity in classical mythology
Fair = beautiful (Roma Gill, William Shakespeare, 1982, pp. 2-12)

Thematic questions: In your experience, why do people not like each other? Why do they get into fights? Why do they insult each other? Do you know of any people who have long-running grudges?

Read Act 1, Sc 1 lines 1-60

   Fill-in-the-blanks (answers below): The play begins with two servants from the ---- family, Sampson and Gregory, joking about raping the ---- women. Some Montague servants then appear. The Capulet servants try to cause a fight with them by making rude gestures which involve biting their ----. The Capulet servants are careful to keep the --- on their side. They become more daring when they see ---- approach and this leads to them ----.
   Flow chart: Devise a chart of the main events in this section.
   Questions: What leads to the servants of the Capulets & Montagues fighting? What shocking things do they say to each other and why? Why do you think they pick fights with each other? Why do you think Shakespeare begins the dramatic action of the play with the servants, who rarely appear in the play?
   Comparison and contrast: Compare the insults that the servants use here with the insults you come across at school or outside school. How and why are they similar and different to the insults you use?
   Analysis: This opening is truly shocking to modern audiences but also very comic in tone. Sampson and Gregory joke about raping the Montague women, but it is clear they are bragging about their sexual prowess and fighting abilities. They are obviously cowards who only become bold enough to fight when they see Tybalt. Shakespeare shows

the audience here how the fight begins not with an "airy word" (which the Prince talks about later on) but with a hand gesture, the biting of the thumb, which was the equivalent of showing the middle finger now. The language the servants use is deeply "misogynistic": this means it reveals a deep hatred of women. The women, or "maids", are viewed as no more than sexual objects who men wield power over.

Creative response: Write your own playscript where some people insult each other and this leads to a fight.

Fill-in-the blanks answers: Capulet; Montague; thumbs; law; Tybalt; fighting.

Activities 1.2

Thematic questions: How do people break up fights? Are there any rules or laws which stop people from fighting?

Read Act 1, Sc 1 lines 61-101

Fill-in-the-blanks (answers below): The fight escalates because all the different generations and ranks from the families --- the fight. Benvolio tries to --- the servants fighting but is then challenged by ----, then officers and citizens from the families join in, followed by the older generation who are the heads of the families: Capulet and Montague. The Prince stops the ----. He tells us that there have been ---- fights recently where blood has been shed. The Prince says he will ----- anyone who starts another one.

Flow chart: Devise a chart of the main events in this section.

Questions: How and why does the fight grow into a bigger fight? How does it escalate? How many fights have there been before this one? Why have they happened? What does the Prince say will happen if the Montagues and the Capulets fight again?

Analysis: This is an extremely dramatic, violent opening to the play and includes a large fight. Shakespeare's audiences would have loved this. It also serves a deeper purpose: it is the back-drop to the love affair. The audience sees how deep the hatred between the families is: they will fight each other for virtually no reason at all. It is difficult here to find out a genuine reason as to why the families are fighting. Indeed, we never learn the real reason for the feud in the first place. This is a culture which loves fighting. Recently, historians have shown that there was a great deal of knife crime in Shakespeare's England and that many people carried knives so this scene could reflect the **context** of the time. The threat of the Prince to execute anyone who starts another fight is very important in generating suspense later on because, of course, Romeo is the person who is threatened with execution when he kills Tybalt. Thus we can see Shakespeare "sowing the seeds" for what is to come.

You & the play: Think about authority figures in your life. Is there anyone like the Prince who can stop fights/arguments like this? How and why do they have authority? Is it because of their position, their age, their wisdom etc?

Creative response: Write the Prince's diary about the trouble he has had to deal with recently between the Montagues and Capulets.

Fill-in-the blanks answers: join, stop, Tybalt, fight, execute.

Act it out: Act out this scene without any words, miming the fight and rude gestures.

Thematic questions: What is typical teenage behavior? How do teenagers get on with their parents? Why do teenagers fall in love?

Activities 1.3

Thematic questions: What is typical teenage behavior? How do teenagers get on with their parents? Why do teenagers fall in love?

Read Act 1, Sc 1 lines 102-236

Fill-in-the-blanks (answers below): Lord and Lady Montague are ----- about Romeo because he has been locking him in his ---- and sitting in the ---, with his curtains closed. He has been ---- a lot and ----- talking to people. Benvolio talks to him and discovers that he is in ---- but that the woman he loves does not ---- his love. He does not tell Benvolio her name but we later learn she is called Rosaline. Romeo says he has tried everything to win her over, including offering her --- to have sex with her, but she has always ---- him.

Flow chart: Devise a chart of the main events in this section.

Questions: Why are Lord and Lady Montague worried about Romeo? What has he been doing which has troubled them? Why do they ask Benvolio for help? When Benvolio talks to Romeo what does he discover? Why is Romeo difficult to talk to? What does Romeo slowly reveal to Benvolio? Why and how does Romeo use such complicated language?

Analysis: This is our first introduction to Romeo. We learn first about him from his parents, Lord and Lady Montague, who are worried for his well-being: we can see that he comes from a caring home. We also learn that Romeo does not like violence: this is important because it makes his killing of Tybalt all the more shocking. As the scene unfolds we become aware that Romeo is possibly rather immature in his attitude to the woman he loves. He talks about his lover for her in "oxymorons" saying it is "brawling love" "loving hate" "cold fire" "sick health": he is putting to opposites together to create surprising, troubling images to describe his love. He is playing with words in a very clever way; possibly this could indicate that he is thinking more about being clever with language than truly expressing his feelings in genuinely passionate language. It is interesting to compare this speech with the sonnet he says when he first sees Juliet, which, while very poetic, is also passionate and heartfelt.

Creative response: Write a description of a person who is depressed using some of the ideas in the descriptions of Romeo. OR: write a story about a person who has been rejected by someone or something, i.e. a rejected lover, or someone who has been rejected by a team, school, a group of people. Call the story "The outsider".

Act it out: In pairs, either act out the conversation between Romeo and Benvolio, or role-play a scene between two friends where one friend is depressed and the other is trying to help him or her. Practice the role-play and then write a script or act it out.

Fill-in-the blanks answers: worried, room, dark, crying, avoiding, love, return, gold, refused.

Act 1, SCENE II. A street.

Important vocabulary: suit = request, usually to marry
Ere = before
Lusty = energetic
E'en = evening
Crush = drink
Ancient = customary
Heretics = people with religious beliefs that were considered evil by the church
Scant = scarcely (Roma Gill, William Shakespeare, 1982, pp. 12-16)

Activities 1.4

Thematic questions: What are your attitudes towards arranged marriages? Do you think teenage girls are more or less free to do what they want than boys?

Read Act 1, Sc II lines 1-37.

Fill-in-the-blanks (answers below): Paris wants to --- Capulet's daughter, Juliet, but Capulet tells him that being ---- years old, she is too young to marry. However, Capulet will listen to what Juliet says. He --- Paris to a party or feast that night so that he can get to ---- Juliet.

Flow chart: Devise a chart of the main events in this section.

Questions: Why is Paris visiting Capulet? Why is Juliet's age a problem? What does Capulet invite Paris to and why?

Analysis: Shakespeare introduces an important narrative "thread" here: Paris's desire to marry Juliet. Later on, in Act 3, this becomes a real problem for Juliet and creates a great deal of tension because Juliet is already married to Romeo. Capulet appears to be loving, caring father here: he is worried that Juliet is too young to marry and wants her to decide who to marry for herself. Later on in the play, he presents a very different persona and orders Juliet to marry Paris. Thus we can see that Shakespeare is presenting us with a complex, "contradictory" character: someone who wants to present a certain "façade" or front to the world but is, at heart, controlling & dictatorial. Juliet's youth is quite shocking to modern audiences but probably would not have been to Shakespeare's. However, it was relatively uncommon for women to marry this young then.

Creative response: Write a poem called "The caring parent" in which you explore what it means to be a caring parent.

Fill-in-the blanks answers: marry, thirteen, invites, know.

Act it out: Hot-seat Capulet and Paris and explore what they are really thinking.

Activities 1.5

Thematic questions: Would you gate-crash the party of your enemy? What kind of people do this?

Read Act 1, Sc II lines 38 to end of the scene.

Fill-in-the-blanks
(answers below): The servant needs Romeo to read the guest-list because he cannot ----. Romeo discovers that ------ has been invited to the party. Benvolio says that Romeo will see women more ------ than Rosaline there but Romeo ------.

Flow chart: Devise a chart of the main events in this section.

Questions: Why does the servant give the guest-list for the feast to Romeo? What does Romeo discover when he reads the list? Why does Benvolio think it would be a good idea for Romeo to go to the party as well?

Analysis: Shakespeare builds up suspense here because we realize that two Montague men are planning to gate-crash a party given by the Capulets so that Romeo can see his beloved, Rosaline. Further suspense is added because Benvolio bets Romeo that he will show Romeo more beautiful women than Rosaline – which, of course, he does. The tone is very comic.

Creative response: Write a short story called 'The Bet' in which a teenager dares his friend to do something dangerous like gate-crash an enemy's party etc.

Answers to fill-in-the-blanks: read, Rosaline, beautiful, disagrees.

Act it out: Put Romeo and Benvolio in the Big Brother Diary Room and get them talking about their lives and what they are looking forward to at the party.

Act 1, SCENE III. A room in Capulet's house.

Important vocabulary: Lammas = Lammas Day is 1st August, the name comes from the Old English word for a loaf of bread, and the festival celebrates harvest. Lammas Eve is the day before Lammas.
Marry = by the Virgin Mary
Dug = breast
I trow = I am sure
I warrant = I'm sure
Stone = testicle
Man of wax = a perfect model of a man
Lineament = line (in a book); feature (on a face) (Roma Gill, William Shakespeare, 1982, pp. 16-20)

Activities 1.6

Thematic questions: What is your attitude towards marriage? Is it a dream of yours? Do you think you can have a happy life without being married? Why do you think parents get embarrassed when they have a chat about grown-up things like sex etc with their children?

Read the whole of the scene.

    Fill-in-the-blanks (answers below): Lady Capulet and the Nurse discuss the fact that Juliet will soon be -----. The Nurse remembers Juliet's age very well because her own daughter was the same age as Juliet, but her daughter, Susan, ---. The Nurse remembers Juliet's birth, on 31st July, almost 14 years ago. The Nurse remembers when Juliet was weaned: the Nurse ------ her. This was common in those days for rich families to have a "--- -----". She remembers another event: when Juliet fell over and hurt herself. Her husband said that Juliet will fall on her --- (i.e. have sex) when she is --- enough. Lady Capulet stops the Nurse from talking and asks Juliet what she thinks about ----- to which Juliet replies she hasn't ----- about it. Lady Capulet then says that Paris wants to ---- Juliet and talks about all his --- qualities in a very artificial way. She says Juliet must get to know him at the ----.

    Flow chart: Devise a chart of the main events in this section.

    Questions: Why do Lady Capulet and the Nurse discuss Juliet's age? What do we learn about the Nurse's daughter, Susan, and Juliet's childhood? What funny incident happened? What reasons does Lady Capulet give as to why Juliet should think about marriage? What does Lady Capulet say about Paris? What do we learn about Juliet's relationship with the Nurse and her mother in this scene?

    Analysis: This scene is in marked contrast to the others because it features only women. We learn about Juliet's privileged but sheltered upbringing. It is clear that the Nurse is much closer to Juliet than her mother, who comes across as a distant figure who is nervous about talking about a tricky matter (marriage) alone with her daughter and asks the Nurse to stay. The Nurse is presented as a rude, cheerful character who is not afraid to joke crudely about sex and breast-feeding. The Nurse also has had a tragedy in her life, the death of her child. Lady Capulet has obviously been talking to her husband and appears keen for Juliet to consider marrying Paris, discussing his great qualities at length. This creates more suspense for the feast at the end of Act 1 because we want to know what will happen between Paris and Juliet; obviously we know she will marry Romeo from the Prologue and so we can see potential conflict here.

Creative response: Write the Nurse's diary for this scene discussing her thoughts and feelings about Juliet and her dead daughter Susan.

Act it out: Improvise a scene in which a parent tells their child that they should marry someone & talks to them about love etc.

Fill-in-the blanks answers: fourteen, died, breast-fed, "wet nurse", back, old, marrying, thought, marry, good, feast.

Act it out: Role play an embarrassing conversation between a parent/guardian who tries to talk to their teenage child about getting married and/or the "facts of life".

Act 1, SCENE IV. A street.

Important vocabulary: lath = wood
Tartar = the Tartars, from central Asia, were famous for shooting bows and arrows
Measure = judge
Heavy = sad
Shaft = arrow
Dun = dark brown
Five wits = five senses: sight, hearing, smell, taste, touch
Masque = party
Wit = sense
Anon = at once
Ambuscados = ambushes
Bosom = heart
Misgives = warns
Expire = put an end to
Forfeit = payment
Untimely = early (Roma Gill, William Shakespeare, 1982, pp. 21-25)

Activities 1.7

Thematic questions: What do teenage boys talk about in your experience or what do you imagine they talk about? Why do some people think sex is always on teenagers' mind? What do you think their attitude towards sex is?

Read the whole of the scene.

    Fill-in-the-blanks (answers below): Romeo is ---- at the beginning of this scene and is worried about gate-crashing a party that they don't have ----- for. Mercutio tries to ---- him up by telling him not to be such a boring person; when Romeo talks about a ---- he had, Mercutio gives a long speech about ----- ---, who is the mid-wife to the fairies, and encourages people to express their ----, which is very ----; it leads to people being ------- in all sorts of ways. Romeo stops him giving the speech because it is clear that he has become upset. Romeo then talks to himself (- ------) and says that something dreadful is going to happen because of this night: he has a feeling that he will die ---- because of the events of this night.

    Flow chart: Devise a chart of the main events in this section.

    Questions: Why is Romeo depressed at the beginning of the scene? How do Benvolio and Mercutio try to cheer him up? What kind of person is Mercutio? How is he different to Benvolio? What does Mercutio say about Queen Mab? Why does he talk about her do you think? What makes Queen Mab dangerous? At the end of the scene, what "foreboding" or sense of doom does Romeo have?

    Analysis: This scene introduces Mercutio, who is a joker and a comedian, and is constantly playing with words and challenging people with his rude thoughts and gestures. Romeo's depression contrasts with Mercutio's high spirits; this is what makes the scene so successful. We see teenage boys inter-acting with each other. The Queen Mab speech is a Shakespearean "tour-de-force", a "set piece" speech, which audiences during his time would have greatly enjoyed for his rude jokes and wordplay. The sense of foreboding and impending doom that Romeo feels at the end of the scene is a running "motif" throughout the play: Romeo has a premonition that this night will cause his death. We see him have a similar premonition after he has killed Tybalt ("I am fortune's fool" Act 3, Sc.1) and when Juliet sees him descend from her balcony and thinks she sees him in a tomb (Act 3, Sc. 5). The Baz Luhrmann film is particularly good at dealing with these moments in the text because we have "flash forwards" in which Romeo is walking towards Juliet's tomb in the candle-lit church.

    Creative response: Role-play a scene in which some teenagers talk about gate-crashing a party: one teenager has his/her doubts and the other really wants to go.

    Analytical response: Answer this question: "What makes the Queen Mab speech so imaginative?"

Fill-in-the-blanks answers: love-sick, invitations, cheer, dream, Queen Mab, desires, dangerous, humiliated, (a soliloquy) early.

Act it out: Have someone read Mercutio's Queen Mab speech and other people miming the actions talked about. Or role play a group of young people getting ready to go to a party.

Act 1, SCENE V. A hall in Capulet's house.

Important vocabulary: trencher = plate
Joint-stools = stools made by a carpenter
Marchpane = marzipan
Walk a bout = dance
Makes dainty = makes a fuss
Visor = mask
Turn the table up = put the tables on top of each other to make more room for dancing
Nuptial = wedding
Forswear = deny
Rude = rough
Kin = family
Princox = rude young man
Gall = poison
Palmers = pilgrims to Jerusalem who brought back palm leaves to show where they'd been
Chinks = lots of money
Foolish = simple
Prodigious = terrible, frightening, suggesting something terrible is going to happen (Roma Gill, William Shakespeare, 1982, pp. 25-30)

Activities 1.8

Thematic questions: What is your attitude towards parties? Do you like them or find them stressful?

Read Act 1, Sc V, lines 1-43

Fill-in-the-blanks (answers below): The servants are very ---- because it is clear, as we see later on from Capulet's behavior, that they have orders to make this a very ------ feast or party. We know from previous scenes that this is the feast in which Capulet wants Paris to --- over Juliet. Capulet is very keen for everyone to get into the ----- atmosphere and to start dancing; he uses jokey blackmail to do this by saying that the ladies have ---- on their feet if they don't dance. Capulet then talks to an ----- Capulet about when it was when they last had a similar party; there is some dispute about this.

Flow chart: Devise a chart of the main events in this section.

Questions: Why are the servants so stressed at the beginning of the scene? How does Capulet persuade the ladies to dance with him? What mood does he present to guests? How does he treat his servants? How does Shakespeare create both tension and comedy in this scene?

Analysis: This opening to the famous scene when Romeo and Juliet meet for the first time is very "frenetic"; it is full of action and movement. It is also comedic and dramatic: it is funny to see all the rushing around on stage. We see the marked contrast between the social classes here as well with the rich people being treated very nicely by Capulet and the servants being shouted out and abused.

Creative response: Write a story about a party in which the host pretends to be very jolly but is actually very stressed that things must go well.

Fill-in-the blanks answers: stressed, successful, win, party, corns, elderly.

Act it out: Role play the servants taking Capulet to a tribunal for being a bullying boss.

Activities 1.9

Thematic questions: Do you think there exists such a thing as falling in love at first sight? What do you think love is? Can young people properly fall in love?

Read Act 1, Sc V lines 43-58.

Fill-in-the-blanks (answers below): Romeo compares Juliet to a very strongly burning "----" (fiery stick), a --- in a black man's ear, and a dove, a --- bird.

Flow chart: Devise a chart of the main events in this section.

Questions: What objects and bird does Romeo compare Juliet to when he first sees her? Why do you think he makes these comparisons?

Analysis: This speech is contrast to the speeches about Rosaline which were more complex and less emotional. Here Juliet is compared to light and "whiteness": this would have a particular significance for Shakespeare's audience as light has religious connotations: God is often compared with light. We also see here how Romeo has fallen in love at first sight: this again was a religious concept. The inner light of Juliet, the "God" in her, speaks to Romeo directly without words, without them meeting. It is a union of minds without any language passing between them. The staging of the scene is important here; the theatre director needs to think very carefully about the positioning of the actors and consider whether Juliet should look at Romeo too. Romeo uses rhyming couplets to emphasize the power of his feelings.

Creative response: Write a poem about love at first sight.

Analytical response: Write a detailed analysis of Romeo's rhyming poem about first seeing Juliet.

Fill-in-the blanks answers: torch, jewel, white.
Act it out: Have someone read Romoe's speech. Other readers can echo important words in the speech, while others could mime actions in response to the imagery.

Activities 1.10

Thematic questions: Do you think there are particular types of people who are always being insulted or who feel insulted even this wasn't what was intended? What are these people like?

Read Act 1, Sc V lines 59-91

Fill-in-the-blanks (answers below): Tybalt is ----- by Romeo's presence at the party because he is a ------ and is wearing an "antic face" or ----- mask. He believes that Romeo has come to the party to mock the Capulets. He says he will --- Romeo. When he tells Capulet about this, Capulet becomes very ---- with him for threatening to cause a --- at the party and tells him that Romeo is a --------- and ---- gentleman. Tybalt backs down but vows to get his ------- at a later date.

Flow chart: Devise a chart of the main events in this section.

Questions: Why is Tybalt so insulted by Romeo's appearance at the party? Why does Capulet get so cross with Tybalt? What does Tybalt promise to Capulet, but promise secretly to himself after he has talked to Capulet?

Analysis: Tybalt's hatred towards Romeo is in marked contrast to the loving speech Romeo has given when he has seen Juliet. We see our first glimpse of Capulet's volcanic temper here: he is very annoyed by Tybalt refusing to listen to his order not to attack Romeo and calls Tybalt a number of names, including "princox". Tybalt backs down in a comic fashion: the "tough teenager" is defeated by the older man.

Creative response: Write a story called 'The gate-crashers'.

Analytical response: How does Shakespeare create both comedy and suspense in his presentation of the confrontation between Tybalt and Capulet?

Answers to fill-in-the-blanks: insulted, Montague, comedy, kill, angry, riot, well-behaved, respected, revenge

Act it out: Role-play Tybalt talking to his Capulet mates about Romeo's appearance at the party.

Activities 1.11

Thematic questions: What do lovers talk about, do you think? Do you think lovers talk differently from other people?

Read Act 1, Sc V lines 92-110.

Fill-in-the-blanks (answers below): Romeo and Juliet ---- hands and ---- with each other, using ------ imagery. Romeo asks Juliet for --- to do what their hands are doing.

Flow chart: Devise a chart of the main events in this section.

Questions: How does Romeo persuade Juliet to kiss him in this section? What imagery does he use?

Analysis: This exchange immediately shows that Romeo and Juliet are on the same wavelength: they "riff off" the other person's images, talking in rhymes, and play together with the idea of the two of them being like "pilgrims" who are worshipping saints by touching palms and lips. Their talk is an example of what Capulet calls "chopped logic": these are words that sound beautiful and nice but actually don't fully make sense. This is because their love isn't entirely logical: they appear to have some sort of telepathic connection with each other which happens immediately. Thus we can see Shakespeare presenting us with lovers who were "meant to be"; destined to love each other.

Creative response: Write a poem called "First Love", or a scene in which two lovers meet for the first time.

Analytical response: How does Shakespeare suggest the genuine love between Romeo and Juliet in this first meeting?

Fill-in-the-blanks answers: touch, flirt, *religious*, lips.

Act it out: Act out Romeo and Juliet's lines in pairs, thinking about what the actors might be doing on stage.

Activities 1.12

Thematic questions: What shocks have you received in your life? Why have these things been shocking?

Read Act 1, Sc V lines 111 to the end of the scene.

Fill-in-the-blanks (answers below): Romeo and Juliet both learn that they are from the families of their -----. Romeo responds by saying that his --- now depends upon his enemy, while Juliet feels that her marriage bed is her ----. They both have terrible "presentiments" (premonitions/visions of the future) that their lives are at risk because of their ---. Romeo has to leave because Benvolio believes that they might be ---- by the Capulets.

Flow chart: Devise a chart of the main events in this section.

Questions: What do Romeo and Juliet learn about each other at the end of the scene? What are their reactions? Why does Romeo have to leave?

Analysis: Shakespeare shows the power of the two lovers' love by their reaction to the news that they are from opposing families: both of them feel their lives are at risk. Romeo's reaction is a little more uncertain than Juliet's: he feels his life depends upon his enemy while Juliet feels her wedding bed is her grave. Thus we can see that although they've only met very briefly, they feel incredibly strongly about each other. Shakespeare creates a great deal of tension because Romeo has to leave and so the two lovers can't linger with each other.

Creative response: Write a poem or story called 'Forbidden Love'.

Analytical response: How does Shakespeare create suspense in Act 1, Scene 5? Consider the following in your answer: the different characters we encounter, the changes in mood and atmosphere, the way he makes the storyline engaging, the dramatic action and the language he uses.

Fill-in-the-blanks answers: enemies, life, grave, love. challenged.

Act it out: Hotseat Romeo and Juliet, asking them what they are thinking and feeling now.

Looking back at Act 1

Focus on structure: put these quotes in the order they happen in the play and write about why Shakespeare ordered them in this way.

> JULIET Prodigious birth of love it is to me,
> That I must love a loathed enemy.

> PRINCE Three civil brawls, bred of an airy word,
> By thee, old Capulet, and Montague,
> Have thrice disturb'd the quiet of our streets

> TYBALT What, drawn, and talk of peace! I hate the word,
> As I hate hell, all Montagues, and thee:
> Have at thee, coward!

> CAPULET My child is yet a stranger in the world;
> She hath not seen the change of fourteen years,
> Let two more summers wither in their pride,
> Ere we may think her ripe to be a bride.

Follow up after you've checked your answers: using a narrator who explains the missing parts of the story, either write up a "story" version of these quotes or work in a group and act out these lines, with a narrator or narrators explaining the story of the Act as a whole and the actors reading these key lines with real expression.

Focus on grammar and lexis: what are the word classes of the following lexis in **CAPS** and why are they significant words?

> ROMEO I FEAR, too early: for my mind misgives

Some CONSEQUENCE yet hanging in the STARS
Shall bitterly begin his fearful date
With this night's REVELS and EXPIRE the term
Of a despised life closed in my breast
By some vile forfeit of UNTIMELY death.

CAPULET Content thee, GENTLE coz, let him alone;
He bears him like a PORTLY gentleman;
And, to say truth, Verona brags of him
To be a VIRTUOUS and WELL-GOVERNED youth:

Focus on characterizations: who said the following and what do we learn about the characters from these quotes?

"If ever you disturb our streets again,
Your lives shall pay the forfeit of the peace."

"She will not stay the siege of loving terms,
Nor bide the encounter of assailing eyes,
Nor ope her lap to saint-seducing gold:"

"A man, young lady! lady, such a man
As all the world--why, he's a man of wax."

"I was your mother much upon these years
That you are now a maid.
Well, think of marriage now; younger than you,
Here in Verona, ladies of esteem,
Are made already mothers: by my count,"
"By giving liberty unto thine eyes;
Examine other beauties."

"My only love sprung from my only hate!
Too early seen unknown, and known too late!"

Follow up after you've checked your answers: Using these quotes as starting points, "hotseat" the relevant characters, i.e interview them in pairs about what they are thinking and feeling at these moments.

Focus on staging: write about how these quotes might be acted out on stage or film, discussing any versions you've seen.

ABRAHAM Do you bite your thumb at us, sir?

ROMEO O, she doth teach the torches to burn bright!
It seems she hangs upon the cheek of night
Like a rich jewel in an Ethiope's ear;

Beauty too rich for use, for earth too dear!

JULIET You kiss by the book.

Focus on imagery: fill in the gaps for the following quotes, then check your answer with Shakespeare's; why do you think Shakespeare made these word choices?

ROMEO Where shall we dine? O me! What --- was here?
Yet tell me not, for I have heard it all.
Here's much to do with hate, but more with love.
Why, then, O ----- ---! O ----- ---!
O any thing, of nothing first create!

ROMEO O, she doth teach the ----- to burn bright!
It seems she hangs upon the cheek of night
Like a rich ---- in an Ethiope's ear;
Beauty too rich for use, for earth too dear!
So shows a snowy ---- trooping with crows,
As yonder lady o'er her fellows shows.

JULIET Good pilgrim, you do wrong your hand too much,
Which mannerly devotion shows in this;
For saints have hands that ------ hands do touch,
And palm to palm is holy ------' kiss.

Focus on rhythm and rhyme: put these quotes into the correct verse form, punctuate them and explain the rhythmic effects of the lines.

TYBALT I will withdraw but this intrusion shall now seeming sweet convert to bitter gall.

ROMEO Is she a capulet o dear account my life is my foes debt

Evaluating Shakespeare's characterisation: put the following statements about Romeo in rank order, with the one you most agree with at the top.

"Shakespeare presents Romeo as an immature young man at the beginning of the play, who has offered money to Rosaline to sleep with him and is frustrated that she continues to reject him."

"Romeo is portrayed as a young man who learns the meaning of true love."

"Romeo is presented as an impulsive character who acts before he thinks."

Evaluating the act: put the following statements in rank order, with the one you most agree with at the top.

"Act One is full of contrasts: Shakespeare is constantly switching focus from the feud to the love story."

"Act One reveals Romeo and Juliet's situations in detail: Romeo's laddishness and Juliet's naivety and youth."

"Act One builds suspense by making us feel sympathy for the two lovers: we come to understand and love them in this act."

Answers

Focus on structure. The correct order is:

TYBALT What, drawn, and talk of peace! I hate the word,
As I hate hell, all Montagues, and thee:
Have at thee, coward!

PRINCE Three civil brawls, bred of an airy word,
By thee, old Capulet, and Montague,
Have thrice disturb'd the quiet of our streets

CAPULET My child is yet a stranger in the world;
She hath not seen the change of fourteen years,
Let two more summers wither in their pride,
Ere we may think her ripe to be a bride.

JULIET Prodigious birth of love it is to me,
That I must love a loathed enemy.

This order of events shows how Shakespeare sets the love affair of Romeo and Juliet in the context of the feud: Shakespeare presents us with the violence of the feud **before** we see Romeo and Juliet fall in love. This increases the sense of **jeopardy** for the lovers: we, the audience, know just how terrifying the consequences of their affair being found out could be.

Focus on grammar and lexis: what are the word classes of the following lexis in **CAPS** and why are they significant words?

ROMEO I FEAR, too early: for my mind misgives

> Some CONSEQUENCE yet hanging in the STARS
> Shall bitterly begin his fearful date
> With this night's REVELS and EXPIRE the term
> Of a despised life closed in my breast
> By some vile forfeit of UNTIMELY death.

Fear = in this context, a verb. It is a dynamic, emotive verb which suggests Romeo's anxious state of mind
Consequence = abstract noun. This is a powerfully suggestive abstract noun which indicates that Romeo is aware that his actions will lead to a terrible tragedy.
Revels = noun meaning parties. Shakespeare conjures a festive atmosphere with lexis that connotes partying.
Expire = a verb which means "end". Again, we have a sense that Romeo is conscious that he will die because of something that happens tonight.
Untimely = an adjective. This adjective tells us that Romeo is aware that he will die well before his time.

> CAPULET Content thee, GENTLE coz, let him alone;
> He bears him like a PORTLY gentleman;
> And, to say truth, Verona brags of him
> To be a VIRTUOUS and WELL-GOVERNED youth:

Gentle = archaic adjective. This adjective is what David Crystal calls a "false friend" because there has been a "semantic shift" in its meaning. In Shakespeare's time it meant that someone behaved in a courtly, polite manner, not that someone was "soft" "kind" etc as gentle means now.
Portly = archaic adjective which means "well-mannered".
Virtuous = adjective. This adjective suggests that Romeo is morally good. This adjective is particularly significant in the mouth of Capulet who is, of course, from an opposing family to Romeo's; this means that Romeo's reputation for being morally good must be well-known.
Well-governed = compound adjective means "disciplined", in control of himself. This adjective is possibly somewhat ironic in the context of the play because Romeo appears to be anything but disciplined at certain junctures: when he kills Tybalt, tries to kill himself in front of Friar Lawrence etc.

Focus on characterizations: who said the following and what do we learn about the characters from these quotes?

> If ever you disturb our streets again,
> Your lives shall pay the forfeit of the peace.

The Prince tells the warring families that he will execute anyone who fights again; we have a sense here that the Prince is desperate to establish peace and has to resort to the most extreme measures to do this.

> She will not stay the siege of loving terms,
> Nor bide the encounter of assailing eyes,
> Nor ope her lap to saint-seducing gold:

Romeo has "sieged" Rosaline with loving words, and has assailed her with his eyes, in other words followed her everywhere, and he has offered her gold to sleep with him. We gain the impression of an immature, slightly unhinged person who is obsessed with Rosaline here.

> A man, young lady! lady, such a man
> As all the world--why, he's a man of wax.

The Nurse is talking to Juliet about Paris, celebrating his perfect qualities: he is a "man of wax". This quote is significant later on because the Nurse tells Juliet that Romeo is a "dishclout" (Act 3, Sc V) compared with Paris and that she should marry him, even though she is already married to Romeo.

> I was your mother much upon these years
> That you are now a maid.
> Well, think of marriage now; younger than you,
> Here in Verona, ladies of esteem,
> Are made already mothers: by my count

Lady Capulet tells us that she had already married Capulet when she was thirteen and was a mother. Some actors playing Lady Capulet have her say these lines in a bitter fashion, indicating that she isn't happy in her marriage.

> By giving liberty unto thine eyes;
> Examine other beauties.

Benvolio tells Romeo to give "freedom" to his eyes and look at beauties other than Rosaline at Capulet's feast, which, of course, Romeo does.

> My only love sprung from my only hate!
> Too early seen unknown, and known too late!

Juliet learns that Romeo is a Montague and uses *antithesis* to emphasize the confusion and shock she feels: "love" and "hate"; "unknown" and "known"; "early" and "late". The antithesis highlights her awareness of the contrast of her feelings for Romeo and what the Capulets feel towards him: she feels "love" and they feel "hate".

Focus on staging: write about how these quotes might be acted out on stage or film, discussing any versions you've seen.

ABRAHAM Do you bite your thumb at us, sir?

The two groups of servants may well be standing looking at each other aggressively at this point and "biting their thumbs" at each other, but with a clear "line" demarking their respective territories.

> ROMEO O, she doth teach the torches to burn bright!
> It seems she hangs upon the cheek of night
> Like a rich jewel in an Ethiope's ear;
> Beauty too rich for use, for earth too dear!

Romeo has seen Juliet at the feast. One way to stage this might to have the rest of the actors freeze as they are dancing etc while Romeo gives the speech, gazing adoringly in Juliet's direction at the opposite side of the stage. Weis writes: "Staging the lovers' first encounter, with the intense intimacy of its rhetoric in the thick of the dance, poses a major problem of choreography". She points out that in the Zeffirelli version, Romeo and Juliet commune on the outside of the dance, behind a pillar (William Shakespeare, René Weis, 2012, p. 173)

> JULIET You kiss by the book.

Romeo and Juliet will probably have taken off their masks and will be kissing each other behind a pillar or in a corner where they can't be seen, possibly at the front of the stage.

Focus on imagery: fill in the gaps for the following quotes, then check your answer with Shakespeare's; why do you think Shakespeare made these word choices?

> ROMEO Where shall we dine? O me! What **fray** was here?
> Yet tell me not, for I have heard it all.
> Here's much to do with hate, but more with love.
> Why, then, O **brawling love**! O **loving hate**!
> O any thing, of nothing first create!

Romeo is talking about the "fray" or feud here and uses oxymoron to describe his own feeling towards Rosaline as "brawling love" and "loving hate" because he believes he loves her but that she despises him.

> ROMEO O, she doth teach the **torches** to burn bright!
> It seems she hangs upon the cheek of night
> Like a rich **jewel** in an Ethiope's ear;
> Beauty too rich for use, for earth too dear!
> So shows a snowy **dove** trooping with crows,
> As yonder lady o'er her fellows shows.

Romeo compares Juliet to a powerful beacon of light which is showing the other "torches" how to burn more brightly. He uses the simile of comparing her to an expensive ear-ring hanging in an Ethiopian's ear; the simile suggests both her "value" and how she makes everyone else look "black". Perhaps a more politically acceptable comparison for us now is when he compares her to a "snowy dove" amongst black crows. Again the imagery emphasizes how she stands out sharply in comparison to everyone else: her beauty, which appears to embody a moral brilliance, makes everyone else look very ordinary.

> JULIET Good pilgrim, you do wrong your hand too much,
> Which mannerly devotion shows in this;
> For saints have hands that **pilgrims'** hands do touch,
> And palm to palm is holy **palmers'** kiss.

Both Romeo and Juliet use religious imagery when talking to each other, comparing themselves to "pilgrims" who are paying devotions to each other; this gives their love both a playful and devotional quality. The play on words regarding "palmers" and "palms" is a reference to the face that pilgrims returning from the Holy Land carried a palm leaf and so were called "palmers" (William Shakespeare, John Seeley, 1993, p. 68). Pilgrims often kiss the shrines they worship; in this case, both Romeo and Juliet kiss the shrines they worship: each other's bodies. The imagery is highly ornate and playful, but carries with an undertow of very strong emotion, the sorts of emotions that pilgrims feel when worshipping God.

Focus on rhythm and rhyme: put these quotes into the correct verse form, punctuate them and explain the rhythmic effects of the lines.

> TYBALT I will withdraw: but this intrusion shall
> Now seeming sweet convert to bitter gall

Tybalt leaves the stage in Act 1, Sc V with this couplet which contains the rhymes "shall" and "gall"; the effect of the half-rhyme emphasizes the word "gall", meaning poison, thus highlighting his hatred of Romeo and the idea that he will have his deadly revenge. The rhythm of the lines is not fully iambic, indicating his disturbed state of mind:

> I WILL withDRAW: BUT this inTRUSion SHALL
> Now SEEMing SWEET conVERT to BITTer GALL

So we have two iambs which are disrupted by the caesura in the middle of the line, making the actor pause before he continues. The heavy beat on "BUT" indicates how strongly Tybalt feels that he must get his revenge. This line is disrupted and not regular in rhythm but the line that follows it is perfectly iambic, showing us now that Tybalt has decided to get revenge, he can now speak in a "regular" rhythm: thus showing us that violence is his habitual, "regular" mode of thought.

> ROMEO Is she a Capulet?
> O dear account! my life is my foe's debt.

This rhyming couplet shows Romeo's shock at learning that Juliet is a Capulet. The rhyme of "Capulet" and "debt" emphasizes how much Romeo feels that he owes the Capulets for producing Juliet; there is a dawning awareness here that his relationship with his enemies can never be the same. The line has a very irregular rhythm because the question is only half of a proper line of blank verse, containing only THREE stresses:

> Is SHE a CAPuLET?
> O DEAR acCOUNT! my LIFE is my FOE's DEBT.

The stresses falling on "foe" and "debts" slows down the reading of the line, forcing the audience and the actor to reflect deeply upon these two monosyllables.

The **evaluation questions** are really a matter of personal judgement backed up with evidence; there are no right or wrong answers.

Act 2, Prologue

Important vocabulary: Gapes = wants
breathe = speak
Tempering = making soft
Extremity = a bad thing, something severe

Activities 2.1

Thematic questions: Why do people fall out of love with certain people and fall in love with others? Why do think love comes very suddenly for certain people?

Read the Prologue for Act 2.

Fill-in-the-blanks (answers below): The Prologue talks how about Romeo was once in love with ---- but now is in love with another person. The problem is that she is the daughter of his ---- and she doesn't have the power to --- as freely as he does.

Questions: What does the Prologue say are the problems that are stopping Romeo and Juliet from loving one another? Why did Shakespeare write this prologue, do you think?

Analysis: The Prologue raises a problem that Juliet never talks about: her lack of freedom to do as she pleases. It is, like the Prologue to

Act 1, a sonnet but it doesn't tell us what is going to happen in the act. Instead, its last line raises a key theme in the play: extremes of passion.
Creative response: Write a story: 'Prisoner in my own home.'
Act it out: In small groups, get someone to read out the poem, and others to mime the key actions talked about.
Analytical response: What purposes do the two prologues serve in the play? Why did Shakespeare not write any more?
Fill-in-the-blanks answers: Rosaline, enemy, move.

Act 2, SCENE I. A lane by the wall of Capulet's orchard.

Important vocabulary: earth = body
Conjure = make appear like magic
Venus = Goddess of love
Befits = suits
Medlar = a small round fruit which was nicknamed "open arse"
Poperin = a pear (Roma Gill, William Shakespeare, 1982, pp. 31-33)

Activities 2.2

Thematic questions: Why do friends make fun of each other? Why can the jokes friends make be very upsetting?

Read the whole scene of Act 2, Sc I.

Fill-in-the-blanks (answers below): Romeo doesn't want to be with his ---- because he wants to find ----, where his heart his. Mercutio and Benvolio think Romeo has gone looking for -----; Mercutio jokes that he can "magick" up Rosaline and excite Romeo's ----. He makes very --- jokes about what he thinks Romeo wants to do with Rosaline.

Flow chart: Devise a chart of the main events in this section.

Questions: Why is Mercutio calling for Romeo? Who does he think Romeo wants to see? How does he make fun of Romeo here?

Analysis: The dramatic irony is very strong here because Mercutio and Benvolio are mistaken in thinking that Romeo is still in love with Rosaline. Mercutio cements his reputation as an obscene joker here by suggesting that Romeo wants to be a "penis-shaped pear" that enters the "arse" of Rosaline. This sort of humour is often "bowdlerized" from Shakespeare: <u>Bowdler</u> was a Victorian critic who tried to cut out all the rude parts of Shakespeare because he was a strict Christian. It appears that people's attitudes towards sex were different in Shakespeare's day: he made sexual jokes which would be considered unacceptable today, especially by religious people. *Romeo and Juliet* is full of very rude jokes, mostly said by Mercutio and the Nurse.

Creative response: Write a story called 'Rude' which is about someone who is very rude.

Act it out: Role-play two friends being rude about their other friend's girlfriend/boyfriend. Or act out the scene.

Analytical response: Write an essay entitled: "Shakespeare: too rude for school?" in which you argue for and against studying the "rude" sections in Shakespeare.

Fill-in-the blanks answers: friends, Juliet, Rosaline, desire, rude.

Act 2, SCENE II. Capulet's orchard.

Important vocabulary: her maid = in classical mythology, Diana was Goddess of the moon and because she was also Goddess of virginity, all virgins were her servants.
Wherefore = why
Doff = shed, get rid of
Prorogued = put off, postponed
Fain would I = I would like to
Jove = Jupiter, chief of the God, who did not take lovers' promises seriously and laughed when they were broken
Contract = engagement
I would = I wish
Bent = intention
Tassel-gentle = the most noble of the falcons
Nyas = a young hawk
Wanton = playful
Gyves = chains
Fleckled = dappled with red blotches like a drunk's face
Titan's wheels = Hyperion, the God of the sun, was sometimes called Titan. He pulled the sun across the sky every day (Roma Gill, William Shakespeare, 1982, pp. 33-40)

Activities 2.3

Thematic questions: Why are the night and the moon associated with love and romance?

Read Act 2, Sc II lines 1-32.

Fill-in-the-blanks (answers below): Romeo compares Juliet to the --- because he feels she emanates a powerful inner light; this is a running "----" throughout the play, Juliet is consistently connected to visions of ----. He feels her eyes are ---- to him. He compares her eyes to --- and imagines what might happen if her eyes swapped places with the ----: the birds would think it was the ----- and begin to sing.

Flow chart: Devise a chart of the main events in this section.

Questions: Why is Juliet like the sun for Romeo? What does Romeo feel Juliet's eyes are doing? What does he compare her eyes to and why?

Analysis: Romeo delivers a powerful soliloquy here which was very much a convention for plays of the time: the central protagonist says in vivid, poetic imagery his feelings of love for a woman. We see Romeo "thinking on his feet" in the speech, which is what makes it so alive: he begins by comparing Juliet to the sun and then imagines that the moon is "envious" of her power, this then leads him to think that Juliet needs to "cast" off the "vestal livery" (the virginal clothing) that the moon has dressed her in. Thus we can see Romeo's strong physical attraction towards Juliet because he is already thinking that Juliet needs to lose her virginity to him. His sexual references contrast very strongly with Mercutio's, which were rude and insulting to women; both Romeo and Juliet talk vividly about sex but in a poetic, sensitive fashion with the best speech about sex coming from Juliet in her "Gallop apace" speech in Act 3, Scene II.

Creative response: Have a go at writing some love poetry in which you use some of the ideas in Romeo's soliloquy comparing a loved one to an object that other objects are jealous of, e.g. a fantastic blue sky that some clouds are jealous of, or an amazing mobile phone which other mobile phones are jealous of. Or do a slideshow which illustrates the imagery in his speech, i.e. stars, sun, etc.

Analytical response: How does Shakespeare make Romeo's discussion of his love for Juliet interesting?

Act it out: Have your group share Romeo's lines and mime the key images spoken about; the sun, the moon etc.

Answers to fill-in-the-blanks: sun, "motif", light, speaking, stars, stars, daytime.

Activities 2.4

Thematic questions: What do you think of your name? What does it tell people about you in terms of your ethnicity, social class, gender, age etc? Would you change it for someone you love?

Read Act 2, Sc II lines 33-141.

Fill-in-the-blanks (answers below): Juliet wonders why Romeo is called by his name because it is his name which is stopping them being as ---; their families are ---- ----. Romeo ---- her because he has been hiding in the ---- underneath the balcony and suddenly speaks, saying that he will take another ----. Juliet is concerned that Romeo will think she is too easily --- over because she has readily admitted her ----- to him, but the main reason why she has done this is because she has been speaking to ---- and didn't know he was ----. Romeo is ------ because he wants them to ----- to marry, which Juliet immediately agrees to. She then takes back that promise so that they can make the ---- again. Both lovers are ----- for different reasons: Juliet is worried their love is too ----- , and Romeo feels it is too like a -----.

Flow chart: Devise a chart of the main events in this section.

Questions: Why is Juliet worried about Romeo's name? Why does Romeo startle her when he speaks? What does he say he will do with his name? Why is Juliet worried that Romeo will think she is too easily won over? Why does Romeo feel "unsatisfied"? What do the two lovers promise to do? Why are both lovers worried about their love affair?

Analysis: Shakespeare maintains interest in this long "love scene" by making it both dramatic and poetic. The scene is dramatic because Juliet is surprised by Romeo's listening to her and doesn't quite know initially who has been listening to her. However, she quickly recognizes Romeo's voice. The scene is poetic because it explores some important images: there's a discussion about what a name means to a person, whether it is that person or whether their body and personality is more important than their name. Both the lovers agree that the family name is unimportant if two people love each other: love defines you, not your family. We see them quickly promising to marry each other.

Creative response: Write a love scene between two lovers in which they agree to either marry/live together or run away together.

Act it out: Role-play two lovers talking in secret and promising to love each other. Or act out these lines with suitable actions.

Analytical response: How does Shakespeare portray love in this part of the scene?

Answers to fill-in-the-blanks: one, mortal enemies, startles, dark, name, won, devotion, herself, there, unsatisfied, promise, promise, worried, sudden, dream.

Activities 2.5

Thematic questions: Why do people agree to marry very suddenly? Do you agree with sex before marriage? Do you think marriage should be religious?

Read Act 2, Sc II lines 132 to the end of the scene.

Fill-in-the-blanks (answers below): Juliet says she will send a messenger tomorrow to ask the --- and ---- of the wedding. Juliet compares Romeo to a "tassel-gentle" or peregrine falcon, the bird of ---- (Gibson, 2006, p. 60). Later Romeo calls Juliet his "nyas", a young fledgling --- (Gibson, 2006, p. 60). These are both birds of --- and may express the two lover's desire to "---" each other. Romeo wants to sleep in order to --- of Juliet.

Flow chart: Devise a chart of the main events in this section.

Questions: Why does Juliet return to the balcony? What does she ask Romeo to do? Why do the two lovers compare themselves to birds? Why does Romeo want to go to sleep?

Analysis: Shakespeare extends the love scene by showing us how the lovers are both thinking practically and wanting to constantly be in each other's company. As we saw in Act 1, Sc V, we see them "playing off" the images each one produces; this is particularly noticeable in the playful way they compare themselves to birds of prey.

Creative response: Write a scene in which two lovers say goodbye to each other. Think of reasons why they might have to say goodbye and show their reluctance to part.

Analytical response: What imagery do the two lovers use in order to express their love for each other?

Act it out: Mime this whole scene in groups of three (Romeo, Juliet, the Nurse) and leave out all the words.

GCSE question: Remind yourself of Act 2 scene 2 in the text and in one or more performed versions of the play.

Explore the ways in which Romeo and Juliet are presented in this scene and elsewhere in Shakespeare's play, and in the performed version(s).

You should consider: the thoughts and feelings Romeo and Juliet express; the ways other characters react to them; what makes the relationship between Romeo and Juliet so moving.

Answers to fill-in-the-blanks: time, place, princes, hawk, prey, devour, dream.

Act 2, SCENE III. Friar Lawrence's cell.

Important vocabulary: osier cage = willow basket
Baleful = harmful
Mickle = much
Canker = cancer, sickness
Ghostly = holy, spiritual
Intercession = prayer, petition
Riddling = confusing
Brine = salt water, tears (Roma Gill, William Shakespeare, 1982, pp. 40-43)

Activities 2.6

Thematic questions: Who are the wise people in your life? What makes them wise?

Read Act 2, Sc III lines 1-26.

Fill-in-the-blanks (answers below): Shakespeare introduces us to Friar Lawrence here through the use of a long ------, establishing a few characteristics that are important to him: his ----- character, his knowledge of ---- and ----, and his ------. The Friar says the earth is both like a ---- and a ----: it is the place where all dead things return to, but the place from which all new life arises.

Flow chart: Devise a chart of the main events in this section.

Questions: Why do you think Shakespeare wrote this long soliloquy for Friar Lawrence? What does Friar Lawrence compare the earth to and why?

Analysis: Friar Lawrence is a complex, multi-faceted character who can be presented as either very benevolent (good) or someone who is slightly sinister. The Baz Luhrmann (DiCaprio, 1996) version emphasizes the Friar's essentially good nature but we also see a darker side to him: he is growing marijuana plants and seems a little deranged. In contrast, the Zeffirelli version (Zeffirelli, 1968) turns the Friar into a well-meaning Irish monk, who tries his best but is rather weak-willed.

Act it out: Have one person read the lines and the other mime the images, add sound effects where appropriate.

Creative response: Write a description of a wise man who is also quite sinister.

Further research: Find out about what people thought of the Catholic Church, which Friars were part of, in Shakespeare's England.

Fill-in-the blanks answers: soliloquy, religious, herbs, potions, philosophizing, tomb, womb.

Activities 2.7

Thematic questions: Who do you trust to tell your problems to? Why do you trust them? What makes them good people to talk to?

Read Act 2, Sc III lines 27 to the end of the scene.

Fill-in-the-blanks (answers below): Friar Lawrence thinks that Romeo has spent the night with -----. He is ---- that Romeo has fallen in love with another woman because he has counselled Romeo so much about Rosaline, watching him --- about the fact that he can't have her. However, he ---- to marry Romeo and Juliet because he believes this might end the ---- between the two families. He advises Romeo to take the romance -----.

Flow chart: Devise a chart of the main events in this section.

Questions: Why is Friar Lawrence shocked by Romeo? Why does he agree to marry Romeo and Juliet? What advice does he give Romeo?

Analysis: We learn here that Romeo has a close relationship with Friar Lawrence and has talked to him about things that he wouldn't talk to his parents about: the Friar knows all about Romeo's love for Rosaline which his parents did not know about. We see here how the Friar is shocked by the fact that Romeo has switched from loving Rosaline to Juliet so suddenly. However, the Friar comes to see that the marriage between the two lovers will ultimately be for the good because it will end the hatred or "rancor" between the two families. There's a grim irony here because the Friar is proved right, but at a terrible cost: the families end their feud after Romeo and Juliet die. We know this to be the case because of what we have been told in the Prologue.

Act it out: Role play a scene between a parental figure listening to a teenager talk about his/her love life and is shocked, but ultimately comes to appreciate the teenager's point of view.

Creative response: Write a scene in which an older person (a teacher/parent/priest etc) is shocked at the behavior of a younger person (a pupil, child etc).

Further research: Do some further research into how and why teenagers fall in love.

Fill-in-the-blanks answers: Rosaline, shocked, cry, agrees, hatred, slowly.

Act 2, SCENE IV. A street.

Important vocabulary: blind bow-boy = Cupid
Butt-shaft = arrow
Prick-song = printed music
Pox = plague
Antic = stupid, absurd
Blade = sword
Dowdy = plain looking woman
Hildings = prostitutes
Slop = wide trousers
Counter-feit = cheat
Pink = perfect example and/or pattern made with holes in leather
Goose = fool
Cheverel = soft, stretchy leather
Bauble = coxcomb, which is the decorated stick of a clown/jester
Prick = point/penis
Bawd = keeper of a brothel or a hare
Hoar = old but also a pun on "whore" (prostitute)
Ropery = joking about
Scurvy knave = rotten man
Deal double = cheat
Shrift = confession
Lay knife abroad = in Shakespeare's time people brought their own knives to dinner and laid them on the table to show they wanted food
Clout = sheet/cloth (Roma Gill, William Shakespeare, 1982, pp. 44-52)

Activities 2.8

Thematic questions: What kind of person annoys or irritates you? Why do you think this type of person can irritate people?

Read Act 2, Sc IV lines 1- 140.

Fill-in-the-blanks (answers below): Benvolio tells Mercutio that Tybalt has sent a ---- to Romeo's home; both Mercutio and Benvolio believe it is a ------- to fight. Benvolio believes Romeo will fight if he is "dared" to, but Mercutio says that Romeo has already been "-----" by Rosaline's "black eye". Mercutio tells us that Tybalt is a very ----- swordsman but he is rather --------. Mercutio has fun in ------- the Nurse, suggesting with a number of puns that she is a "bawd" – a female ---- – and a prostitute herself; he sings a song which puns on the words "hare" and "hoar", thereby suggesting the Nurse is a "----- -----".

Flow chart: Devise a chart of the main events in this section.

Questions: What does Benvolio say Tybalt has sent to Romeo? What do Benvolio and Mercutio say Romeo will do about Tybalt's challenge? When Romeo appears, what do he and Mercutio joke about? How and why does Mercutio make fun of the Nurse?

Analysis: We see just how "yobbish" Mercutio is here: he appears to have nothing but contempt for Tybalt's fashionable fencing techniques, he trades rude jokes with Romeo and takes real delight in humiliating the Nurse. He is though frequently portrayed as a sympathetic character both in the Luhrmann film (DiCaprio, 1996), where he is played as a cross-dressing homosexual who has a crush on Romeo, and in the Zeffirelli film (Zeffirelli, 1968) where he is shown to be "one of the lads". The Zeffirelli film is particularly good at showing the world of Verona: its heat and the apparent lack of anything for young people to do.

Creative response: Write a story called 'The Yob' or 'Rude' in which you show a young person being rude to older people.

Analytical response: Research and investigate the puns in this scene, looking up their meanings and thinking why Shakespeare's audiences might have found them so funny.

Act it out: Role play a group of young people telling each rude jokes, and making fun of an older person.

GCSE question: *Explore the ways in which Romeo and Mercutio are presented in this scene and elsewhere in the play, and in the performed versions.* Consider: the thoughts and feelings Romeo and Mercutio express; the way other characters react to them; what makes the relationship between Romeo and Mercutio so important.

Answers to fill-in-the-blanks: letter, challenge, stabbed, skilful, effeminate, mocking, pimp, "hairy whore".

Activities 2.9

Read Act 2, Sc IV lines 141 to the end of the scene.

Thematic questions: Have you ever made secret arrangements in your life? What was it like? Do you like having secrets? What is your attitude towards secrets?

Fill-in-the-blanks (answers below): The Nurse is very ---- at the way Mercutio has treated her and the ------ names he has called her, suggesting that she is a woman of ---- morals, a "flirt-gill". Romeo says that Mercutio ---- more in a minute than he would ever -- in a month, in other words his bark is bigger than his ---. Romeo says that Juliet needs to come to ------ that afternoon where he will marry her. After that Romeo's servant will bring the Nurse a --- ----- that will enable Romeo to climb up to Juliet's bedroom at ----.

Flow chart: Devise a chart of the main events in this section.

Questions: Why is the Nurse so upset with Mercutio and how does Romeo excuse his behavior? What does the Nurse warn Romeo he must not do? What arrangements does Romeo say he has made for the wedding and after it?

Analysis: The Nurse is rightly very annoyed by Mercutio's treatment of her and his suggestion that she is a whore; Romeo though just sees this as Mercutio's joke. Thus we can see that the two generations don't really understand each other and are potentially in conflict; this is a running theme throughout the play where the older generation consistently comes into conflict with the younger. We see it when Romeo argues with Friar Lawrence after he is banished, and most forcibly when Juliet refuses to marry Paris and incurs the anger of her father, Capulet.

Creative response: Write the Nurse's diary about what she thinks of the situation: her views on Juliet, Paris, Romeo and Mercutio.

Act it out: Improvise a scene which has a lover giving an important message to an older person about his/her loved one.

Further research: Find out more about the conflict between the older and younger generations in the play.

Fill-in-the blanks answers: upset, insulting, loose, speaks, do, bite, confession, rope ladder, night.

Act 2, SCENE V. Capulet's orchard.

Important vocabulary: Perchance = perhaps
Nimble-pinioned doves = quick flying doves, who in classical mythology, drew the chariot of Venus, the goddess of love
Jaunt = long trip
Wanton = uncontrolled, passionate (Roma Gill, William Shakespeare, 1982, pp. 52-54)

Activities 2.10

Thematic questions: When have you been very impatient in your life? Why were you impatient? Do you think old and young people understand each other?

Read Act 2, Sc V the whole scene.

    Fill-in-the-blanks (answers below): Juliet is very ----- at the beginning of the scene to hear the news from Romeo and really wants to know what he's ----. She believes that the older generation don't ----- the younger generation because the Nurse is so --- at conveying messages between the lovers; she feels that the older generation have little understanding of what it means to be in ---. When the Nurse appears however Juliet is very nice to her, calling her "honey" Nurse and is desperate to hear the Nurse's news. The Nurse teases Juliet and holds back from giving her the important ---; Juliet gets very frustrated and ------- with the Nurse, who appears to ---- the power she has over Juliet. Eventually, the Nurse tells Juliet that when she goes to confession she will be -----.
    Flow chart: Devise a chart of the main events in this section.
    Questions: Why is Juliet so impatient at the beginning of the scene? Why does she feel that the Nurse and the older generation as a whole don't understand her? How does her treatment of the Nurse contrast with the way she has been talking about the Nurse? How does the Nurse wind up Juliet? What news does the Nurse eventually tell Juliet?
    Analysis: Shakespeare develops the theme of the conflict between the older and younger generations here with Juliet's soliloquy which reveals her impatience with the Nurse's lateness and her lack of understanding as to what it means to be in love. The tone though, like the previous scene, is comic and "light touch": much comedy is generated when Juliet repeatedly questions the Nurse about what news she has and only receives complaints about her health and strange comments back. Shakespeare uses dramatic irony to comic effect here because we and the Nurse know what Romeo has said and know that Juliet need not be so anxious.
    Creative response: Write a story/poem/play called "Waiting to hear" in which a teenager is waiting to hear some important news and is very impatient to hear it. Describe the person's response when they finally hear the news.
    Act it out: Improvise a scene between an older parental figure talking to a younger person about his/her loved one. The older person should know some vital information about the other lover which he/she is reluctant to reveal.
    Analytical response: How does Shakespeare generate comedy in this scene?
    Answers to fill-in-the-blanks: impatient, said, understand, slow, love, news, irritable, enjoy, married.

Act 2, SCENE VI. Friar Lawrence's cell.

Important vocabulary: Countervail = equal
Tardy = late
Wanton = playful
Conceit = imagination
Sum up sum = add up the total (Roma Gill, William Shakespeare, 1982, pp. 55-56)

Activities 2.11

Thematic questions: What are your attitudes towards weddings? Do you think they are important? Do you think secret weddings are a good idea? Do you think it is good to be very passionate in a marriage or not?

Read Act 2, Sc VI the whole scene.

Fill-in-the-blanks (answers below): Romeo feels he will not be afraid of ----- after he has married Juliet; he can die ----- just knowing he has spent a minute in her company. Friar Lawrence warns Romeo against loving too ----- because it can lead to two people "exploding" like mixing ---- and --------. Juliet finds Romeo's analogy about his love in which he compares it to dancing, air and music far too --------- and ------. She herself can't begin to put into ----- what she feels.

Flow chart: Devise a chart of the main events in this section.

Questions: When and why is Romeo not afraid of death? What does Friar Lawrence warn Romeo about at the beginning of the scene? What happens when the two lovers meet? Why does Juliet criticize Romeo's way of talking about their love?

Analysis: This short scene before the marriage explores two important themes. First, Friar Lawrence discusses the dangers of feeling and acting too violently and in too an extreme a fashion. This is a running theme in the play: the young people in the play – and some of the older generation – let their feelings "get the better of them" and don't act rationally. We see this happen to Mercutio and Romeo in the next scene when they get involved with fighting the Capulets, and we see it with the two lovers in their responses to being separated from one another. You could argue that the whole play is a warning against the dangers of excessive, irrational emotions: the feud is irrational and violent, as is, you could argue, Romeo and Juliet's love. The second theme that's explored is the power of love and the difficulty of putting "real love" into words; the failure of language to suggest feelings and emotions. This is a point that Juliet raises when criticizing Romeo's flowery explanation of his love.

Creative response: Write a story called 'The Secret Wedding'. Or write a character's diary for this scene: Romeo, Juliet, and Friar Lawrence.

Act it out: Improvise a scene working in a group of four in which two lovers get married in secret.

Analytical response: Write a speech for your class: "Can feelings be put into words?"

Answers to fill-in-the-blanks: death, happy, violently, fire gunpowder, complicated, flowery, words.

Looking Back At Act 2

Focus on structure: put these quotes in the order they happen in the play and write about why Shakespeare ordered them in this way.

NURSE Then hie you hence to Friar Lawrence's cell;
There stays a husband to make you a wife:
Now comes the wanton blood up in your cheeks,
They'll be in scarlet straight at any news.

ROMEO And stay, good nurse, behind the abbey wall:
Within this hour my man shall be with thee
And bring thee cords made like a tackled stair;
Which to the high top-gallant of my joy
Must be my convoy in the secret night.

ROMEO The exchange of thy love's faithful vow for mine.

FRIAR LAWRENCE In one respect I'll thy assistant be;
For this alliance may so happy prove,
To turn your households' rancour to pure love.

JULIET O Romeo, Romeo! wherefore art thou Romeo?
Deny thy father and refuse thy name;

Follow up after you've checked your answers: using a narrator who explains the missing parts of the story, either write up a "story" version of these quotes or work in a group and act out these lines, with a narrator or narrators explaining the story of the Act as a whole and the actors reading these key lines with real expression.

Focus on grammar and lexis: what are the word classes of the following lexis in **CAPS** and why are they significant words?

MERCUTIO I conjure THEE by Rosaline's bright eyes,

By her high FOREHEAD and her SCARLET lip,
By her fine FOOT, straight LEG and quivering THIGH

Focus on characterizations: who said the following and what do we learn about the characters from these quotes?

If thou dost love, pronounce it faithfully:
Or if thou think'st I am too quickly won,
I'll frown and be perverse an say thee nay,
So thou wilt woo; but else, not for the world.

Holy Saint Francis, what a change is here!
Is Rosaline, whom thou didst love so dear,
So soon forsaken? young men's love then lies
Not truly in their hearts, but in their eyes.

More than prince of cats, I can tell you. O, he is
the courageous captain of compliments. He fights as
you sing prick-song, keeps time, distance, and
proportion;

Had she affections and warm youthful blood,
She would be as swift in motion as a ball;
My words would bandy her to my sweet love,
And his to me: But old folks, many feign as they were dead;
Unwieldy, slow, heavy and pale as lead.

These violent delights have violent ends
And in their triumph die, like fire and powder,
Which as they kiss consume: the sweetest honey
Is loathsome in his own deliciousness

Follow up after you've checked your answers: Using these quotes as a starting point, "hotseat" the relevant characters, i.e interview them in pairs about what they are thinking and feeling at these moments.

Focus on staging: write about how these quotes might be acted out on stage or film, discussing any versions you've seen.

ROMEO O, wilt thou leave me so unsatisfied?

JULIET If that thy bent of love be honourable,
Thy purpose marriage, send me word to-morrow,
By one that I'll procure to come to thee,
Where and what time thou wilt perform the rite;

MERCUTIO A bawd, a bawd, a bawd! so ho!

NURSE Now, afore God, I am so vexed, that every part about
me quivers. Scurvy knave! Pray you, sir, a word:
and as I told you, my young lady bade me inquire you
out; what she bade me say, I will keep to myself:
but first let me tell ye, if ye should lead her into
a fool's paradise, as they say, it were a very gross
kind of behaviour,

Focus on imagery: fill in the gaps for the following quotes, then check your answer with Shakespeare's; why do you think Shakespeare made these word choices?

ROMEO Her eye discourses; I will answer it.
I am too bold, 'tis not to me she speaks:
Two of the fairest stars in all the heaven,
Having some business, do entreat her eyes
To twinkle in their spheres till they return.

Focus on rhythm: put these quotes into the correct verse form, punctuate them and explain their poetic effects.

Act 2, Sc II JULIET o romeo, romeo wherefore art thou
Romeo deny thy father and refuse thy name

Answers

Focus on structure: this is the correct order for the quotes

ROMEO The exchange of thy love's faithful vow for mine.

FRIAR LAWRENCE In one respect I'll thy assistant be;
For this alliance may so happy prove,
To turn your households' rancour to pure love.

ROMEO And stay, good nurse, behind the abbey wall:
Within this hour my man shall be with thee
And bring thee cords made like a tackled stair;
Which to the high top-gallant of my joy
Must be my convoy in the secret night.

NURSE Then hie you hence to Friar Lawrence's cell;
There stays a husband to make you a wife:
Now comes the wanton blood up in your cheeks,
They'll be in scarlet straight at any news.

These quotes show how the whole of Act 2 is structured around the issue of Romeo and Juliet's marriage: every scene, every speech has some connection with their marriage. The feud, which had dominated Act 1, is rarely mentioned. Romeo's request to "exchange" vows means that he is asking to marry Juliet. When Friar Lawrence learns about Romeo's intentions he is shocked at first, but then agrees to the marriage because he believes that it may "turn" the "rancour" or hatred of the families into "pure love". Romeo meets the Nurse in the market square and makes arrangements so that he can sleep with Juliet on his wedding night; this involves his servant giving the Nurse a rope ladder later on. When the Nurse returns home, she finally tells Juliet that when Juliet goes to confession, she will be married to Romeo there: the Nurse jokes that she can see Juliet's cheeks turning red at this news.

Focus on grammar and lexis:

> MERCUTIO I conjure THEE by Rosaline's bright eyes,
> By her high FOREHEAD and her SCARLET lip,
> By her fine FOOT, straight LEG and quivering THIGH

Thee = archaic second person pronoun singular. The use of "thee" here is important because Mercutio is not being polite in the way he talks about Romeo, if he was being polite, he would have used the pronoun "you" which was usually considered the proper way for one gentleman to address another gentleman.
Forehead, foot, leg, thigh = concrete nouns. These concrete nouns evoke Rosaline's body in a very sexual fashion, objectifying her as a sexual plaything.
Scarlet = adjective. This adjective has heavily sexual connotations in the context; the colour indicates both sexual desire and availability.

Focus on characterizations: who said the following and what do we learn about the characters from these quotes?

> If thou dost love, pronounce it faithfully:
> Or if thou think'st I am too quickly won,
> I'll frown and be perverse an say thee nay,
> So thou wilt woo; but else, not for the world.

This is Juliet talking to Romeo in Act 2, Sc II, imploring Romeo to be sincere with her and say in good faith that he loves her. She is also worried that he will think that she is "too quickly won"; she says that if he feels this way, she'll play hard to get by frowning and saying no to him, but if he doesn't think this of her, she wouldn't behave like this for all the world.

> Holy Saint Francis, what a change is here!
> Is Rosaline, whom thou didst love so dear,
> So soon forsaken? young men's love then lies
> Not truly in their hearts, but in their eyes.

Friar Lawrence is very shocked at Romeo's switching of affections from Rosaline to Juliet; he states that young men don't love with their hearts but with their eyes; in other words, they're only interested in the next attractive girl.

> More than prince of cats, I can tell you. O, he is
> the courageous captain of compliments. He fights as
> you sing prick-song, keeps time, distance, and
> proportion;

Mercutio is talking with Benvolio about Tybalt and is making fun of him, saying that Tybalt is truly brave when it comes to "sucking up" to people with "compliments". He fights in a very particular way like a singer reading notes from the page ("prick-song") rather than a singer who sings from memory. In other words, he is very artificial and forced in the way he fights.

> Had she affections and warm youthful blood,
> She would be as swift in motion as a ball;
> My words would bandy her to my sweet love,
> And his to me: But old folks, many feign as they were dead;
> Unwieldy, slow, heavy and pale as lead.

Here Juliet is complaining about the Nurse and saying that if she was young, she come and tell her the news about Romeo's marriage arrangements very quickly, but she feels that "old folks" are almost like the "dead": very slow and lacking in passion "pale as lead".

> "These violent delights have violent ends
> And in their triumph die, like fire and powder,
> Which as they kiss consume: the sweetest honey
> Is loathsome in his own deliciousness"

Just before Friar Lawrence marries Romeo and Juliet at the end of the act, he warns them that if they are too passionate with each other, if they love each other "too physically", they will come to a violent end because it will be like mixing gunpowder and fire. If they indulge in what they like too much – i.e. sex – they will end up hating it, finding it "loathsome", because they grow sick of it like someone eating too much sweet honey.

Focus on staging: write about how these quotes might be acted out on stage or film, discussing any versions you've seen.

ROMEO O, wilt thou leave me so unsatisfied?

This is a critical line during Act 2, Sc II because it leads to Romeo promising to marry Juliet. The film versions of the play both put heavy emphasis on it with the Zeffirelli version having Juliet look in shock at Romeo because she assumes he is asking to sleep with her (Zeffirelli, 1968). He may well be, but we never quite know. I imagine that they will be very much entwined with each other's bodies at this point on stage.

JULIET If that thy bent of love be honourable,
Thy purpose marriage, send me word to-morrow,
By one that I'll procure to come to thee,
Where and what time thou wilt perform the rite;

Juliet has gone inside and then returned; on stage, she may well have sought out Romeo as he leaving the Capulet orchard and then he will have returned to the balcony. The Zeffirelli version creates dramatic and comic tension by the way Romeo leaves and comes back again. There will be a look of concern on Juliet's face because she is very worried about getting married quickly.

MERCUTIO A bawd, a bawd, a bawd! so ho!

Mercutio has been abusing the Nurse in the market square. The Zeffirelli version has Mercutio grabbing the Nurse's head-dress and prancing around with it. His insult to the Nurse here is extreme: he is joking that she is a woman who "procures" prostitutes for young men, a "bawd".

NURSE Now, afore God, I am so vexed, that every part about
me quivers. Scurvy knave! Pray you, sir, a word:
and as I told you, my young lady bade me inquire you
out; what she bade me say, I will keep to myself:
but first let me tell ye, if ye should lead her into
a fool's paradise, as they say, it were a very gross
kind of behavior...

The Nurse is very upset about the antics of Mercutio who has abused her with his words. Then, she turns on Romeo, saying that if Romeo leads Juliet into a "fool's paradise", it would be a terrible thing. The Nurse could possibly be grabbing Romeo as she says this to indicate her strength of feeling.

Focus on imagery: fill in the gaps for the following quotes, then check your answer with Shakespeare's; why do you think Shakespeare made these word choices?

> ROMEO Her eye discourses; I will answer it.
> I am too bold, 'tis not to me she speaks:
> Two of the fairest stars in all the heaven,
> Having some business, do entreat her eyes
> To twinkle in their spheres till they return.

The imagery here is all about Juliet's eyes and how they are speaking or "discoursing" to him. However, he is not certain about this and this leads him to personify the stars in the sky as wanting Juliet's eyes to take over their role of twinkling in the sky during the day until they return the next night. Throughout the play, Juliet is associated with different forms of heavenly light and whiteness: she appears to shine with an inner, God-like light for Romeo. As a consequence, the imagery is suggestive of Juliet's beauty, her inner power and her divine radiance.

Focus on rhythm: put these quotes into the correct verse form, punctuate them and explain their poetic effects.

> JULIET O Romeo, Romeo! wherefore art thou Romeo?
> Deny thy father and refuse thy name;

The rhythm of these famous lines are very striking:
O ROMeo, ROMeo! WHEREfore ART thou ROMeo?
The effect of a passionate reading of the line means that "ROMeo" has a "falling" rhythm, with the heavy stress on ROM and two soft stresses on "eo". This gives the line its famous yearning, regretful quality. The exclamation mark creates a break or pause in the line, what is known as a caesura, and then Juliet asks the key question: why is he called Romeo? There are two trochees here, followed by the dactyl on "Romeo"; these are "falling" units of rhythm which add to the plaintive nature of Juliet's call. The next line though is more regular:
DeNY thy FATHer AND reFUSE thy NAME
Shakespeare returns to the use of iambic pentameter here as Juliet develops her thoughts on what Romeo should do to remedy the situation.

Act 3, SCENE I. A public place.

Important vocabulary: Meat = food
Draws him = draws his sword on him
Doublet = sleeveless jacket
Riband = ribbon
Fee simple = absolute possession (legal term)
Fiddle-stick = bow or sword
Livery = uniform
Villain = peasant, pleb, riff-raff (a terrible insult to a posh person like Romeo)
Devise = imagine
Pilcher = case
Forbear = stop
Sped = killed
Spleen = temper
Stout = brave
Amerce = punish
Purchase out = buy pardon for (Roma Gill, William Shakespeare, 1982, pp. 57-64)

Activities 3.1

Thematic questions: Do you think that men/boys get into more fights than women? If so, why? When someone says "be like a man" what do they mean? When someone says "you're being a woman" what do they mean? Do you think men are expected to be violent in our society, while women aren't?

Read Act 3, Sc I lines 1-54.

Fill-in-the-blanks (answers below): Mercutio makes --- of Benvolio by accusing him of being a man with a very ---- temper who easily gets into fights; quarrelling, for example, with someone who has one more hair in his beard than he has. Mercutio appears hot and bothered: even for him his joking seems ---- and irritable. Benvolio says that if he argued as much as Mercutio did, he would be ----. Tybalt arrives and says that Mercutio "-----" with Romeo, i.e. knows or plays with him. Mercutio takes offence at this word, because he feels that it makes him and Romeo sound like ------ ----. Benvolio advises them to go somewhere private where they can't be seen; they are in the ---- square at the moment.

Flow chart: Devise a chart of the main events in this section.

Questions: How does Mercutio make fun of Benvolio at the beginning of the scene? What do you think Mercutio's mood? How does Benvolio respond? Who is Tybalt looking for and why? What does Benvolio advise them to do? Why does Mercutio become upset with Tybalt?

Analysis: Here we see how Mercutio's bad temper leads to him fighting with Tybalt; we can already see at the beginning of the scene that he is taking offence at Tybalt and trying to pick a fight with him, saying he would like to have a word and a "blow" (i.e. fight) with him. His manner is highly aggressive. We can see also that Tybalt isn't particularly interested in fighting Mercutio at this point; his argument is with Romeo for gate-crashing the party. Interestingly enough, Tybalt doesn't seem to have seen Benvolio or Mercutio at the party.

Creative response: Write a short story/poem/play called 'The hot day' in which you describe in vivid detail a very hot day, similar to the weather in this scene.

Analytical response: Write an article for a magazine called 'Teenage arguments and violence' in which you explore the reasons why teenagers argue and fight with each other.

Act it out: Role play a scene in which two gangs of youths wind each other up.

Answers to fill-in-the-blanks: fun, quick, extreme, dead, "consorts", travelling musicians, public

Activities 3.2

Thematic questions: why do people blame other people for things that are actually their fault? Can you think of any times when this has happened in your own life?

Read Act 3, Sc I lines 55-108.

Fill-in-the-blanks (answers below): Tybalt is mystified by Romeo saying that he loves ---- more than he could possibly know; this is completely ------ to the way the two families talk to each other. We know the reason why: Romeo has married Tybalt's -----. Mercutio believes Romeo's gestures of love amount to a "dishonourable, vile -------"; in other words, he has given in and is behaving like a -----. As a result, Mercutio feels duty bound to take up Romeo's fight on his -----. Mercutio blames two things for his death: the fact that Romeo came between him and Tybalt and that he was stabbed underneath his ---; and the --- between the two families. A careful reading of the scene pretty much shows that Mercutio is to ---- for his own death: he didn't have to fight ----, who was not looking to fight him but ----.

Flow chart: Devise a chart of the main events in this section.

Questions: Why is Tybalt mystified by Romeo's answer to his challenge? Why is Mercutio very angry about what Romeo says? Who or what causes the fight between Tybalt and Mercutio? Who does Mercutio blame for his death? Who do you think is to blame yourself?

Analysis: The mood of the play changes in this scene; whereas Acts 1 and 2 had been full of love and light comedy, now the mood darkens with the death of Mercutio. The atmosphere is hot and tense. Shakespeare once again uses dramatic irony to powerful effect in the scene when

Romeo professes his love for Tybalt and this leaves the men totally mystified – and angry. We see how Shakespeare is painting a portrait of masculinity here: being a man involves fighting when you're required to fight, stepping outside this way of talking amounts to a "submission". Mercutio's blaming of Romeo and the feud for his death is tragically ironic because it is clear he has brought his own death upon himself.

Creative response: Write a poem or short story called 'The Fight' in which you describe a violent fight between two people in detail.

Analytical response: Who is to blame for Mercutio's death in this scene?

Answers to fill-in-the-blanks: Tybalt, different, cousin, submission, coward, behalf, arm, feud, blame, Tybalt, Romeo.

Activities 3.3

Thematic questions: Do you think getting revenge is a good idea?

Read Act 3, Sc I lines 108-137.

Fill-in-the-blanks (answers below): Romeo fights Tybalt in ---- for Mercutio's death. His mood quickly changes from one of love towards his cousin-in-law, Tybalt, to one of "fire-eyed fury". Romeo is very, very -----; he believes his love for Juliet has made him "effeminate" – i.e. too like a -----. After he has killed Tybalt, he realizes that he is "fortune's ---"; in other words, he is the idiot of "----", a key idea set out in the Prologue.

Flow chart: Devise a chart of the main events in this section.

Questions: Why does Romeo fight Tybalt? Who does he blame for Mercutio's death? How does he respond after Tybalt has died?

Analysis: It is fascinating to look at the presentation of the fights in various productions and films of the play. In the Zeffirelli version, Mercutio's fight with Tybalt is quite playful until an accident, with Romeo intervening, leaves him dead; the fight with Tybalt and Romeo is much more violent. In the Luhrmann version, Mercutio is goaded into fighting Tybalt because Tybalt is already attacking Romeo – something which is not written about in the play. The fights are also separated out in time: the fight between Mercutio and Tybalt takes place during the day, while Romeo's rage against Tybalt is at night and involves a car chase. There's no doubt that many people in Shakespeare's audience would come to see the plays especially to see the fights; what is a very short stage direction can be extended into a long piece of action on stage.

Creative response: Write a poem or story called 'Fury' in which a character is furious about something.

Act it out: Act out the fight between Tybalt and Romeo.

Analytical response: Do some further research about why it is largely men who get involved in violent fights.

Fill-in-the-blanks answers: revenge, angry; woman, fool, fate.

Activities 3.4

Thematic questions: In your experience, how do teachers or other authority figures such as parents deal with misbehavior? Do they issue punishments and threats etc? Do these threats work?

Read Act 3, Sc I lines 138 to the end of the scene.

Fill-in-the-blanks (answers below): Benvolio's long speech ---- Tybalt for everything: he says that Romeo was being very nice to Tybalt when Tybalt then ----- Mercutio. He says that Tybalt returned to ---- Romeo, who got his revenge. Lady Capulet doubts Benvolio's account because he is a ----- and bound to be ---- against Tybalt. She then calls for Romeo to be ----. The Prince decides to ---- Romeo from Verona.

Flow chart: Devise a chart of the main events in this section.

Questions: Who does Benvolio blame for the deaths? Why does Lady Capulet doubt the truth of Benvolio's observations? What sentence does the Prince pass on Romeo?

Analysis: It is fascinating to see how Shakespeare's explores the topic of "bias" in this section: both sides, as represented by Benvolio and Lady Capulet, are very biased and both are incapable of arriving at a fair account or judgement of the situation. Benvolio is clearly biased in that he leaves out any mention of Mercutio's goading of Tybalt and Mercutio's insistence upon fighting him. He also doesn't emphasize Romeo's desire to fight Tybalt as the primary reason for the duel between Tybalt and Romeo. Similarly, Lady Capulet, who has not witnessed the events, is very quick to blame Romeo without any proper evidence he was the main cause of the fights.

Creative response: Write two accounts of the same fight from different perspectives; one which favours one opponent and the other which favours the other.

Act it out: Devise a radio or TV report about the deaths.

Analytical response: How does Shakespeare make the fights so dramatic?

Answers to fill-in-the-blanks: blames, attacked, fight, Montague, biased, executed, exile.

Act 3, SCENE II. Capulet's orchard.

Important vocabulary: Apace = quickly
Steeds = horses who draw the chariot of the sun-god, Phoebus Apollo
Phaeton = the son of Phoebus Apollo; he was allowed to drive his father's chariot for a day but went too fast and was killed by Jupiter

Civil = respectable
Hood...mantle = as with Act 2, Sc II, Juliet uses the language of falconry. Hoods had to be put over tethered hawks who are moving their wings (bating) because they are not used to men (unmanned)
Mantle = cloak
Cords = rope ladder
Cockatrice = a fantasy snake who killed people if it looked at them
Beguil'd = cheated
Wot = know (Roma Gill, William Shakespeare, 1982, pp. 64-68)

Activities 3.5

Thematic questions: Can you express your feelings of love in words? Is it possible? Do you think we talk about sex enough?

Read Act 3, Sc II lines 1-33.

    Fill-in-the-blanks (answers below): Juliet wants the ----to come quickly so that she can be with -----; she wants it to hide her and Romeo so that they can lose their -------. She isn't aware that Romeo has killed -----. She feels she has bought "the mansion of a love" – a ---- ---- of love – but she doesn't ------ this house yet; she hasn't ---- in.
    Flow chart: Devise a chart of the main events in this section.
    Questions: Why does Juliet want the night to come quickly? Why does she want the night hide her and Romeo? What does she not know about yet? What she has bought but doesn't own?
    Analysis: This famous soliloquy expresses Juliet's impatience to have sex with Romeo; to consummate their marriage; she plays with the imagery of the night, the night-sky and the sun throughout the speech to suggest the strength of her desire and love for Romeo.
    Creative response: Write a poem/story called "Impatience" or "Waiting for the night".
    Act it out: Improvise a monologue giving by a lover, waiting for her/his lover to arrive.
    Analytical response: How does Shakespeare present Juliet's sexuality in this speech?
    Fill-in-the-blanks answers: night, Romeo, virginities, Tybalt, huge house, possess, moved.

Activities 3.6

Thematic questions: What are some of the ways in which people deal with bad news? How do they react?

Read Act 3, Sc II lines 34 to the end of the scene.

    Fill-in-the-blanks (answers below): The Nurse is upset because Tybalt has ----, and doesn't seem very upset about Romeo's -----. She speaks in a confused, grief-stricken fashion and does not clearly ---- what has happened; this is probably not deliberate but because she is so -----. When Juliet learns fully what has happened, that Tybalt is dead and Romeo has been sent into exile, she responds firstly by ----- Romeo, saying that his beautiful form hid a -----, and then she criticizes herself for ----- Romeo. She says that she has only been married three hours and already she is ----- him. The Nurse says at the end of the scene that she is going to visit Romeo who is ----- in Friar Lawrence's room. Juliet asks her to give Romeo a ----.

Flow chart: Devise a chart of the main events in this section.

Questions: Why is the Nurse so upset? How and why does she confuse Juliet? When Juliet learns what has happened, how does she respond? Why is she cross with herself? What does the Nurse say she is going to do at the end of the scene?

Analysis: This scene very quickly changes mood when the Nurse enters because Juliet had been very happy and excited at the thought of Romeo coming to her bed. However, the Nurse's distressed state brings confusion and dismay into the scene and makes Juliet very upset. In a previous scene in Act 2, Sc V, we had seen how the Nurse can be a very frustrating person; she refuses to give Juliet vital information about the marriage arrangements. Here, she is equally frustrating and also misleading, showing little sympathy or empathy for what Juliet might be feeling because she doesn't tell Juliet that who has died and who is alive immediately.

Creative response: Write a story called 'The Shocking News'.

Act it out: Improvise a scene in which an older person gives a younger person bad news about their loved one.

Analytical response: What do we learn about the characters of Juliet and the Nurse in this scene?

Answers to fill-in-the-blanks: died, situation, explain, distraught, criticizing, serpent, criticizing, cursing, doubting, hiding, ring.

Act 3, SCENE III. Friar Lawrence's cell.

Important vocabulary: vestal = virgin
Sharp-ground = sharpened by grinding
Fond = foolish
Blaze = announce
Chide = tell off
Sojourn = stay (Roma Gill, William Shakespeare, 1982, pp. 69-74)

Activities 3.7

Thematic questions: Why is being "excluded" or sent away from a particular place such as home/school so upsetting for some people? Why is it the ultimate sanction in schools? Do you think "exclusion" works?

Read Act 3, Sc III lines 1-80.

    Fill-in-the-blanks (answers below): Romeo is ----- to learn that he has been exiled from ----- because this is where Juliet lives. Friar Lawrence tries to reassure him with -----. Romeo dismisses the Friar's advice, saying that it is useless to help him unless it can bring Juliet --- to him. He then throws himself on the floor and has a ------ fit.
    Flow chart: Devise a chart of the main events in this section.
    Questions: Why is Romeo so upset when he learns he has been banished? How does Friar Lawrence try to reassure him? What is his response?
    Analysis: We see here the conflict between the two generations here: the younger, represented by Romeo, and the older, represented by Friar Lawrence. Romeo feels that the Friar can't understand him because he has no knowledge of what it means to be in love, while the Friar believes that philosophy can assist Romeo. We also see the ways in which extreme emotions can distort thought processes: Romeo works himself up into a furious hysteria because he feels he won't ever be able to see Juliet while even a Verona fly can.
    Creative response: Write Romeo's diary for this scene, explaining why he is so unhappy.
    Act it out: Improvise a scene in which an older person tries to calm down a younger person but fails.
    Analytical response: Write a character study of Romeo, examining the ways in which he is ruled by his emotions.
    Answers to fill-in-the-blanks: devastated, Verona, philosophy, back, hysterical

Activities 3.8

Thematic questions: Why do some people attempt suicide in front of other people? Do you think it is a cry for help? What is the best way to calm down people who are very upset?

Read Act 3, Sc III lines 81 to the end of the scene.

    Fill-in-the-blanks (answers below): We learn from the Nurse that Juliet is distraught too about the death of Tybalt and Romeo's -------. As a result of hearing this, Romeo tries to --- himself but the Nurse and the Friar --- him. The Friar tells Romeo that he must get control of himself: suicide is a --- sin and if he kills himself he will kill ---- too. He says that Romeo should be happy that he is alive and that he has not been executed; it means he will be able to --- Juliet again. He says that Romeo should see Juliet tonight, and then go to ---- while the Friar ---- everything out. The Nurse gives Romeo Juliet's --- and they make arrangements for Romeo to spend the --- with Juliet.

Flow chart: Devise a chart of the main events in this section.

Questions: What do we learn from the Nurse about Juliet's behavior? Why does Romeo try to kill himself? How does Friar Lawrence reassure him? What is agreed by the end of the scene?

Analysis: The Friar mixes condemnation, religious philosophy and advice in his long speech to Romeo, emphasizing a number of times that Romeo should be happy. His condemnation for Romeo is that he should try and kill himself, which was regarded as a mortal sin; a sin which meant you could go to Hell. He talks about how both heaven and earth exist in Romeo's body and that as long as he is alive there is hope.

Creative response: Write Friar Lawrence's diary for this scene, looking carefully at his speeches to Romeo in order to get ideas as to what he is really thinking.

Act it out: Improvise a scene in which an older person gives good advice to a younger person, which he/she listens to.

Analytical response: How does Shakespeare present the dangers of extreme emotions in this scene?

Answers to fill-in-the-blanks: banishment, kill, stop, mortal, Juliet, see, Mantua, sorts, ring, night.

Act 3, SCENE IV. A room in Capulet's house.

Important vocabulary: tender = offer (Roma Gill, William Shakespeare, 1982, p. 75)

Activities 3.9

Thematic questions: Do you think people need to be distracted from being upset? Do they need things to take their minds off their worries and concerns?

Read Act 3, Sc IV the whole of the scene.

Fill-in-the-blanks (answers below): Capulet tells Paris that the death of Tybalt has meant that they haven't had time to "move" or persuade Juliet to ---- him, thus indicating to Paris that marriage at the moment is ----. Paris agrees that it's very difficult to win someone over at such a sad time. But as Paris is leaving, Capulet says he will speak for

Juliet and that she will be "----" by him in "all respects". Possibly Capulet believes that the marriage needs to happen quickly because life is so -----. At first, he says that Lady Capulet should tell Juliet that the marriage will take place on -------, but he changes his mind and makes it ------.

Flow chart: Devise a chart of the main events in this section.

Questions: At the beginning of the scene, how does Capulet indicate to Paris that marrying Juliet is unlikely? How does Paris respond? And how and why does Capulet change his mind, do you think?

Analysis: Capulet's change of mind here is surprising but it creates suspense; he appears very anxious to have Paris as a son-in-law, and believes his daughter will be "ruled" by him "in all respects". We see in Capulet again a representation of the older generation who are nervous of their position as a parent: he doesn't quite know whether Juliet should be the one to decide who she marries or it should be him. In the end, he decides Juliet must obey him. His hesitancy about everything is also reflected upon his inability to decide exactly what day the wedding should be on.

Creative response: Write a poem/story called 'The Arranged Marriage' or 'The Strict Parent'.

Act it out: Improvise a scene in which a parent and a suitor talk about an arranged marriage.

Analytical response: How effectively does Shakespeare represent Capulet in this scene?

Fill-in-the-blanks answers: marry, unlikely, "ruled", fragile, Wednesday, Thursday.

Act 3, SCENE V. Capulet's orchard.

Important vocabulary: exhales = breathes out. People in Shakespeare's time believed that the sun sucked up gases from the earth and sets fire to them, and so breathed out or "exhaled" shooting stars.
Reflex = reflection
Ill-divining = predicting disaster
Unaccustomed = unexpected
Dram = little drink
Conduit = water-pipe
Counterfeit'st = copy
Bark = boat
Decree = decision
Bride = bridegroom
Chop-logic = nonsensical way of speaking
Minion = naughty girl
Green-sickness = very pale, anaemic
Hilding = worthless girl

Demesnes = property
Whining mammet = crying doll
Dishclout = dishcloth
Ancient damnation = damned old woman (Roma Gill, William Shakespeare, 1982, pp. 76-83)

Activities 3.10

Thematic questions: Why are couples happy together? What makes them happy?

Read Act 3, Sc V lines 1-59.

   Fill-in-the-blanks (answers below): Juliet believes it is the nightingale which is singing, which indicates it is still ------ -----. Romeo points out that it is the ---, the bird that signals it is morning time but when Juliet says it is a ----- in the sky which is making it light, Romeo laughs and says if she says it is night-time then it is, and he welcomes ---- if that's what Juliet wants. At this, Juliet realizes that it is the ---, and that Romeo must go -----. Juliet worries that she will never --- Romeo again, to which he replies that he is certain that they will meet again and these times will make interesting conversations in the days they spend together. As Romeo descends the ladder Juliet believes she sees him in a ---.

   Flow chart: Devise a chart of the main events in this section.
   Questions: Why does Juliet say that Romeo must stay? What does Romeo say in response? What does Juliet then realize and what does she tell Romeo to do? What worries does Juliet have and how does Romeo reassure her? What premonition does Juliet have as he descends the ladder?
   Analysis: Romeo and Juliet have consummated the marriage and clearly are feeling very loving towards each other, particularly Juliet who is desperate for Romeo to stay. The Zeferrilli and the Luhrmann films linger on this moment, taking care to show that Romeo and Juliet's relationship is passionate. They are less flirtatious with each other here but possibly more loving. Juliet, in particular, expresses her worries but Romeo tries to show real bravado, reassuring Juliet that they will see each other again. However, it is important that Juliet notices that he is pale: he is more anxious than he lets on.
   Creative response: Imagine you are Romeo leaving the Capulet house, describe his departure and the thoughts that race through his mind as he escapes. Or write a poem/story called 'The Parting'.
   Act it out: Improvise a scene in which two lovers say goodbye to each other.
   Analytical response: How does Shakespeare represent the passion between the two lovers in this scene?
   Fill-in-the-blanks (answers below): night-time, lark, meteorite, death, day, immediately, see, tomb.

Thematic questions: Why do children disobey their parents? Who are the most powerful people in families: the father, mother or child? Why do parents lose their tempers with children?

Activities 3.11

Thematic questions: Why do children disobey their parents? Who are the most powerful people in families: the father, mother or child? Why do parents lose their tempers with children?

Read Act 3, Sc V lines 60 to the end of the scene.

Fill-in-the-blanks (answers below): Lady Capulet thinks it shows a "want of wit" (a lack of common ----) for someone to cry so ----. She then says that she is going to ---- Romeo when she has the chance. Juliet annoys her by responding in a paradoxical fashion, saying that she would rather ---- Romeo, who she knows her mother hates, than ----. Capulet arrives and voices his ----- that she is crying so much. When he learns that she won't obey his "decree", which means ----, he loses his ---- and says that he will ---- her and cast her out into the streets, calling her rude names in the process. Lady Capulet and the Nurse try to stop him ---- Juliet without much effect. Juliet turns in her distress to her mother to help her make her father reconsider but Lady Capulet ---- her. Then she turns to the Nurse who advises her to go ahead and ---- Paris because Romeo is a "----" compared with the noble Count. Juliet says ------- that the Nurse has helped her "marvellous much" and says she is going to see Friar Lawrence to make her confession. Finally, when left alone, she curses the Nurse, who she feels really ----- her because she is now criticizing Romeo who she has previously ------ thousands of times. She says that either she will get help from Friar Lawrence or --- herself.

Flow chart: Devise a chart of the main events in this section.

Questions: Why does Lady Capulet think that Juliet is behaving like an idiot? What does Lady Capulet say she is going to do to Romeo and why? How does Juliet respond to this? How does Juliet behave in a disobedient fashion? Why is Capulet irritated by Juliet? What does he say will happen if Juliet does not obey him? What is his mood and how do the other characters respond to it? Juliet turns for comfort to her mother and then the Nurse? What do they say to her? What is Juliet's response when they've all left?

Analysis: Some critics have wondered why Juliet does not escape with Romeo in this scene, given that she seems an independent person. However, we can see that Shakespeare was keen to write this powerful, disturbing scene which shows the brutal authoritarian nature of Capulet and the callousness of Lady Capulet. Juliet is threatened with being thrown into the streets and is hit by her father because she won't obey the order of her father. Once again, we see inter-generational conflict caused by a young person's refusal to accept the authority of the older person.

Creative response: Write a poem/scene in which a parent becomes very angry with their child because they have disobeyed their orders. Or write Juliet's diary entry for this scene.
Analytical response: How does Shakespeare create suspense in this scene?
Act it out: Improvise a scene in which a parents gets very angry with a teenage child because they won't obey them.
Answers to fill-in-the-blanks: sense, much, poison, marry, Paris, irritation, order, temper, disown, hitting, disowns, marry, dishcloth, sarcastically, betrayed, praised, kill.

Looking back at Act 3

Focus on structure: put these quotes in the order they happen in the play and write about why Shakespeare ordered them in this way.

CAPULET Hang thee, young baggage! disobedient wretch!
I tell thee what: get thee to church o' Thursday,
Or never after look me in the face:
Speak not, reply not, do not answer me;
My fingers itch.

MERCUTIO Why the devil came you between us? I
was hurt under your arm... A plague o' both your houses!
They have made worms' meat of me:

FRIAR LAWRENCE There art thou happy: Tybalt would kill thee,
But thou slew'st Tybalt; there are thou happy too:
The law that threaten'd death becomes thy friend
And turns it to exile; there art thou happy:

JULIET O serpent heart, hid with a flowering face!
Did ever dragon keep so fair a cave?

ROMEO I do protest, I never injured thee,
But love thee better than thou canst devise,
Till thou shalt know the reason of my love:

TYBALT Romeo, the hate I bear thee can afford
No better term than this,--thou art a villain.

PRINCE let Romeo hence in haste,
Else, when he's found, that hour is his last.

Follow up after you've checked your answers: using a narrator who explains the missing parts of the story, either write up a "story" version of these quotes or work in a group and act out these lines, with a narrator or narrators explaining the story of the Act as a whole and the actors reading these key lines with real expression.

Focus on grammar and lexis: what are the word classes of the following lexis in **CAPS** and why are they significant words?

> FRIAR LAWRENCE There art THOU happy: Tybalt
> WOULD KILL thee,
> But THOU slew'st Tybalt; there are THOU happy too:
> The law that threaten'd death becomes THY friend
> And turns it to exile; there art thou HAPPY:

Focus on characterizations: who said the following and what do we learn about the characters from these quotes?

> Alive, in triumph! and Mercutio slain!
> Away to heaven, respective lenity,
> And fire-eyed fury be my conduct now!

> He is a kinsman to the Montague;
> Affection makes him false; he speaks not true:

> O, I have bought the mansion of a love,
> But not possess'd it, and, though I am sold,
> Not yet enjoy'd:

> Monday! ha, ha! Well, Wednesday is too soon,
> O' Thursday let it be: o' Thursday, tell her,
> She shall be married to this noble earl.

> I think it best you married with the county.
> O, he's a lovely gentleman!
> Romeo's a dishclout to him:

Follow up after you've checked your answers: Using these quotes as a starting point, "hotseat" the relevant characters, i.e interview them in pairs about what they are thinking and feeling at these moments.

Focus on staging: write about how these quotes might be acted out on stage or film, discussing any versions you've seen.

> MERCUTIO O calm, dishonourable, vile submission!

BENVOLIO Tybalt, here slain, whom Romeo's hand did slay;
Romeo that spoke him fair, bade him bethink
How nice the quarrel was, and urged withal
Your high displeasure:

JULIET Blister'd be thy tongue
For such a wish! he was not born to shame:
Upon his brow shame is ashamed to sit;

ROMEO In what vile part of this anatomy
Doth my name lodge? tell me, that I may sack
The hateful mansion.

ROMEO Let me be ta'en, let me be put to death;
I am content, so thou wilt have it so.

JULIET
O God, I have an ill-divining soul!
Methinks I see thee, now thou art below,
As one dead in the bottom of a tomb:

Focus on imagery: fill in the gaps for the following quotes, then check your answer with Shakespeare's; why do you think Shakespeare made these word choices?

BENVOLIO The day is hot, the Capulets abroad,
And, if we meet, we shall not scape a brawl;

ROMEO There is no world without Verona walls,
But purgatory, torture, hell itself.

LADY CAPULET I'll send to one in Mantua,
Where that same banish'd runagate doth live,
Shall give him such an unaccustom'd dram,
That he shall soon keep Tybalt company:

JULIET Ancient damnation! O most wicked fiend!
Is it more sin to wish me thus forsworn,
Or to dispraise my lord with that same tongue
Which she hath praised him with above compare
So many thousand times?

Focus on rhythm: put these quotes into the correct verse form and write about the rhythmic effects of the lines.

MONTAGUE Not romeo prince he was Mercutio's friend

his fault concludes but what the law should end the life of Tybalt

JULIET I will not marry yet and when I do I swear it shall be Romeo, whom you know I hate rather than Paris these are news indeed

Answers

Focus on structure. This is the correct order for the quotes.

TYBALT Romeo, the hate I bear thee can afford
No better term than this,--thou art a villain.

ROMEO I do protest, I never injured thee,
But love thee better than thou canst devise,
Till thou shalt know the reason of my love:

MERCUTIO Why the devil came you between us? I
was hurt under your arm... A plague o' both your houses!
They have made worms' meat of me:

PRINCE let Romeo hence in haste,
Else, when he's found, that hour is his last.

JULIET O serpent heart, hid with a flowering face!
Did ever dragon keep so fair a cave?

FRIAR LAWRENCE There art thou happy: Tybalt would kill thee,
But thou slew'st Tybalt; there are thou happy too:
The law that threaten'd death becomes thy friend
And turns it to exile; there art thou happy:

CAPULET Hang thee, young baggage! disobedient wretch!
I tell thee what: get thee to church o' Thursday,
Or never after look me in the face:
Speak not, reply not, do not answer me;
My fingers itch.

The sequence of these quotes is excellent at illustrating how the feud dominates Act 3, hijacking the love story which occupied Act 2. Tybalt calls Romeo a "villain" which I translated as "pleb" in my modern translation because I think this conveys the fact that the word used to mean someone who was lower class, born from a bad family and rude or common in the way they behaved. Romeo though protests that he never harmed Tybalt and that he loves Tybalt more than he could know; Mercutio sees this as a "vile submission" and fights in place of Romeo. When Mercutio dies, he blames Romeo for coming between them in the fight and the two families for feuding; his death compels Romeo to kill Tybalt for which the Prince exiles him, saying if "he's found" in Verona, he will die. Romeo's exile brings the love story back into play: Juliet is initially horrified that Romeo has killed her cousin and she says that his "flowering face" hid a "serpent heart" before changing her mind. Meanwhile Friar Lawrence has to stop Romeo killing himself after he learns that Juliet is so upset about his behaviour; Friar Lawrence begins to devise a plan which will soon occupy much of the plot: Romeo will spend the night with Juliet and then go to Mantua while the Friar fixes things so that he can return in triumph. This leaves Juliet to weather the rage of her father when she refuses to marry Paris. The arranged marriage between Paris and Juliet had been a minor sub-plot in the first Act but is made particularly important by Capulet's impatience to get Juliet married.

Focus on grammar and lexis: what are the word classes of the following lexis in **CAPS** and why are they significant words?

> FRIAR LAWRENCE There art THOU happy: Tybalt
> WOULD KILL thee,
> But THOU slew'st Tybalt; there are THOU happy too:
> The law that threaten'd death becomes THY friend
> And turns it to exile; there art thou HAPPY:

Thou and thy = archaic second person singular pronoun meaning "you". Friar Lawrence doesn't use the polite form "you" because he is so angry at Romeo's "beast-like" behaviour in trying to kill himself. The more familiar form "thou" is used both to show the Friar's power over Romeo and to be more intimate.
Would kill = conditional verb. Here Friar Lawrence discusses what "might" have happened if he hadn't killed Tybalt; Romeo would have been killed himself and therefore is still alive to see Juliet. This grammatical construction allows Friar Lawrence to show Romeo a different future, a future where he might not exist.

Focus on characterizations: who said the following and what do we learn about the characters from these quotes?

> Alive, in triumph! and Mercutio slain!
> Away to heaven, respective lenity,
> And fire-eyed fury be my conduct now!

This is Romeo's first reaction when he hears Tybalt is showing off about Mercutio death is that his "lenity" – his inclination to think better of people – should be sent to heaven with Mercutio, and "fire-eyed fury" should inform his "conduct", his behaviour now. The alliteration of "fire-eyed fury" emphasizes Romeo's anger; with the "f" sound being particularly effective at showing Romeo's extreme anger.

> He is a kinsman to the Montague;
> Affection makes him false; he speaks not true:

Lady Capulet questions Benvolio's account of the death of Tybalt because it exclusively blamed Tybalt for beginning the fight with Mercutio and Romeo. She says his "affection" makes him "false" or lie. She is possibly presented as the most upset by the death of Tybalt and becomes fixated upon revenge against Romeo as a consequence.

> O, I have bought the mansion of a love,
> But not possess'd it, and, though I am sold,
> Not yet enjoy'd:

Here Juliet in her famous "gallop apace" speech talks about her physical yearning to have sex with Romeo. She uses the metaphor of "buying" the "mansion of love" but not "possessing" it; the mansion is, of course, Romeo's body, which is, she said in Act 2, Sc II, is the "god of her idolatry". She worships his physical being as a God. She then compares herself to a product or food which having been sold has not been enjoyed. We see an important side to her character here: she is a sensual, sexual being.

> Monday! ha, ha! Well, Wednesday is too soon,
> O' Thursday let it be: o' Thursday, tell her,
> She shall be married to this noble earl.

Capulet's impulsive patriarchal nature is revealed here. The "ha, ha!" reveals someone who is very excitable, while the debating about the different days show how he is calculating everything in his mind, but still isn't quite sure as to the best mode of action. When Juliet tells him later on that she will marry Paris, he changes the day again to Wednesday, bringing it forward by a day, despite his wife warning him not to because things aren't properly prepared. The description of Paris as a "noble earl" is important because Capulet is, above all, someone who feels it is important to have a high social standing, something this marriage will bring.

> I think it best you married with the county.
> O, he's a lovely gentleman!
> Romeo's a dishclout to him:

This is the ultimate betrayal for Juliet, the Nurse advises her to marry

Paris, and saying that Romeo is a "dish-clout" compared with Paris. The Nurse is, above all, a very practical person but not a particularly moral person: she will do what is "expedient", i.e. in someone's best and easiest interests. This is an approach to life which is entirely opposite to Juliet's, who is an idealist, a dreamer, a romantic.

Focus on staging: write about how these quotes might be acted out on stage or film, discussing any versions you've seen.

> MERCUTIO O calm, dishonourable, vile submission!

Mercutio's disgust at Romeo saying he loves Tybalt in the market square needs to be conveyed here, with Mercutio possibly shaking his head and waving his sword about as he does so. This is a moment of high suspense because the Capulets and Montagues have been stunned by Romeo's saying that he doesn't want to fight Tybalt. It is mistakenly interpreted as cowardice by Mercutio when we know it is, in fact, because Romeo has married Juliet; this is a moment of intense dramatic irony.

> BENVOLIO Tybalt, here slain, whom Romeo's hand did slay;
> Romeo that spoke him fair, bade him bethink
> How nice the quarrel was, and urged withal
> Your high displeasure:

The scene on stage will be very crowded with the Capulets, the Montagues, the Prince and the dead bodies of Mercutio and Tybalt lying there. Benvolio will point to Tybalt's body as he explains that Tybalt began the fight. He may well turn then to face the Prince as he says that Romeo tried to stop the fight.

> JULIET Blister'd be thy tongue
> For such a wish! he was not born to shame:
> Upon his brow shame is ashamed to sit;

I almost imagine that Juliet might be on the verge of hitting the Nurse here when she says that Romeo should be shamed for killing Tybalt. Although she has herself criticised Romeo, she says that the Nurse's tongue should be covered in blisters for saying something horrible about Romeo.

> ROMEO In what vile part of this anatomy
> Doth my name lodge? tell me, that I may sack
> The hateful mansion.

Here Romeo grabs a knife and tries to kill himself, looking for the part of his body, his "anatomy", which contains his name, the root of all his problems. He says his body is a "hateful mansion"; he could be hitting himself as he says these words to show his extreme self-loathing.

> ROMEO Let me be ta'en, let me be put to death;
> I am content, so thou wilt have it so.

Here Romeo is lying in bed with Juliet and saying that if Juliet believes it is night, even though it isn't, he is willing to be put to death. I imagine he may well kiss her at this point.

> JULIET
> O God, I have an ill-divining soul!
> Methinks I see thee, now thou art below,
> As one dead in the bottom of a tomb:

Juliet is looking down at Romeo climbing down the balcony and has a promotion of seeing him dead at the bottom of a tomb.

Focus on imagery: fill in the gaps for the following quotes, and then check your answer with Shakespeare's; why do you think Shakespeare made these word choices?

> BENVOLIO The day is hot, the Capulets abroad,
> And, if we meet, we shall not scape a brawl;

The imagery here is all about the day being "hot" both literally and metaphorically: tempers are high, Benvolio knows that Tybalt has sent a letter to Romeo's house and is aware there could be trouble. He is convinced that they will no escape from a fight.

> ROMEO There is no world without Verona walls,
> But purgatory, torture, hell itself.

The imagery evoked by Romeo here is the imagery inside his head: he sees no other world than those in Verona with Juliet. Beyond Verona there is only "purgatory, torture, hell", indicating that he is tortured by the hellish thought that he can never be with Juliet.

> LADY CAPULET I'll send to one in Mantua,
> Where that same banish'd runagate doth live,
> Shall give him such an unaccustom'd dram,
> That he shall soon keep Tybalt company:

Lady Capulet's image of the "unaccustom'd dram", the unexpected poison, which will make Romeo "keep company" with Tybalt is effective because it is euphemistic; she doesn't state baldly that she is going to have Romeo murdered but this is what it amounts to. We see the sneaky, vindictive side to Lady Capulet in these images.

> JULIET Ancient damnation! O most wicked fiend!
> Is it more sin to wish me thus forsworn,
> Or to dispraise my lord with that same tongue
> Which she hath praised him with above compare
> So many thousand times?

The imagery that Juliet deploys when talking about the Nurse is both religious and condemnatory; she sees the Nurse as a form of "damnation" and as a "wicked fiend". With her words that the Juliet should marry Paris, the Nurse has changed from being Juliet's closest friend and confidante to being a devil who deserves damnation. Juliet asks what is more sinful of the Nurse to encourage her to commit bigamy or to criticise the very person she has praised "so many thousand times".

Focus on rhythm: put these quotes into the correct verse form and write about the rhythmic effects of the lines.

> MONTAGUE NOT ROMeo, PRINCE, HE was MERcutio's FRIEND;
> His FAULT concLUDES but WHAT the LAW should END,
> The LIFE of TYBalt

Montague's desperate plea for the life of his son is highlighted in the disrupted rhythm of the first line quoted above; the heavy stress comes upon the word "Not" because Montague is desperate to make sure that Romeo isn't executed; the other stresses in the line fall on key ideas he wants to emphasize: the Prince and the fact that Romeo was Mercutio's friend. The next line is perfectly regular because Montague has constructed a clear argument to justify his case: Romeo's killing of Tybalt was justice.

> JULIET I will not marry yet; and, when I do, I swear,
> It shall be Romeo, whom you know I hate,
> Rather than Paris. These are news indeed!

The pauses in the lines here are very important. Juliet pauses after "yet"; and then she appears to speak slowly after this. The rhythm of the lines is irregular and disrupted, highlighting Juliet's rebelliousness:
I will NOT MARry YET (pause): AND, when I DO, I SWEAR,
It SHALL be ROMeo, WHOM you KNOW I HATE,
RATHer than PARis. THESE are NEWS indeed!
It is the pauses in the lines which give heavy, angry emphasis to Juliet's defiant words.

Act 4, SCENE I. Friar Lawrence's cell.

Important vocabulary: inundation = flooding
Will I rouse ye = in Shakespeare's time the wedding day started when the bridegroom, with musicians playing beside him, fetched his bride from her bed and took her to church
Label = the wax seal attached to a document to make it legal
Charnel-house = the place for bones dug up in the course of digging new graves in the churchyard
Vial = small bottle
Surcease = stop
Eyes' windows = eyelids
Abate = lessen/weaken (Roma Gill, William Shakespeare, 1982, pp. 84-88)

Activities 4.1

Read Act 4, Sc I lines 1-43.

Thematic questions: Why do people fall in love with people who don't love them? Why are some very people very insensitive to other people's feelings?

Fill-in-the-blanks (answers below): Paris thinks Juliet is upset because of Tybalt's ----. He explains to Friar Lawrence that Capulet has ----- up the marriage because he thinks the wedding will ----- her and stop her from being so depressed. Juliet talks in a very terse way to Paris, giving ---- ---- answers such as "what must be shall be". Her manner towards him seems cold and ----. Paris claims Juliet's face for his own because he is about to marry "it" and he doesn't like the way Juliet ---- her looks. Juliet agrees that her face is not her ----; again a double-edged answer.

Flow chart: Devise a chart of the main events in this section.

Questions: Why does Paris think Juliet is so upset? Why, in his view, has Capulet hurried up the marriage? Why is Friar Lawrence so uncomfortable? How does Juliet respond to Paris? Why do Paris and Juliet talk about her face?

Analysis: Shakespeare reveals something of Paris's character here: he is no monster but seems to have genuine affection for Juliet, even if he doesn't understand her. He believes the marriage will stop her being depressed. And yet, he claims her for his own before he is married to her, and doesn't seem to want to know if she really wants to marry him. Possibly, he is used to women wanting him and assumes that Juliet does too. The scene is full of dramatic irony: we know that Friar Lawrence and Juliet find Paris's presence excruciatingly painful, but he seems unaware of this.

Act it out: Improvise a scene between someone who loves another person, who doesn't return that love.

Creative response: Write Paris's diary here, discussing his feelings for Juliet.

Analytical response: How does Shakespeare create suspense here?

Answers to fill-in-the-blanks: death, hurried, distract, double-edged, distant, criticizes, own.

Activities 4.2

Thematic questions: Why do women have so little power in some societies?

Read Act 4, Sc I lines 44 to the end of the scene.

Fill-in-the-blanks (answers below): Juliet threatens to --- herself if the Friar doesn't --- her marrying Paris. Because she's so desperate, the Friar considers a ----- solution. He will give her a ---- which will make her look like she is dead for --- hours; this will mean she will be given a ------. The Friar will send a letter to Romeo who come and fetch her from the tomb and take her to ----.

Flow chart: Devise a chart of the main events in this section.

Questions: What does Juliet threaten to do if Friar Lawrence doesn't find a solution for her? What does this make him think could be a possible solution?

Analysis: The Friar's solution is somewhat ridiculous for modern audiences but it was very much a dramatic convention of Elizabethan theatre to include some sort of potion as a plot-device. While, as has been said, it is implausible that Juliet didn't go with Romeo in the first place, the plot-device of the potion provides the play with some of its most powerful scenes: the scene in which Juliet craves death rather than marrying Paris, and the scene when she takes the potion, which for me, is the most powerful soliloquy in the play. These scenes provide us with real evidence that Juliet is both very brave and very alone.

Act it out: Improvise a scene between an older person who persuades a younger person to do something dangerous.

Creative response: Write a poem or story called 'The Drug'.

Analytical response: Is Friar Lawrence's potion a ridiculous plot-device, or a brilliant way of increasing the suspense?

Fill-in-the-blanks answers: kill, stop, desperate, potion, 42, funeral, Mantua.

Act 4, SCENE II. Hall in Capulet's house.

Important vocabulary: cunning = skillful
Harlotry = worthless woman
Deck up = dress up (Roma Gill, William Shakespeare, 1982, pp. 88-90)

Activities 4.3

Thematic questions: Why do people deceive others? Why are so many stories about deception?

Read Act 4, Sc II the whole of the scene.

    Fill-in-the-blanks (answers below): Capulet is busy making arrangements for the ----- at the beginning of the scene and is telling people to ---- up, and also cursing Juliet for being a stubborn "----", which is slang for ---- or ----- ----. He doesn't literally mean she is but he just uses it as a term of abuse here. Juliet says that the Friar has asked her to fall "prostrate" (face first) before him and be "---" by him, i.e. --- his every word. He is delighted and immediately says that Paris needs to be --- of this. He then decides to make the wedding -------: Lady Capulet is doubtful that they have enough ---- and ---- for the party. However, Capulet says he will stay up all night and "play the ----" so that everything will be ready.
    Flow chart: Devise a chart of the main events in this section.
    Questions: What evidence is there that Capulet is very stressed at the beginning of the scene? What does Juliet tell him that delights him? What does he re-arrange about the wedding? Why is Lady Capulet doubtful about this re-arrangement?
    Analysis: It is interesting to note that Capulet is carrying on with the wedding preparations anyway, despite the fact that Juliet has not agreed to be married. In other words, he is convinced that it will happen: he is an impulsive man who is inclined to take risks. His impatience is shown by the way he brings the wedding forward: maybe he has done this because he is worried that Juliet will change her mind again. His joy that she has changed her mind is genuine: this is a man who loves his daughter – but on certain conditions. The dramatic irony here is powerful because we know that Juliet is not obeying him at all but doing the exact opposite: she will look as though she is dead tomorrow.
    Creative response: Write a dialogue between two Capulet servants who are gossiping about all the arrangements that are happening regarding Juliet and Paris's wedding.
    Act it out: Improvise a scene in which a child pretends to be obeying

their parent when secretly they are not.
   Analytical response: How is suspense generated in this scene?
   Fill-in-the-blanks answers: wedding, hurry, harlot, prostitute, difficult woman, ruled, obey, told, tomorrow, food, drink, housewife.

Act 4, SCENE III. Juliet's chamber.

Important vocabulary: attires = clothes
Orisons = prayers
Mandrakes = plants which had roots that looked like men. People believed mandrakes screamed when they were pulled up and people who heard them went mad. (Roma Gill, William Shakespeare, 1982, p. 91)

Activities 4.4

Thematic questions: Why do people do very risky things like sky-diving, jumping off cliffs, or taking drugs etc?

Read Act 4, Sc III the whole of the scene.

   Fill-in-the-blanks (answers below): Juliet wants to sleep ---- so that she can take the ----. Juliet has a number of fears about taking the potion, which she explores during the long -----. She worries first of all that the potion won't work and that she'll have to ---- Paris. She sets aside this worry because she has a ---- which she will kill herself with if the potion doesn't work. Then she worries that the potion is poison which the Friar has given her because he would be "----" if it was known that he married Romeo and Juliet. She rejects this worry because she knows he is a --- man. Then she worries that she will ----- to death when she wakes up in the vault. She is also concerned that she will be terrified by the spirits and bones of the dead and will be driven out of her mind, and will club herself to death in her madness with an old ---. In her panic, she sees the ---- of Tybalt looking for Romeo, but, even with all these fears, she takes the potion because she is doing it for ----.
   Flow chart: Devise a chart of the main events in this section.
   Questions: Why does Juliet want to sleep alone tonight? What worries does Juliet have about taking the potion?
   Analysis: This, for me, is the best soliloquy in the play because it is so dramatic. We see Juliet's mind working "over-time" here; she is besieged by terrifying anxieties about what might happen to her. She dismisses some of her worries but can't escape them all, especially a vision of Tybalt seeking out Romeo. Even so, she takes the potion. Thus we see Shakespeare showing the depth of Juliet's love: she only takes the

potion because she loves Romeo and her love is more powerful than her many fears.
Act it out: Act out this speech in a group of four, with people miming the actions/images spoken about.
Creative response: Using Juliet's speech as a starting point, write her diary.
Analytical response: How does Shakespeare create feelings of drama and terror in Juliet's soliloquy?
Fill-in-the-blanks answers: alone, potion, soliloquy, marry, dagger, "dishonoured", holy, suffocate, bone, ghost, Romeo.

Act 4, SCENE IV. Hall in Capulet's house.

Important vocabulary: curfew bell = the bell marking the beginning and end of the day
Cot-quean = a man who does women's work, i.e. housework
Mouse-hunt = woman chaser
Hood = woman
(Roma Gill, William Shakespeare, 1982, pp. 92-93)

Activities 4.5

Thematic questions: Why are some people in such a hurry? Why are they always rushing things? What sort of atmosphere do they create?

Read Act 4, Sc IV the whole of the scene.

Fill-in-the-blanks (answers below): The Capulet household is in a state of real ----- and panic because the wedding is going to happen that ---. Paris has already ----- in the expectation that he will be married. This is all highly ironic because we know that they will soon find Juliet looking as though she is ----.
Flow chart: Devise a chart of the main events in this section.
Questions: Why is the Capulet household in such a state of excitement and activity here? Why is their activity highly ironic?
Analysis: This scene serves as a contrast in mood to the previous scenes because it has comic elements with the family and servants flying about the stage, stressed out by making everything ready in time.
Creative response: Write a story called 'The Wedding That Went Wrong'.
Act it out: Improvise a scene in which a family prepares for a wedding.
Analytical response: Why is this scene in the play?
Fill-in-the-blanks answers: anxiety, day, arrived, dead.

Act 4, Scene V. Juliet's Chamber.

Important vocabulary: solemnity = ceremony
Rosemary = the herb of remembrance, worn at weddings and funerals
Gleek = a nasty gesture
Pate = head
Dry-beat = hit someone without drawing blood
Catling = the string of a small lute
Soundpost = wooden peg fixed below the bridge of a violin
Tarry = wait for
(Roma Gill, William Shakespeare, 1982, pp. 93-98)

Activities 4.6

Thematic questions: What feelings does death provoke? Why are some religious people less upset by death?

Read Act 4, Sc V the whole of the scene.

    Fill-in-the-blanks (answers below): The Nurse is too ----- to say anything other than that Juliet is ----, but Capulet talks at length about his feelings of ---. He says that death has taken her in the same way the frost in a field kills off the most beautiful -----. His language contrasts greatly with Act 3, ScV, in which he called her many horrible names, including "green sickness -----". Paris appears to be stunned and asks why he is seeing this sight on his ---- day, while Lady Capulet says this is the worst day since time ----. Friar Lawrence calms them down by saying that they should be pleased because Juliet has gone to ---- and that long marriages never work out; it is best to die ------.
    Flow chart: Devise a chart of the main events in this section.
    Questions: How does the family respond when they find Juliet dead? What reasons does Friar Lawrence give as to why the family should not be so upset? Why are the Musicians asked to leave? How does Peter insult musicians?
    Analysis: There are multiple levels of irony in this scene. First, we know that Juliet is not dead and so people's grief is just as misplaced as their belief that Juliet will be married in the previous scene. Second, their reactions to her death contrast greatly with their treatment of Juliet when she refused to be married: Capulet threatened to throw her on the streets, Lady Capulet disowned her, and the Nurse said that Juliet's true love was a "dish-cloth". They are, thus, exposed as hypocrites.
    Creative response: Write the Nurse and the Friar Lawrence's diary entries for this scene, given that they know a great deal more than the other characters.
    Act it out: We never see Juliet's funeral. Act it out, with Capulet and

Friar Lawrence giving the speeches.
Analytical response: How does Shakespeare explore the theme of hypocrisy in the play?
Fill-in-the-blanks answers: distraught, dead, grief, flower, carrion, wedding, began, heaven, young.

Looking back at Act 4

Focus on structure: put these quotes in the order they happen in the play and write about why Shakespeare ordered them in this way.

> CAPULET Why, I am glad on't; this is well: stand up:
> This is as't should be. Let me see the county;
> Ay, marry, go, I say, and fetch him hither.
> Now, afore God! this reverend holy friar,
> Our whole city is much bound to him.
>
> JULIET O, look! methinks I see my cousin's ghost
> Seeking out Romeo, that did spit his body
> Upon a rapier's point: stay, Tybalt, stay!
> Romeo, I come! this do I drink to thee.
>
> FRIAR LAWRENCE And in this borrow'd likeness of shrunk death
> Thou shalt continue two and forty hours,
> And then awake as from a pleasant sleep.
>
> PARIS Immoderately she weeps for Tybalt's death,
> And therefore have I little talk'd of love;
> For Venus smiles not in a house of tears.

Follow up after you've checked your answers: using a narrator who explains the missing parts of the story, either write up a "story" version of these quotes or work in a group and act out these lines, with a narrator or narrators explaining the story of the Act as a whole and the actors reading these key lines with real expression.

Focus on grammar and lexis: what are the word classes of the following lexis in **CAPS** and why are they significant words?

> NURSE O day! O day! O day! O HATEFUL day!
> Never was seen so BLACK a day as this:
> O WOFUL day, O WOFUL day!
>
> FRIAR LAWRENCE Hold; get you gone, be strong and

> prosperous
> In this RESOLVE: I'll send a friar with speed
> To Mantua, with my LETTERS to thy LORD.

Focus on characterizations: who said the following and what do we learn about the characters from these quotes?

> "Thy face is mine, and thou hast slander'd it."

> "Or bid me go into a new-made grave
> And hide me with a dead man in his shroud;
> Things that, to hear them told, have made me tremble;"

> "Death is my son-in-law, Death is my heir;
> My daughter he hath wedded: I will die,
> And leave him all; life, living, all is Death's."

Follow up after you've checked your answers: using these quotes as a starting point, "hotseat" the relevant characters, i.e interview them in pairs about what they are thinking and feeling at these moments.

Focus on staging: write about how these quotes might be acted out on stage or film, discussing any versions you've seen.

> JULIET: Come, vial.
> What if this mixture do not work at all?
> Shall I be married then to-morrow morning?
> No, no: this shall forbid it: lie thou there.

Focus on imagery: fill in the gaps for the following quotes, then check your answer with Shakespeare's; why do you think Shakespeare made these word choices?

> CAPULET Death lies on her like an untimely frost
> Upon the sweetest flower of all the field.

Focus on rhythm: put these quotes into the correct verse form and write about the rhythmic effects of the lines.

> LADY CAPULET we shall be short in our provision tis now near night.

> FRIAR LAWRENCE shes not well married that lives married long but shes best married that dies married young dry up your tears, and stick your rosemary on this fair corse and as the custom is in all her best array bear her to church

Answers

Focus on structure. The correct order is this:

> PARIS Immoderately she weeps for Tybalt's death,
> And therefore have I little talk'd of love;
> For Venus smiles not in a house of tears.
>
> FRIAR LAWRENCE And in this borrow'd likeness of shrunk death
> Thou shalt continue two and forty hours,
> And then awake as from a pleasant sleep.
>
> CAPULET Why, I am glad on't; this is well: stand up:
> This is as't should be. Let me see the county;
> Ay, marry, go, I say, and fetch him hither.
> Now, afore God! this reverend holy friar,
> Our whole city is much bound to him.
>
> JULIET O, look! methinks I see my cousin's ghost
> Seeking out Romeo, that did spit his body
> Upon a rapier's point: stay, Tybalt, stay!
> Romeo, I come! this do I drink to thee.

Act 4 almost exclusively explores Juliet's plight in being left behind by Romeo and abandoned by her family and the Nurse. The dramatic irony that pervades the act is mostly related to the fact that we, the audience, know that Juliet is married to Romeo and yet many others do not, including Paris who believes, like her family, that she's showing "immoderate" grief for the death of Tybalt. Friar Lawrence had told Romeo that he would sort everything out, and now he has to pursue the plan in a desperate fashion; by making Juliet look like she's dead for forty two hours. This plan comforts Juliet and she agrees to marry Paris to her father, knowing full well that she won't. Capulet, as we see in the above quote, is delighted and feels very grateful to the friar, pointing out that the whole city should be. Finally, we see Juliet having many doubts about taking the potion; she's clearly frightened by the consequences of waking up in the tomb and seeing the dead bodies of her ancestors. Just before she drinks the potion, she sees the ghost of Tybalt.

Focus on grammar and lexis: what are the word classes of the following lexis in **CAPS** and why are they significant words?

> NURSE O day! O day! O day! O HATEFUL day!
> Never was seen so BLACK a day as this:
> O WOFUL day, O WOFUL day!

Hateful, black, woful = adjectives. These are highly emotive adjectives spoken by the Nurse and show her grief that Juliet is dead. There's a heavy irony to them because, of course, Juliet isn't dead. The lexis of the last two acts is laced with this sort of emotive vocabulary.

> FRIAR LAWRENCE Hold; get you gone, be strong and prosperous
> In this RESOLVE: I'll send a friar with SPEED
> To Mantua, with my LETTERS to thy LORD.

Resolve, speed, letters, lord = all nouns. Speed and resolve are abstract nouns which are important because they embody the two vital plot elements: Juliet's firm decision to pretend to be dead in order to escape marrying Paris (her 'resolve') and the necessity for Romeo to be informed quickly of what is happening ('speed'). **Letters** play an important role in the story: Romeo's ignored letters to Rosaline, Tybalt's ignored letter to Romeo, the letter that doesn't reach Romeo from Friar Lawrence, and the letter he writes to his father before he kills himself which clears the name of Friar Lawrence. The noun "lord" shows how Friar Lawrence is aware of the central importance of Romeo in Juliet's life.

Focus on characterizations: who said the following and what do we learn about the characters from these quotes?

> Thy face is mine, and thou hast slander'd it.

Paris is talking about Juliet as though he is already married to Juliet and as though he owns her face and therefore she has no right to talk about her own face in a critical fashion.

> Or bid me go into a new-made grave
> And hide me with a dead man in his shroud;
> Things that, to hear them told, have made me tremble;

Juliet shows how brave she is here, saying she would willingly be hidden with a dead man, a thought that has always made her "tremble".

> Death is my son-in-law, Death is my heir;
> My daughter he hath wedded: I will die,
> And leave him all; life, living, all is Death's.

Capulet is devastated that his daughter married death rather than Paris. He realises now that he will never have son and heir and that death will inherit everything.

Focus on staging: write about how these quotes might be acted out on stage or film, discussing any versions you've seen.

> JULIET: Come, vial.
> What if this mixture do not work at all?
> Shall I be married then to-morrow morning?
> No, no: this shall forbid it: lie thou there.

This is a fascinating point in the play: here we have Juliet about to take Friar Lawrence's potion. In terms of the staging, I imagine her standing at the front of the stage with the "vial" – the glass with the potion in – in her hand, thinking about whether to take it or not. The soliloquy will be full of gestures as Juliet thinks things through in her mind. When she asks the question as to whether the mixture will work and considers the point, I imagine that she picks up the dagger at this point and holds it in her hand, looking at it. Then she will put it possibly in her dress. I think this could be acted out with real tension as she looks at the knife and the potion.

Focus on imagery: fill in the gaps for the following quotes, then check your answer with Shakespeare's; why do you think Shakespeare made these word choices?

> CAPULET Death lies on her like an untimely frost
> Upon the sweetest flower of all the field.

Capulet uses the simile of comparing the death that has come upon Juliet as an "untimely frost". The adjective "untimely" is an echo of Romeo's commenting on the fact that he feels going to Capulet's party (Act I, Sc IV) will lead to his "untimely" death. There is heavy irony in the way he compares his daughter in this extended simile to the "sweetest flower" when he has just recently called her a "green sickness carrion" and threatened to throw her out into the streets.

Focus on rhythm: put these quotes into the correct verse form and write about the rhythmic effects of the lines.

> LADY CAPULET We shall be short in our provision:
> 'Tis now near night.

Lady Capulet curt "put-down" of Capulet has a quick, urgent rhythm echoing her panic that things may not work out properly for the wedding.

> FRIAR LAWRENCE: She's not WELL MARRied that LIVES MARRied LONG;
> But she's BEST MARRried that DIES MARRied YOUNG.
> DRY up your TEARS, and STICK your ROSEmary
> On this FAIR CORSE; AND, as the CUStom is,
> In ALL her BEST arRAY BEAR her to CHURCH:

There's real rhythmic vitality to the Friar's speech her because he uses a blend of rising and falling rhythms to both upbraid (tell off) and encourage the weeping family. The first two lines combine anapaests and trochees to create an aphorism of surprising vitality; the rhythm is rising on the phrase "she's not WELL" but then falls away with the verb "MARRied"; the rising rhythm creates a feeling of hope in contrast to the words themselves while the trochee causes a falling cadence. This pattern of a pacey rising rhythm contrasting with a much slower falling trochaic one is repeated throughout the two lines. These lines are text-book cases of balanced clauses with the words either mirroring each other through antithesis or repetition. Friar Lawrence then issues his imperative "DRY up your TEARS": the dactyl at the beginning of this line "DRY up your" gives energy and pace to the line and stirs the grief-stricken family into action.

Act 5, SCENE I. Mantua. A street.

Important vocabulary: took post = travelled with the horses that carried the mail, which were changed at inns along the route and so were always faster (Roma Gill, William Shakespeare, 1982, p. 99)
Bladders = used for storing liquids
Mischief = evil deed, harmful scheme,
Caitiff = miserable
Ducat = small, valuable gold coin
Cordial = medicine that helps your heart
(Roma Gill, William Shakespeare, 1982, p. 102)

Activities 5.1

Thematic questions: Why do people find it so difficult to break bad news? Why do people commit suicide? What is society's attitude towards suicide? Why do some people sell drugs when they know they shouldn't?

Read Act 5, Sc I lines 1 to the end of the scene.

Fill-in-the-blanks (answers below): Romeo has a dream that Juliet found him ---- and brought him to life with her ----. Initially, Balthasar says that Juliet is well and that he saw her sleeping in the tomb of the Capulets because he doesn't want to tell Romeo what he thinks is the ----: that she is dead. But then it becomes clear to Romeo that she must be dead because she is in a ----. Romeo decides to go to "defy the ---" and go to Juliet and lie with her. He visits a chemist, an apothecary, and buys ---- from him. It is against the --- to sell poison in Mantua and the sentence is death, but the apothecary agrees to give it to him because he is so ----, he needs the ---.

Flow chart: Devise a chart of the main events in this section.

Questions: What strange dream did Romeo have? What news does Balthasar bring Romeo? Why does he first say that he saw Juliet sleeping and then change his story? What is Romeo's reaction? What does he ask the Apothecary for and why does the Apothecary agree to give it to him?

Analysis: It is tragically ironic that Romeo thinks that he is defying the fate mapped out for him by killing himself by Juliet's side, when we know from the Prologue that he is actually fulfilling his fate by killing himself. Romeo's description of the apothecary's shop is a masterpiece of evocative writing: the hanging tortoise, the stuffed alligator, the weirdly shaped fishes and the atmosphere of poverty and decay are marvelously evoked, giving the powerful sense of a trapped personality who wants to do good in the world, but can't because he is so poor.

Act it out: Act out Romeo's interaction with the apothecary.

Creative response: Write a day in the life of the apothecary.

Further research: Do some research into the chemicals, potions and poisons that the Elizabethans used.

Fill-in-the-blanks answers: dead, kisses, truth, tomb, stars, poison, law, poor, money.

Act 5, Scene II. Friar Lawrence's Cell.

Important vocabulary: crow = crowbar
Beshrew = curse
(Roma Gill, William Shakespeare, 1982, pp. 102-103)

Activities 5.2

Thematic questions: Why do bad things happen in life? Is it God's plan, is it fate (destined to happen), or just bad luck/coincidence because we live in a meaningless universe?

Read Act 5, Sc II the whole of the scene.

Fill-in-the-blanks (answers below): Friar John who was delivering Friar Lawrence's letter to ---- visited another Friar who was staying in a house which was suspected to be a ---- house, and had to stay in ---- until it was clear that no one was ----. As a result, he had to turn back. Friar Lawrence curses his ------- and decides to write again to Mantua; he decides that he will fetch ---- and keep her at his cell until ---- arrives.

Flow chart: Devise a chart of the main events in this section.

Questions: Why was the letter to Romeo not delivered? What is Friar Lawrence going to do now?
Analysis: Again we have an unlikely plot-twist, but as has been said in the Prologue, the lovers are "star-crossed": it has been written in the stars that they are doomed to die.
Act it out: Improvise a scene in which two people realize something has gone badly wrong.
Creative response: Write a story or poem called 'The Unlucky Lovers' or write Friar Lawrence's new letter to Romeo.
Analytical response: What role does fate play in the tragedy?
Fill-in-the-blanks answers: Romeo, plague, quarantine, infected, ill-fortune, Juliet, Romeo.

Act 5, SCENE III. A churchyard; in it a tomb belonging to the Capulets.

Important vocabulary: aloof = at a distance
Maw = stomach, which is a metaphor for the vault
Ensign = flag
Inauspicious = unlucky, ill-fated
Descry = see, perceive
Winking at = ignoring
(Roma Gill, William Shakespeare, 1982, pp. 103-114)

Activities 5.3

Thematic questions: Why are people buried in graveyards or put in tombs? Why do people visit dead loved ones in graveyards etc?

Read Act 5, Sc III lines 1-73.

Fill-in-the-blanks (answers below): Paris has come to the tomb to pay his respects to Juliet by putting ---- on her tomb. He intends to come every ---- and --- over her. Romeo tells Balthasar that he is visiting Juliet to see her face and get a ---- that she is wearing which means a lot to him. He threatens to tear Balthasar limb from limb if he comes to --- on him. Paris thinks that Romeo has come to ----- the bodies in the tomb because he is a -----. Romeo tells Paris not to "tempt a ----- man" and that he has come to kill himself. Paris defies Romeo and tries to ---- him. They fight and Paris is ----.

Flow chart: Devise a chart of the main events in this section.
Questions: Why has Paris come to the tomb? What reasons does Romeo give Balthasar as to why he is going into the tomb? What does he

threaten Balthasar if he interrupts him? What does Paris think Romeo is doing at the tomb? What warning does Romeo give Paris? What is Paris's response?

Analysis: We see here how Paris is genuinely in love with Juliet, intending to pay homage to her every night. His death is frequently omitted from filmed versions of the play, but it is important because it adds to the tragedy of the play.

Act it out: Improvise a scene in which two characters visit the grave of their loved one at midnight.

Creative response: Write the diary of Paris's page for this section of the play.

Analytical response: What role does Paris play in the tragedy?

Fill-in-the-blanks nswers: flowers, night, cry ring, spy, desecrate, Montague, desperate, arrest, killed.

Activities 5.4

Thematic questions: Why do people talk to themselves? Who is their audience? Why do people write suicide notes or letters? Do you think suicide can ever be the right thing to do?

Read Act 5, Sc III lines 74-120.

Fill-in-the-blanks (answers below): When he looks closely, Romeo is shocked that he has killed ----, and wonders whether what he heard about Paris was actually ----, that he was going to marry Juliet, or whether it was a -----. Romeo looks hard at Juliet's body and feels that it makes the tomb a festival of ----, and that she looks as if she is ----. He wonders if Death is keeping her for his "------" and wanting to make ---- to her himself; in which case, Romeo intends to stay with Juliet and ---- her from -----.

Flow chart: Devise a chart of the main events in this section.

Questions: What are the important things that Romeo says before he kills himself?

Analysis: It is heavily and tragically ironic that Romeo thinks that Juliet looks almost as if she is alive, when, of course, she is.

Creative response: Imagine you are "Death" observing the events in the last act, write your account of the end of the play.

Act it out: Act out this section of the scene in small groups.

Analytical response: How does Shakespeare maintain interest and suspense during Romeo's soliloquy?

Fill-in-the-blanks answers: Paris, true, dream, light, alive, paramour, love, protect, Death.

Activities 5.5

Thematic questions: Why do people panic? When have you panicked in your life?

Read Act 5, Sc III lines 121-169.

Fill-in-the-blanks (answers below): The Friar speaks to Balthasar and discovers that Romeo has entered the ---- and worries that something --- has happened. He finds ---- on the steps of the tomb, and then finds the dead bodies of --- and ----. When Juliet wakes he urges her to leave the tomb with him, and tells her that Romeo and Paris are dead, and that he will place her in a ----. He hears the Watch approaching and runs away because he --- no longer stay. Juliet tries to drink Romeo's poison but it has all ----, instead she stabs herself with her ---- she had hidden on herself in case she was forced to marry -----.

Flow chart: Devise a chart of the main events in this section.

Questions: What does Friar Lawrence discover when he arrives on the scene? What does he tell Juliet when he wakes her? Why does he run away? What does Juliet say before she kills herself?

Analysis: Friar Lawrence's cowardice is highly problematic because it seems out of character but, of course, if he didn't flee, Juliet wouldn't have the same chance to kill herself. Her soliloquy is much shorter than Romeo's, and in a certain sense, she had already given her "death speech" when she took the potion.

Act it out: Act out this section of the scene in small groups, or improvise a scene in which a lover finds their loved one dead. What do they do?

Creative response: Write a poem about Juliet's "happy dagger" or write a story called 'I Won't Be Left Behind'.

Analytical response: How does Shakespeare make Juliet's death such a tense and dramatic moment?

Fill-in-the-blanks answers: tomb, terrible, blood, Romeo, Paris, nunnery, dare, gone, dagger, Paris.

Activities 5.6

Thematic questions: Why and how do people stop fighting each other?

Read Act 5, Sc III lines 170 to the end of the play.

Fill-in-the-blanks (answers below): The Watch find Count Paris and Romeo ----, and Juliet --- dead, even though she was supposed to be dead for --- days. They then find Balthasar, looking very frightened, and the Friar, who is ----. We learn from Lady Capulet that the sight of her dead daughter is her own "sepulcher" or ----, while Montague tells us that his wife died that night because of Romeo's ----. The Friar then explains that he married Romeo and Juliet in ---- in the hope that he would ----

the two warring families but that things went wrong when Capulet ---- Juliet to marry Paris, and he had to give her the ---- that made her look dead and so stopped her from marrying Paris. He then explains that his ---- about Juliet didn't reach Romeo and he arrived at the ---- to find Romeo and Paris dead. He was scared away by a ---- and Juliet ---- herself. A letter written by Romeo to his ---- is given to the Prince and backs up the Friar's account. The Prince then criticizes the two families, blaming the --- for all the tragic deaths. Montague says he will pay for a gold ---- of Juliet and Capulet says he will pay for one of Romeo to ---- beside her; the feud ---. The Prince concludes the play by saying there was never a more ------- tale than that of Romeo and Juliet.

Flow chart: Devise a chart of the main events in this section.

Questions: What do the Watch discover? What are people crying out on the streets? What do the parents of Romeo and Juliet say? What are the main points Friar Lawrence makes in his explanation of events? What evidence is found to back up the Friar's account? What do the two families agree to do? How does the Prince conclude the play?

Analysis: The end of the play is very frenetic, with the Watch and then the Prince piecing together the truth about what happened. The Prince's criticism of the two families is important and brings the play to a powerful conclusion, although a careful examination of the play has to question whether ultimately it was the feud which was to blame for the deaths of Romeo and Juliet.

Creative response: Write Romeo's letter to his father.

Act it out: Improvise a scene in which a policeman finds three dead bodies and has to work out what is going on. Double-up roles if necessary.

Analytical response: Who or what was to blame for the tragedy of Romeo and Juliet?

Act it out: Act out all the action in this scene without the words; miming the important incidents such as the deaths. Or imagine the statues of Romeo and Juliet come to life; what do they say?

Answers to fill-in-the-blanks: dead, freshly, two, weeping, tomb, exile, secret, unite, forced, potion, letter, tomb, noise, killed, father, feud, statue, lie, ends, sorrowful.

Looking back at Act 5

Focus on structure: put these quotes in the order they happen in the play and write about why Shakespeare ordered them in this way.

> PARIS This is that banish'd haughty Montague,
> That murder'd my love's cousin, with which grief,
> It is supposed, the fair creature died;

JULIET Yea, noise? then I'll be brief. O happy dagger!
This is thy sheath; there rust, and let me die.

ROMEO ...here, here will I remain
With worms that are thy chamber-maids; O, here
Will I set up my everlasting rest,
And shake the yoke of inauspicious stars
From this world-wearied flesh. Eyes, look your last!

FRIAR LAWRENCE All this I know; and to the marriage
Her nurse is privy: and, if aught in this
Miscarried by my fault, let my old life
Be sacrificed, some hour before his time,
Unto the rigour of severest law.

PRINCE Where be these enemies? Capulet! Montague!
See, what a scourge is laid upon your hate,
That heaven finds means to kill your joys with love.

APOTHECARY My poverty, but not my will, consents.

FRIAR JOHN Suspecting that we both were in a house
Where the infectious pestilence did reign,
Seal'd up the doors, and would not let us forth;
So that my speed to Mantua there was stay'd.

ROMEO I dreamt my lady came and found me dead--
Strange dream, that gives a dead man leave
to think!--
And breathed such life with kisses in my lips,
That I revived, and was an emperor.

Follow up after you've checked your answers: using a narrator who explains the missing parts of the story, either write up a "story" version of these quotes or work in a group and act out these lines, with a narrator or narrators explaining the story of the Act as a whole and the actors reading these key lines with real expression.

Focus on grammar and lexis: what are the word classes of the following lexis in **CAPS** and why are they significant words?

FRIAR LAWRENCE COME, I'll DISPOSE of thee
Among a sisterhood of holy NUNS:
Stay not to question, for the watch is COMING;

Focus on characterizations: who said the following and what do we learn about the characters from these quotes?

> Is it even so? then I defy you, stars!
>
> ...here is come to do some villanous shame
> To the dead bodies: I will apprehend him.
>
> Alas, my liege, my wife is dead to-night;
> Grief of my son's exile hath stopp'd her breath:
>
> And I for winking at your discords too
> Have lost a brace of kinsmen: all are punish'd.

Follow up after you've checked your answers: using these quotes as a starting point, "hotseat" the relevant characters, i.e. interview them in pairs about what they are thinking and feeling at these moments.

Focus on staging: write about how these quotes might be acted out on stage or film, discussing any versions you've seen.

> BALTHASAR Then she is well, and nothing can be ill:
> ... O, pardon me for bringing these ill news,
> Since you did leave it for my office, sir.
>
> ROMEO In faith, I will. Let me peruse this face.
> Mercutio's kinsman, noble County Paris!
> What said my man, when my betossed soul
> Did not attend him as we rode? I think
> He told me Paris should have married Juliet:
> Said he not so? or did I dream it so?
>
> PRINCE This letter doth make good the friar's words,
> Their course of love, the tidings of her death:

Focus on imagery: fill in the gaps for the following quotes, and then check your answer with Shakespeare's; why do you think Shakespeare made these word choices?

> LADY CAPULET O me! this sight of death is as a bell,
> That warns my old age to a sepulchre.
>
> PARIS Sweet flower, with flowers thy bridal bed I strew,--
> O woe! thy canopy is dust and stones;--
> Which with sweet water nightly I will dew,
> Or, wanting that, with tears distill'd by moans:
> The obsequies that I for thee will keep
> Nightly shall be to strew thy grave and weep.

ROMEO But if thou, jealous, dost return to pry
In what I further shall intend to do,
By heaven, I will tear thee joint by joint
And strew this hungry churchyard with thy limbs:

JULIET Yea, noise? then I'll be brief. O happy dagger!
This is thy sheath; there rust, and let me die.

MONTAGUE But I can give thee more:
For I will raise her statue in pure gold;

Focus on rhythm: put these quotes into the correct verse form and write about the rhythmic effects of the lines.

PRINCE For never was a story of more woe
Than this of Juliet and her Romeo.

Answers

Focus on structure. This is the correct order for the quotes.

ROMEO I dreamt my lady came and found me dead--
Strange dream, that gives a dead man leave
to think!--
And breathed such life with kisses in my lips,
That I revived, and was an emperor.

APOTHECARY My poverty, but not my will, consents.

FRIAR JOHN Suspecting that we both were in a house
Where the infectious pestilence did reign,
Seal'd up the doors, and would not let us forth;
So that my speed to Mantua there was stay'd.

PARIS This is that banish'd haughty Montague,
That murder'd my love's cousin, with which grief,
It is supposed, the fair creature died;

ROMEO ...here, here will I remain
With worms that are thy chamber-maids; O, here
Will I set up my everlasting rest,
And shake the yoke of inauspicious stars
From this world-wearied flesh. Eyes, look your last!

JULIET Yea, noise? then I'll be brief. O happy dagger!
This is thy sheath; there rust, and let me die.

> FRIAR LAWRENCE All this I know; and to the marriage
> Her Nurse is privy: and, if aught in this
> Miscarried by my fault, let my old life
> Be sacrificed, some hour before his time,
> Unto the rigour of severest law.
>
> PRINCE Where be these enemies? Capulet! Montague!
> See, what a scourge is laid upon your hate,
> That heaven finds means to kill your joys with love.

The Act opens with Romeo talking about how he has dreamt that Juliet has found him dead and breathed life into him with her kisses; a highly ironic dream in the light of what happens. His feelings of optimism are quickly stopped when he learns from Balthasar that Juliet is lying dead in the tomb of the Capulets. He buys poison from an apothecary who only agrees to give him it because he is so poor: the apothecary knows Romeo means to kill himself. The sense of impending doom is then strengthened when Friar John tells Friar Lawrence that he was put in quarantine in a plague house and couldn't deliver the vital letter which explained that Juliet was alive. As a result, Romeo goes to the tomb having decided to kill himself; he kills Paris outside the tomb because Paris challenges him and believes he has come to desecrate Tybalt's body. More tragedy. Shakespeare structures things so that Romeo gives a much longer death speech than Juliet; this is possibly because Juliet has already given a long soliloquy before she took the potion. Friar Lawrence has been implausibly frightened by the Watch and is caught and brought to account for himself before the Prince. He explains everything with honesty and asks to be executed if found guilty. The Prince, having read a letter from Romeo to his father about his plans, does not do this but tells everyone that they are punished for their endless feud.

Focus on grammar and lexis: what are the word classes of the following lexis in **CAPS** and why are they significant words?

> FRIAR LAWRENCE COME, I'll DISPOSE of thee
> Among a sisterhood of holy NUNS:
> Stay not to question, for the watch is COMING;

Come = a verb, an imperative. Friar Lawrence's urgent imperative verb is spoken because he is desperate to leave the tomb, fearing that the Watch will catch him.
Dispose = a verb. This verb suggests that he is thinking in his panic of Juliet as an object who can be "disposed" of, got rid of.
Nuns = noun. This collective noun has a chilling connotation here; nuns are celibate and stereotypically passionless, the exact opposite to Juliet.
Coming = present continuous verb. Friar Lawrence's panic rises as footsteps approach; this present continuous verse hints at his panic.

Focus on characterizations: who said the following and what do we learn about the characters from these quotes?

> ROMEO Is it even so? then I defy you, stars!

Here Romeo learns from Balthasar that Juliet is dead – as Balthasar believes her to be. A running theme with Romeo in the last act is his belief that he can defy his fate by killing himself; this is, of course, tragically ironic because he is actually fulfilling his fate by killing himself.

> PARIS...here is come to do some villanous shame
> To the dead bodies: I will apprehend him.

Paris is shown to be someone who genuinely cares for Juliet in the last act and is genuinely grief-stricken at her death; he is also revealed to be someone who will defend the Capulet honour. Here he tries to arrest Romeo for, as he believes, trying to desecrate the Capulet tomb by vandalizing the bodies of the dead.

> MONTAGUE Alas, my liege, my wife is dead to-night;
> Grief of my son's exile hath stopp'd her breath:

Romeo's parents are presented as very caring about their son: here we learn that Montague's wife has died because of the shame of Romeo's exile.

> PRINCE And I for winking at your discords too
> Have lost a brace of kinsmen: all are punish'd.

The Prince is fiercely angry with himself for "winking" at the "discords" of the feuding families, in other words he believes he didn't do enough to stop the feud and has been punished for it.

Focus on staging: write about how these quotes might be acted out on stage or film, discussing any versions you've seen.

> BALTHASAR Then she is well, and nothing can be ill:
> ... O, pardon me for bringing these ill news,
> Since you did leave it for my office, sir.

Here we imagine Balthasar as trying to seem like things are OK and then hanging his head in shame at having initially lied to Romeo and admitting in a woebegone fashion that he has "ill news". We can imagine Romeo's responses as he speaks: first Romeo may be very happy and then gradually his body language will jolt with shock as he realises what Balthasar is saying.

> ROMEO In faith, I will. Let me peruse this face.
> Mercutio's kinsman, noble County Paris!
> What said my man, when my betossed soul
> Did not attend him as we rode? I think
> He told me Paris should have married Juliet:
> Said he not so? or did I dream it so?

This is an excellent dramatic moment: Romeo turns over Paris's dead body to see who he is. He will be in shock as he realises what he has done and wonders why Paris is here.

> PRINCE This letter doth make good the friar's words,
> Their course of love, the tidings of her death:

The Prince will read the letter on stage and then look much more kindly upon Friar Lawrence because he realises that the Friar is more or less innocent.

Focus on imagery: fill in the gaps for the following quotes, then check your answer with Shakespeare's; why do you think Shakespeare made these word choices?

> LADY CAPULET O me! this sight of death is as a bell,
> That warns my old age to a sepulchre.

This powerful simile conveys the fact that Lady Capulet believes she will be in a "sepulchre" before she is old; in other words she will be dead. The simile is gloomy and filled with a sense of doom.

> PARIS Sweet flower, with flowers thy bridal bed I strew,--
> O woe! thy canopy is dust and stones;--
> Which with sweet water nightly I will dew,
> Or, wanting that, with tears distill'd by moans:
> The obsequies that I for thee will keep
> Nightly shall be to strew thy grave and weep.

Paris compares Juliet to a "sweet flower", echoing the extended simile that Capulet used to describe Juliet in death. Whereas Capulet envisaged Juliet as being killed off by an "untimely frost", here we see Paris noting that her "canopy is dust and stones", powerful imagery which connotes death and barrenness.

> ROMEO But if thou, jealous, dost return to pry
> In what I further shall intend to do,
> By heaven, I will tear thee joint by joint
> And strew this hungry churchyard with thy limbs:

Romeo personifies the church as "hungry" for dead limbs, which he will provide if Balthasar "pries" into his business.

> JULIET Yea, noise? then I'll be brief. O happy dagger!
> This is thy sheath; there rust, and let me die.

Juliet personifies the dagger as "happy" because it will enable her to be at one with Romeo: dead.

> MONTAGUE But I can give thee more:
> For I will raise her statue in pure gold;

This is one of the last images of the play: that of golden statues being erected to commemorate Romeo and Juliet's death suggesting that they have attained immortality as the lovers who ended the feud.

Focus on rhythm: put these quotes into the correct verse form and write about the rhythmic effects of the lines.

> PRINCE For never was a story of more woe
> Than this of Juliet and her Romeo.

This closing rhyming couplet encapsulates the overall tone of the last act which is soaked in misery, doom and death. However, it does not reflect the opening of the play which is notably comedic and full of hope. The rhythm of the first line is classically iambic:

> For NEVer WAS a STORy OF more WOE

There is a certainty of tone here, but the rhythm of the second line is disrupted by the "dactylic" quality of their two names, which creates a falling rhythm and a sadder, more uncertain mood:

> Than THIS of JULiet AND her ROMeo.

Summary of the whole play

Prologue

The Prologue tells us that the play is set in Verona and is about two feuding families who give birth to two lovers. Romeo and Juliet will die because it is their fate – it is written in the stars.

Act 1, Sc I

The play begins with two servants from the Capulet family, Sampson and Gregory, joking about raping the Montague virgins. Some Montague servants then appear and the Capulet servants to try to cause a fight with them by making rude gestures which involve biting their thumbs. The Capulet servants are careful to keep the law on their side. They become more daring when they see Tybalt Capulet approach and this leads to them fighting. Benvolio Montague tries to stop the servants fighting but is then challenged by Tybalt, then officers and citizens from the families join in, followed by the older generation who are the heads of the families: Capulet and Montague. The Prince stops the fight. He tells us that there have been three fights recently where blood has been shed. The Prince says he will execute anyone who starts another one.

Lord and Lady Montague are worried about Romeo because he has been locking himself in his room and sitting in the dark, with his curtains closed. He has been crying a lot and avoiding talking to people. Benvolio talks to him and discovers that he is in love but that the woman he loves does not return his love. He does not tell Benvolio her name but we later learn she is called Rosaline. Romeo says he has tried everything to win her over, including offering her gold to have sex with her, but she has always refused him.

Act 1, Sc II

Paris wants to marry Capulet's daughter, Juliet, but Capulet tells him that being thirteen years old she is too young to marry. However, Capulet will listen to what Juliet says. He invites Paris to a party or feast that night so that he can get to know Juliet.

A Capulet servant carrying Capulet's letter about the party needs Romeo to read the guest-list because he cannot read. Romeo discovers that Rosaline has been invited to the party. Benvolio says that Romeo will see women more beautiful than Rosaline at the party but Romeo disagrees.

Act 1, Sc III

Lady Capulet and the Nurse discuss the fact that Juliet will soon be fourteen. The Nurse remembers Juliet's age very well because her own daughter, Susan, was the same age as Juliet, but Susan died. The Nurse remembers Juliet's birth, on 31st July, almost 14 years ago. The Nurse remembers when Juliet was weaned – i.e. stopped breast-feeding. The Nurse breast-fed her. It was common in those days for rich families to have a "wet nurse" who would breast-feed their children. The Nurse remembers another funny event: when Juliet fell over and hurt herself. Her husband said that Juliet would fall on her back (i.e. have sex) when she is old enough. Lady Capulet stops the Nurse from talking and asks Juliet what she thinks about marrying to which Juliet replies she hasn't thought about it. Lady Capulet then says that Paris wants to marry Juliet and talks about all his good qualities in a very artificial way. She says Juliet must get to know him at the feast.

Act 1, Sc IV

Romeo is love-sick at the beginning of this scene and is worried about gate-crashing a party. Mercutio tries to cheer him up by telling him not to be such a boring person. When Romeo talks about a dream he had, Mercutio gives a long speech about Queen Mab, who is the mid-wife to the fairies and encourages people to express their desires, which is very dangerous; it leads to people being humiliated in all sorts of ways. Romeo stops him giving the speech because it is clear that he has become upset. Romeo then talks to himself (a soliloquy) and says that something dreadful is going to happen because of this night: he has a feeling that he will die young because of the events of this night.

Act 1, Sc V

The servants are very stressed as they prepare for the feast. Their master, Capulet wants this to be a very successful party. We know from previous scenes that this is the feast in which Capulet wants Paris to win over Juliet. Capulet is very keen for everyone to get into the party atmosphere and to start dancing; he uses jokey blackmail to do this by saying that the ladies must have corns on their feet if they don't dance. Capulet then talks to an elderly relative about when it was when they last had a similar party; there is some dispute about this.

When Romeo first sees Juliet, he compares her to a very strongly burning "torch" (fiery stick), a jewel in a black man's ear, and a dove, a white bird amongst black crows.

Tybalt is insulted by Romeo's presence at the party because Romeo is a Montague and is wearing an "antic face" or comedy mask. He believes that Romeo has come to the party to mock the Capulets. He says he will kill Romeo. When he tells Capulet about this, Capulet becomes very angry with him for threatening to cause a riot at the party and tells him that Romeo is a well-behaved and respected gentleman. Tybalt backs down but vows to get his revenge on Romeo at a later date.

Romeo and Juliet touch hands and flirt with each other, speaking to each other using religious imagery. Romeo asks Juliet for lips to do what their hands are doing, i.e. kiss.

After they've parted, Romeo and Juliet both learn that they are from the families of their enemies. Romeo responds by saying that his life now depends upon his enemy, while Juliet feels that her marriage bed is her grave. They both have terrible "presentiments" (premonitions/visions of the future) that their lives are at risk because of their love. Romeo has to leave because Benvolio believes that they might be caught.

Act 2, Prologue

The Prologue talks how about Romeo was once in love with Rosaline but now is in love with another person. The problem is that she is the daughter of his enemy and she doesn't have the power to move as freely as he does.

Act 2, Sc I

Romeo doesn't want to be with his friends because he wants to find Juliet, where his heart his. Mercutio and Benvolio think Romeo has gone looking for Rosaline; Mercutio jokes that he can "magick" up Rosaline and excite Romeo's desire. He makes very rude jokes about what he thinks Romeo wants to do with Rosaline.

Act 2, Sc II

Romeo compares Juliet to the sun because he feels she emanates a powerful inner light; this is a running "motif" throughout the play, Juliet is consistently connected to visions of light. He feels her eyes are talking to him. He compares her eyes to stars and imagines what might happen if her eyes swapped places with the stars: the birds would think it was the daytime and begin to sing.

Juliet wonders why Romeo is called by his name because it is his name which is stopping them being as one; their families are mortal enemies. Romeo startles her because he has been hiding in the dark underneath the balcony and suddenly speaks, saying that he will take another name. Juliet is concerned that Romeo will think she is too easily won over because she has readily admitted her devotion to him, but the main reason why she has done this is because she was speaking to herself and didn't know he was there. Romeo is unsatisfied because he wants them to promise to marry, which Juliet immediately agrees to. She then takes back that promise so that they can make the promise again. Both lovers are worried for different reasons: Juliet is worried their love is too sudden, and Romeo feels it is too like a dream.

Juliet returns to the balcony because she says she will send a messenger tomorrow to ask the time and place of the wedding. Juliet compares Romeo to a "tassel-gentle" or peregrine falcon, the bird of princes (Gibson, 2006, p. 60). Later Romeo calls Juliet his "nyas", a young fledgling hawk (Gibson, 2006, p. 60). These are both birds of prey and may express the two lover's desire to "devour" each other. After leaving Juliet, Romeo wants to sleep in order to dream of Juliet.

Act 2, Sc III

Shakespeare introduces us to Friar Lawrence here through the use of a long soliloquy, establishing a few characteristics that are important to him: his religious character, his knowledge of herbs and potions, and his philosophizing. The Friar says the earth is both like a tomb and a womb: it is the place where all dead things return to, but the place from which all new life arises.

Friar Lawrence thinks that Romeo has spent the night with Rosaline. When Romeo confesses to him, he is shocked that Romeo has fallen in love with another woman because he has counselled Romeo so much about Rosaline, watching him cry about the fact that he can't have her. However, he agrees to marry Romeo and Juliet because he believes this might end the hatred between the two families. He advises Romeo to take the romance slowly.

Act 2, Sc IV

Benvolio tells Mercutio that Tybalt has sent a letter to Romeo's home; both Mercutio and Benvolio believe it is a challenge to fight. Benvolio believes Romeo will fight if he is "dared" to, but Mercutio says that Romeo has already been "stabbed" by Rosaline's "black eye". Mercutio tells us that Tybalt is a very skilful swordsman but he is vain. Mercutio has fun in mocking the Nurse, suggesting with a number of puns that she is a "bawd" – a female pimp – and a prostitute herself; he sings a song which puns on the words "hare" and "hoar", thereby suggesting the Nurse is a "hairy whore".

The Nurse is very upset at the way Mercutio has treated her and the insulting names he has called her, suggesting that she is a woman of loose morals, a "flirt-gill". Romeo says that Mercutio says more in a minute than he would ever do in a month, in other words his bark is bigger than his bite. Romeo says that Juliet needs to come to confession that afternoon where he will marry her, after that Romeo's servant will bring the Nurse: a rope ladder that will enable Romeo to climb up to Juliet's bedroom at night.

Act 2, Sc V

Juliet is very impatient at the beginning of the scene to hear the news from Romeo and really wants to know what he's said. She believes that the older generation doesn't understand the younger generation because the Nurse is so slow at conveying messages between the lovers; she feels that the older generation have little understanding of what it means to be in love. When the Nurse appears however she is very nice to her, calling her "honey" Nurse and is desperate to hear the Nurse's news. The Nurse teases Juliet and holds back giving her the important news; Juliet gets very frustrated and irritable with the Nurse, who appears to enjoy the power she has over Juliet. Eventually, the Nurse tells Juliet that when she goes to confession she will be married.

Act 2, Sc VI

Romeo will not be afraid of death after he has married Juliet; he can die happy just knowing he has spent a minute in her company. Friar Lawrence warns Romeo against loving too violently because it can lead to two people "exploding" like mixing fire and gunpowder. Juliet finds Romeo's analogy about his love in which he compares it to dancing, air and music far too complicated and flowery. She herself can't begin to put into words what she feels.

Act 3, Sc I

Mercutio makes fun of Benvolio by accusing him of being a man with a very quick temper who easily gets into fights; quarrelling, for example, with someone who has one more hair in his beard than he has. Mercutio appears hot and bothered: even for him his joking seems extreme and irritable. Benvolio says that if he argued as much as Mercutio did, he would be dead. Tybalt arrives and says that Mercutio "consorts" with Romeo, i.e. knows or plays with him. Mercutio takes offence at this word, because he feels that it makes him and Romeo sound like travelling musicians, an insult in his eyes. Benvolio advises them to go someone private where they can't be seen; they are in the public square at the moment.

Tybalt is mystified when Romeo appears and says that he loves Tybalt more than he could possibly know; this is completely different to the way the two families talk to each other. We know the reason why: Romeo has married Tybalt's cousin. Mercutio believes Romeo's gestures of love amount to a "dishonourable, vile submission"; in other words, he has given in and is behaving like a coward. As a result, Mercutio feels duty bound to take up Romeo's fight on his behalf. Unfortunately, Tybalt fatally stabs Mercutio, who blames two things for his death: the fact that Romeo came between him and Tybalt and he was stabbed underneath his arm, and the feud between the two families. A careful reading of the scene pretty much shows that Mercutio is to blame for his own death: he didn't have to fight Tybalt, who was not looking to fight him but Romeo.

Romeo fights Tybalt in revenge for Mercutio's death. His mood quickly changes from one of love towards his cousin-in-law, Tybalt, to one of "fire-eyed fury". Romeo is very, very angry; he believes his love for Juliet has made him "effeminate" – i.e. too like a woman. After he has killed Tybalt, he realizes that he is "fortune's fool"; in other words, he is the idiot of "fate", a key idea set out in the Prologue.

Benvolio's long speech blames Tybalt for everything: he says that Romeo was being very nice to Tybalt when Tybalt then attacked Mercutio. He then says that Tybalt returned to fight Romeo, who got his revenge. Lady Capulet doubts Benvolio's account because he is a Montague and bound to be biased against Tybalt. She then calls for Romeo to be executed. The Prince decides to exile Romeo from Verona.

Act 3, Sc II

Juliet wants the night to come quickly so that she can be with Romeo; she wants it to hide her and Romeo so that they can lose their virginities. She isn't aware that Romeo has killed Tybalt. She feels she has bought "the mansion of a love" – a huge house of love – but she doesn't possess this house yet; she hasn't moved in.

The Nurse appears, upset because Tybalt has died, but doesn't seem very concerned about Romeo's situation. She speaks in a confused, grief-stricken fashion and does not clearly explain what has happened; this is probably not deliberate but because she is so distraught. When Juliet learns fully what has happened, that Tybalt is dead and Romeo has been sent into exile, she responds firstly by criticizing Romeo, saying that his beautiful form hid a serpent, and then she criticizes herself for criticizing Romeo. She says that she has only been married three hours and already she doubts him. She tells off the Nurse for criticizing Romeo too. The Nurse says at the end of the scene that she is going to visit Romeo, who is hiding in Friar Lawrence's room. Juliet asks her to give Romeo a ring.

Act 3, Sc III

Romeo is devastated to learn that he has been exiled from Verona because this is where Juliet lives. Friar Lawrence tries to reassure him with philosophy. Romeo dismisses the Friar's advice, saying that it is useless to help him unless it can bring Juliet back to him. He then throws himself on the floor and has a hysterical fit.

We learn from the Nurse that Juliet is distraught too about the death of Tybalt and Romeo's banishment. As a result of hearing this, Romeo tries to kill himself but the Nurse and the Friar stop him. The Friar tells Romeo that he must get control of himself: suicide is a mortal sin and if he kills himself he will kill Juliet too. He says that Romeo should be happy that he is alive and that he has not been executed; it means he will be able to see Juliet again. He says that Romeo should see Juliet tonight, and then go to Mantua while the Friar sorts everything out. The Nurse gives Romeo Juliet's ring and they make arrangements for Romeo to spend the night with Juliet.

Act 3, Sc IV

Capulet tells Paris that the death of Tybalt has meant that they haven't had time to "move" or persuade Juliet to marry him, thus indicating to Paris that marriage at the moment is unlikely. Paris agrees that it's very difficult to win someone over at such a sad time. But as Paris is leaving, Capulet says he will speak for Juliet and that she will be "ruled" by him in "all respects". Possibly Capulet believes that the marriage needs to happen quickly because life is so fragile. At first, he says that Lady Capulet should tell Juliet that the marriage will take place on Wednesday, but he changes his mind and makes it Thursday.

Act 3, Sc V

Juliet believes it is the nightingale which is singing, which indicates it is still night-time. Romeo points out that it is the lark, the bird that signals it is morning time, but when Juliet says it is a meteorite in the sky which is making it light, Romeo laughs and says if she says it is night-time then it is, and he welcomes death if that's what Juliet wants. At this, Juliet realizes that it is the day, and that Romeo must go immediately. Juliet worries that she will never see Romeo again, to which he replies that he is certain that they will meet again and these times will be interesting to remember in the days they spend together. As Romeo descends the ladder Juliet believes she sees him in a tomb.

Lady Capulet appears, saying it shows a "want of wit" (a lack of common sense) for someone to cry so much. She then says that she is going to poison Romeo when she has the chance. Juliet annoys her by responding in a paradoxical fashion, saying that she would rather marry Romeo, who she knows her mother hates, than Paris. Capulet arrives and voices his irritation that she is crying so much. When he learns that she won't obey his "decree", which means order, he loses his temper and says that he will disown her and cast her out into the streets, calling her rude names in the process. Lady Capulet and the Nurse try to stop him hitting Juliet without much effect. Juliet turns in her distress to her mother to help her make her father reconsider but Lady Capulet disowns her. Then she turns to the Nurse who advises her to go ahead and marry Paris because Romeo is a "dishcloth" compared with the noble Count. Juliet says sarcastically that the Nurse has helped her "marvellous much" and says she is going to see Friar Lawrence to make her confession. Finally, when left alone, she curses the Nurse, who she feels really betrayed her because the Nurse is now criticizing Romeo who she has previously praised thousands of times. She says that either she will get help from Friar Lawrence or kill herself.

Act 4, Sc I

Paris thinks Juliet is upset because of Tybalt's death. He explains to Friar Lawrence that Capulet has hurried up the marriage because he thinks the wedding will distract her and stop her from being so depressed. Juliet talks in a very terse way to Paris, giving double-edged answers such as "what must be shall be". Her manner towards him seems cold and distant. Paris claims Juliet's face for his own because he is about to marry "it" and he doesn't like the way Juliet criticizes her looks. Juliet agrees that her face is not her own; again a double-edged answer.

Juliet threatens to kill herself if the Friar doesn't stop her marrying Paris. Because she's so desperate, the Friar considers a desperate solution. He will give her a potion which will make her look like she is dead for 42 hours; this will mean she will be given a funeral. The Friar will send a letter to Romeo who come and fetch her from the tomb and take her to Mantua.

Act 4, Sc II

Capulet is busy making arrangements for the wedding at the beginning of the scene and is telling people to hurry up, and also cursing Juliet for being a stubborn "harlot", which is slang for prostitute or difficult woman. He doesn't literally mean she is but he just uses it as a term of abuse here. Juliet says that the Friar has asked her to fall "prostrate" (face first) before him and be "ruled" by him, i.e. obey his every word. He is delighted and immediately says that Paris needs to be told of this. He then decides to make the wedding tomorrow: Lady Capulet is doubtful that they have enough food and drink for the party. However, Capulet says he will stay up all night and "play the housewife" so that everything is ready.

Act 4, Sc III

Juliet wants to sleep alone so that she can take the potion. Juliet has a number of fears about taking the potion, which she explores during the long soliloquy. She worries first of all that the potion won't work and that she'll have to marry Paris. She sets aside this worry because she has a dagger with which she will kill herself if the potion doesn't work. Then she worries that the potion is poison which the Friar has given her because he would "dishonoured" if it was known that he married Romeo and Juliet. She rejects this worry because she knows he is a holy man. Then she worries that she will suffocate to death when she wakes up in the vault. She goes on to worry that she will be terrified by the spirits and bones of the dead and will be driven out of her mind, and will club herself to death in her madness with an old bone. In her terror, she sees the ghost of Tybalt looking for Romeo, but, even with all these fears, she takes the potion because she is doing it for Romeo.

Act 4, Sc IV

The Capulet household is in a state of panic because the wedding is going to happen that day and they are not really ready. Paris has already arrived with the musicians. This is all highly ironic because we know that they will soon find Juliet looking as though she is dead.

When she sees Juliet, the Nurse becomes distraught. Seeing his daughter, Capulet talks at length about his feelings of grief. He says that death has taken her like the frost in a field which kills off the most beautiful flower. His language contrasts greatly with Act 3, ScV, in which he called her many horrible names, including "green sickness carrion". Paris appears to be stunned and asks why he is seeing this sight on his wedding day, while Lady Capulet says this is the worst day since time began. Friar Lawrence calms them down by saying that they should be pleased because Juliet has gone to heaven and that long marriages never work out; it is best to die young. Some musicians pack up their instruments which they were planning to play at the wedding; they make rude jokes about each other.

Act 5, Sc I

Romeo has a dream that Juliet found him dead and brought him to life with her kisses. Initially, Balthasar says that Juliet is well and that he saw her sleeping in the tomb of the Capulets because he doesn't want to tell Romeo what he thinks is the truth: that she is dead. But then it becomes clear to Romeo that she must be dead because she is in a tomb. Romeo decides to "defy the stars" and go to Juliet and lie with her. He visits a chemist, an apothecary, and buys poison from him. It is against the law to sell poison in Mantua and the sentence is death, but the apothecary agrees to give it to him because he is so poor; he needs the money.

Act 5, Sc II

Friar John -- who was delivering Friar Lawrence's letter to Romeo -- visited another Friar; the latter was staying in a house which was suspected to be a plague house. And so, Friar John has to stay in quarantine until the house is given the all clear. As a result, he has to turn back and the letter is not delivered to Romeo. When he learns of this, Friar Lawrence curses his ill-fortune and decides to write again to Romeo in Mantua; he decides that he will fetch Juliet and keep her at his cell until Romeo arrives.

Act 5, Sc III

Paris has come to the tomb to pay his respects to Juliet by putting flowers on her tomb. He intends to come every night and cry over her. Romeo tells Balthasar that he is visiting Juliet to see her face and get a ring that she is wearing that means a lot to him. He threatens to tear Balthasar limb from limb if he comes to spy on him. Paris thinks that Romeo has come to vandalize the bodies in the tomb because he is a Montague. Romeo tells Paris not to "tempt a desperate man" and that he has come to kill himself. Paris defies Romeo and tries to arrest him. They fight and Paris is killed. Romeo is shocked to learn that he has killed Paris, and wonders whether what he heard about Paris was actually true, that he was going to marry Juliet, or whether it was a dream. Romeo looks hard at Juliet's body and feels that it makes the tomb a festival of light, and that she looks as if she is alive. He wonders if Death is keeping her for his "paramour" and wanting to make love to her himself; in which case, Romeo intends to stay with Juliet and protect her from Death. Then he takes the poison and dies.

    The Friar speaks to Balthasar and discovers that Romeo has entered the tomb and worries that something terrible has happened. He finds blood on the steps of the tomb, and then finds the dead bodies of Romeo and Paris. When Juliet wakes he urges her to leave the tomb with him, and tells her that Romeo and Paris are dead, and that he will place her in a nunnery. He hears the Watch approaching and runs away because he dare no longer stay. Juliet tries to drink Romeo's poison but it has all gone; instead she stabs herself with her dagger she had hidden on herself in case she was forced to marry Paris.

The Watch find Count Paris and Romeo dead, and Juliet freshly dead, even though she was supposed to be dead for two days. They then find Balthasar, looking very frightened, and the Friar, who is weeping. We learn from Lady Capulet that the sight of her dead daughter is her own "sepulcher" or tomb, while Montague tells us that his wife died that night because of Romeo's exile. The Friar then explains that he married Romeo and Juliet in secret in the hope that he would unite the two warring families but that things went wrong when Capulet forced Juliet to marry Paris, and he had to give her the potion. He then explains that his letter about Juliet didn't reach Romeo and he arrived at the tomb to find Romeo and Paris dead. He was scared away by a noise and Juliet killed herself. A letter by Romeo to his father is given to the Prince and backs up the Friar's account. The Prince then criticizes the two families, blaming the feud for all the tragic deaths. Montague says he will pay for a gold statue of Juliet. Capulet says he will pay for one of Romeo to lie beside her. And so the family feud ends. The Prince concludes the play by saying there was never a more sorrowful tale than that of Romeo and Juliet.

Speaking and listening activities

Act out a shortened version of the play: Collect all the quotes in the sequencing activities at the end of every act and use them as the basis to tell the story of Romeo and Juliet in 20 minutes, with a narrator filling in all the gaps or using the above summary as a guideline. Work in a small group of four or five and present your shortened, dramatic version to the class.

Devise a chat-show in which the main characters in the play appear. Work in a group of four or five and choose the five most important characters, with a chat-show host asking good questions.

Hold an inquest into the deaths of Romeo and Juliet and investigate who might be to blame.

Put Friar Lawrence or the families (you decide which) **on trial** on the charge of criminal negligence for their role in the deaths of Romeo and Juliet.

Improvise a modern version of the play or a particular scene in a small group, using modern language. Then write a **script** or story version of your play.

Devise a **radio/TV documentary or news report** about what has happened at the end of the play, interviewing all the major players.

Literary Criticism

Literary criticism of the play should be a **"starting off" point** for your own thoughts. You should avoid blindly agreeing with everything various critics have said. This is why I have put questions at the end of every section.

Early critics

In 1662, nearly seventy years after the play was written, the diarist Samuel Pepys became the first known critic of the play and was very negative, saying: "it is a play of itself the worst that I ever heard in my life." His analysis didn't go much further than that! Later on, other critics in the 18th century said that the main messages of the play were that the families were punished because of their feud. Some critics argued that the play was flawed because it didn't follow Aristotle's rules for classic tragedies in that the main characters didn't have major "flaws" which led to their deaths, and that the tragedy happened because of fate, not because of the main characters' actions. Remember, Aristotle had said the best tragedies relied on the action being driven by characters' actions, not by accidents of fate.

Many critics for the next two hundred years debated the **moral message** of the play; some critics **placed the blame** for the tragedy heavily on Romeo because he was wild (he had had previously been in love with Rosaline and he murdered Tybalt very recklessly) and because he abandoned Juliet rather than taking her to Mantua. Other critics argued that Friar Lawrence was actually Shakespeare speaking because the Friar warns against too much haste, which they felt is probably what Shakespeare thought.

Question: to what extent do you agree with these interpretations? Justify your opinions with evidence from the play and good arguments.

Nicholas Brooke

The academic Nicholas Brooke writes an important chapter about *Romeo and Juliet* in his book *Shakespeare's Early Tragedies* (1968) and offers a number of points that are worthy of consideration. He comments upon the **emotional impact** of the play when he says:

> The most moving scene in the play, in a sense, is not this final pavan of death at all (note: Romeo and Juliet's deaths) but the

> death of Mercutio in Act III, scene I, which is in prose, and the sequel to a passage of very trivial comedy. (Brooke, 1968, p. 82)

It's worth thinking about this in some depth, particularly if you are analyzing the scene. Is Mercutio's death moving? Some critics might argue that Mercutio is unsympathetic because he appears to have stirred up the fight himself and then blames everyone else for it. Brooke notes, as many critics have, that Act 3, Sc I, is a **major turning point** in the play. Brooke writes: "The shock of this scene is used to precipitate a change of key in the play: it becomes immediately more serious and decisively tragic where before it had been predominantly comic." (Brooke, 1968, p. 83).

Brooke feels that the first two acts are **largely comic** in tone and that it is the scenes with the Nurse which are the most comic. He describes the Nurse's comic speech about her husband laughing regarding the Juliet falling on her back when she was a child in Act 1, sc III as "earthy, sentimental, warm-blooded, bawdy, repetitious" (Brooke, 1968, p. 93). For Brooke and many critics the Nurse is one of the most vibrant characters in the play: her playfulness, her "bawdiness" (joking about sex) and loyalty make her a moving but funny figure. Some critics disagree because ultimately the Nurse betrays Juliet in Act 3, Sc V.

Like many critics, Brooke notes how **immature** both lovers are at the beginning of the play. Brooke says: "Juliet is introduced between her mother and the nurse and thus has, from the start, a fuller humanity than Romeo has yet displayed...Juliet, then, is a child growing up; immature, obviously, but in a very different way from Romeo who is evidently older; he is continually revealed as 'immature' in the sense of being less grown-up than he seems...With Juliet, it is rather the other round."

Brooke then goes on to show that the lovers mature quickly in the play, and highlights Juliet's "Gallop apace" speech (Act 3, Sc II), in which Juliet anticipates having sex with Romeo, as being one of the most impressive in the play, noting its sexual content. He writes:

> 'Gallop apace' is put *after* Mercutio's death, but *before* she has heard of it. It is, as *we* see it, an experience of 'what might have been'. In itself it is a magnificently full-bodied evocation of sexual desire, enacting a series of paradoxes that are already more or less familiar...The focal image throughout is the day-night contrast, and Juliet's desire for night becomes a cluster of powerfully associated ideas: night, of course, is sex-time; it is blindness; it is the 'madame' of a brothel...The core of this in Juliet's discovery that in most wanting her true love with Romeo she must experience the wish to be a whore in the fullest sense... (Brooke, 1968, p. 100)

In summing up, Brooke says: "The play is overall suspended between two major ceremonies: the dance-betrothal of Act I, and the wedding-funeral of Act V. Between them it projects a double climax in Act III, which is in both parts entirely unceremonial: Mercutio's death and Romeo and

Juliet's clandestine consummation (with the rope ladder to the balcony and so it has the air of stolen love)." (Brooke, 1968, p. 106).

Question: to what extent do you agree with these interpretations? Justify your opinions with evidence from the play and good arguments.

Feminist criticism

Many feminist critics have pointed out that *Romeo and Juliet*, like most of Shakespeare's plays, presents us with a patriarchal society: a society where men have the power. They argue, as we saw when we looked at Romeo's character, that he is the victim of a very strict "male" or "masculine" code which demands that he behaves in a violent way and keeps to the rules of the feud. We see evidence of this when he says after Mercutio's murder that his love for Juliet has made him "effeminate": too like a woman. The women in the play have varying degrees of power but they are all far less free to do what they want than the men; some feminists have argued that they are "oppressed" – treated very badly – by the patriarchal society that they live in. The critic Coppelia Kahn writes:

> In patriarchal Verona, men bear names and stand to fight for them; women, "the weaker vessels", bear children and "fall backward" to conceive them, as the Nurse's husband once told the young Juliet...Unlike its sons, Verona's daughters have, in effect, no adolescence, no sanctioned period of experiment with adult identities or activities. (Kahn, 1993, p. 345)

We have already seen how the critic Dymna Callaghan argues that the play is really about the shift from a society which is controlled by the leading men in the families to a society which is controlled by the laws of the government as embodied by the Prince Escalus (Callaghan, 2001). Callaghan writes in conclusion to her essay about the play, *The Ideology of Romantic Love*: "Romeo and Juliet are simultaneously sacrificed to the old feudal order of Montague and Capulet and to patriarchy's new order of the unified power of the state represented by Escalus." (Callaghan, 2001, p. 107). By the end of the play, it has been established that people can marry who they like and don't have to obey the leading men, the patriarchs, of the families. It is now the Prince who sets the rules for who marries who; he represents the law of the government.

Question: to what extent do you agree with these interpretations? Justify your opinions with evidence from the play and good arguments.

Marxist and cultural materialist criticism

The Marxist theatre director and playwright, Bertold Brecht, focused upon the role of the "lower social classes" in the play: he noted that they are largely ignored and not allowed to have love lives. He believed though that if you look carefully you can see how they are oppressed by their "social superiors". He felt this was unfair. As a result, he wrote his own play which illustrates their oppression fully. In his play, Romeo rejects a plea for some money from a tenant who is starving to death. Juliet talks to a maid, comparing her love for Romeo with the maid's love for Thurio (Brecht, 2001). The point that Brecht makes through this creative response is that the text makes "ordinary" people, the working classes, the underclass, totally invisible and doesn't highlight the terrible treatment they received.

Cultural materialist critics, who often use Marx's analysis of society to guide their work, have investigated in some depth the world the play arose from, noting that the violence in the play mirrors the violence in Shakespeare's society where there was an epidemic of gun crime. (The British Museum, n.d.). The best place to learn about this is to listen to the Shakespeare's Restless World podcast Swordplay and Swagger. There is also a transcript of this programme.

Question: to what extent do you agree with these interpretations? Justify your opinions with evidence from the play and good arguments.

Queer criticism

Some critics have looked at the play from the perspective of "Queer Theory"; this is an approach which examines the role of homosexuality in texts. The critic Jonathan Goldberg argues that there is a hidden homosexual attraction between Mercutio and Romeo. Goldberg writes at length about Act 2, Sc I, which takes place immediately after the party; Mercutio and Benvolio have lost Romeo because he is seeking out Juliet. Mercutio believes Romeo is looking for Rosaline and so "conjures" her up for Romeo, describing her in sexual terms, emphasizing how Romeo could have anal sex with her now that Mercutio has "conjured" her up. Goldberg says:

> Mercutio's conjuring also conjures him (Romeo) into the magic circle, an O that is not, as most commentators would have it be, the vaginal opening, for this is how Mercutio voices – through Rosaline – his desire for Romeo, her version, that is, of Benvolio's more benign voicing of the place she can have between men. Mercutio is calling Romeo up for him, as he does throughout the opening acts of the play, a deflection of Romeo's desire from the unresponsive beloved, to one who, as much as Juliet later, want to share a bed with Romeo. (Goldberg, 2001, p. 206)

Mercutio's homosexual love for Romeo is an idea that Baz Luhrmann, the film director, picks up upon. He presents Mercutio as being very jealous when he suspects Romeo has gone off with Rosaline. Goldberg also argues that Rosaline may actually be Shakespeare's code for a man and that Romeo at the beginning of the play is lusting after the beauty of a man, in the same way Shakespeare himself writes love poetry about a man in his sonnets (Goldberg, 2001, p. 200). We also have to remember that Juliet herself would have been played by a teenage boy so there would have been many homosexual elements to the play when people watched it in Shakespeare's time.

The critic Barbara Hodgson when commenting upon Baz Luhrmann's film notes how Luhrmann emphasizes the homosexual under-currents in the play by casting Leonardo DiCaprio as Romeo. She writes:

> In a culture fascinated by youth and in a subculture where one is most interesting if one's sexuality cannot be defined, DiCaprio's pale androgynous beauty – sharp Aryan looks and hint of exotic heritage, a quintessential Greek boy god – makes him a polysexual figure, equally attractive to young women and to gay and straight men. (Hodgson, 2001, p. 135)

Question: to what extent do you agree with these interpretations? Justify your opinions with evidence from the play and good arguments.

Tasks

Map out in the form of a **flow diagram** the overall views of these critics, summarizing their points in a few words.

What are the **similarities and differences** between these opinions?

Rank these opinions by putting the ones you agree with at the top of your list and those you least agree with at the bottom.

Hold a **group discussion** about these views, with students defending different viewpoints (even if they don't agree with them).

Try to **integrate** some of these views into one of your essays.

Essays

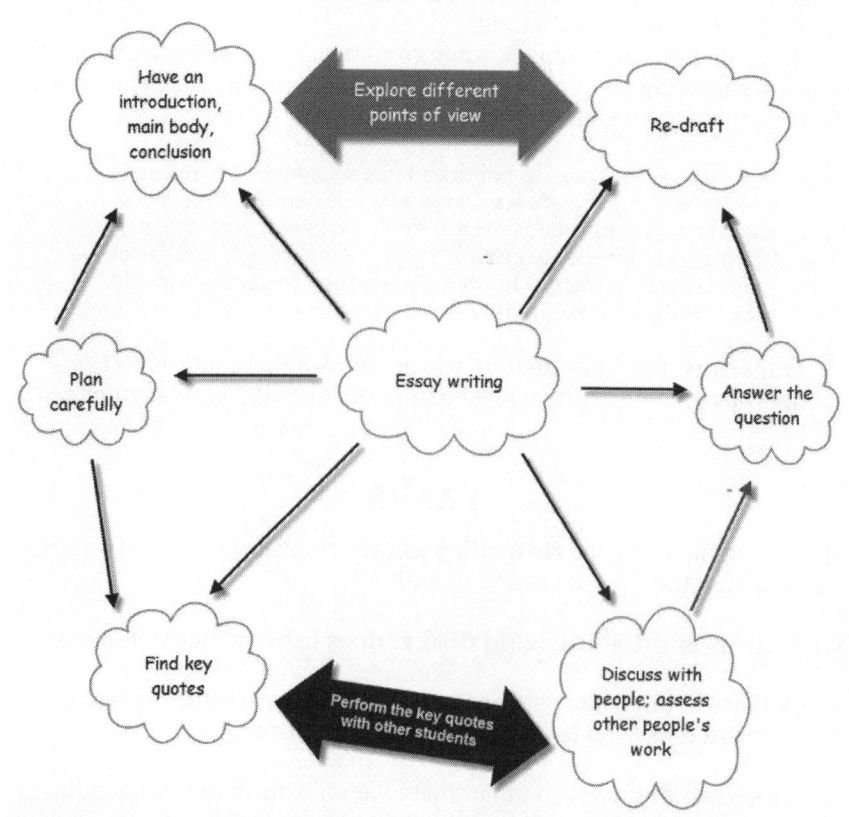

Figure 16 How to get good at essay writing: you can find a larger version of this diagram on the Romeo and Juliet Reloaded website here

Let's face it, writing essays on Shakespeare is probably one of the most difficult things you will do in English. The problem is that Shakespeare is difficult to understand and even when you understand his work well, there's always more to know; the scholarship on Shakespeare is exhaustive. But there are some key pointers that will help you. Before you write any essay on the play, you need to be secure in these areas:

> You need to know the **story, characters, themes** and the **key quotes** in the play well. If you think your knowledge is a bit shaky, then I would recommend going back over the exercises I have set at the end of each act, which cover the key elements of the plot, characters and language.

> You need to be **familiar with the type of question** you are being confronted with. There are usually two types of essay

question on Shakespeare: questions which ask you to comment and **analyze the whole play**, and questions which ask you to focus upon **one particular scene or passage**. We will cover both types of questions in this section.

You need to be familiar with how you might **structure an essay question**. By and large, essays follow a set format: they have introduction, a main body, and a conclusion. In the **introduction**, the candidate usually explores what the question means to them; it offers an interesting interpretation of the question and outlines the ways in which the essay will explore the question. It shouldn't be too detailed but offer "broad brushstrokes" as to how the topics will be covered: be careful of writing conclusions in an introduction. Starting with a key quote which triggers a discussion of the question is a good way around this. The **main body** needs to explore the question in depth, offering argument and counter-argument; you need to suggest how one critic might see an issue in a particular way while another might have a different point of view. Finally, the **conclusion** needs to sum up the findings in your essay; it should not introduce new points.

Now we've covered the basics, we're ready to start looking at a specific essay. What follows is a candidate's essay for GCSE on a familiar topic. The essay is far from perfect and would have achieved a D grade at GCSE. I want to show it to you so that you can learn from the candidate's mistakes and see how the essay could be taken up to an A grade with a little bit more work.

Dissecting a sub-standard essay

This is the title of the essay: *"Romeo and Juliet is as much about hate as it is about love. To what extent do you agree with this statement?"*

This is the candidate's introduction:

This play is as much about hate, as it is about love. For this piece of writing I am going to analyse how the theme of hatred is explored in Shakespeare's play, discussing how it is represented in the language of the play and could be presented dramatically. To do this I am going to use and analyse quotes from the play.

> This introduction could be significantly improved if the candidate had got more of an overview of the question. First the candidate writes his conclusion as his first sentence: "This play is as much about hate, as it is about love." This is a statement which possibly sums up his findings and should be at the end of the essay. It would be much better if he had said something like "In the popular imagination, many people think of *Romeo and Juliet* as being a love story, telling the tragic tale of two 'star-crossed lovers' rather than a story which is full of hatred -- and yet we must remember

that hatred does play a pivotal role in the drama. But just how much? Does the hatred dramatized in the play really make it a play which is as much about negative emotions as it is about the positive emotions of love? This essay will explore whether this statement can really be justified when the text is analysed in depth." Here, I've not come to any firm conclusions, but used the introduction to explore the question and to ask questions of the question. This is perfectly acceptable in an introduction which should "open out a topic" for discussion rather than narrow it down with conclusions. Let's now look at the rest of the essay:

'What, drawn and talk of peace! I hate the word, as I hate hell, all Montague's and thee. Have at thee coward.'
The above is a quote from Tybalt, this quote shows Tybalt's hate for the Montague family and any sort of peace deal between the two families. In the last sentence of the quote, 'Have at thee coward' Tybalt is effectively taunting Romeo by calling him a coward and trying to make him fight sort of saying come on then The irony of this quote is that despite this hate for Romeo, Romeo is now married to a close family member, Juliet, and because of this Romeo refuses to fight Tybalt, Mercutio instead takes up the fight and ends up being killed.

> First, let's look at what the candidate has got right. The use of the quotation is appropriate because it is about the topic of "hatred" and the idea that you should analyse the quote is appropriate too. However, the candidate falls down because he has not explored the quotation in any real depth and he has made a mistake! This quote is taken from Act 1, Sc 1 and is when Tybalt confronts Benvolio, not Romeo. You must **avoid factual errors** of this sort to get a good mark. Check, double-check, and check again! The candidate could have got a better mark by discussing the quote when Tybalt confronts Romeo in Act 3, Sc I when he calls him a "villain" and then is stunned by Romeo telling him that he loves him more than he can possibly know. He could have also gained more marks by saying that it's important with this first quote in Act 1, Sc 1 to realise that Tybalt's hatred "frames" the play: we are aware of Tybalt's hatred before anything else. Shakespeare differed from his source, the long poem by Brooke, in that he introduced the hate-filled figure of Tybalt early; thus you could say that the theme of hatred was uppermost in Shakespeare's mind.

Shakespeare begins the play with a dramatization of a brutal fight, between the servants of the two families, thus telling the audience that hatred is a key theme in the play.
During the play Shakespeare soaks the play with incidents which are characterised by hatred, these incidents intensify the irony of Romeo and Juliet's relationship. Near the beginning of the play Romeo attends a Capulet party, in the knowledge that he's love interest at the time Rosaline was there, although at the party he meets and instantly falls in love with Juliet. This incident of love is however contradicted by an

incident of hatred also during the party when Tybalt, a Capulet and Juliet's cousin who has much hatred for any Montague, see's and becomes very angry at the presence of Romeo at the party and threatens to kill him, although Capulet, Juliet's father confronts him and tells him to leave Romeo alone.

> There are some interesting points here about how the hatred in the play intensifies the "irony of Romeo and Juliet's relationship", although you sense that the candidate hasn't really understood this idea fully. Possibly they've got it from the internet or a teacher. The crucial thing to remember is to comment on things **you understand** and avoid talking about things you don't. The point about Tybalt's hatred "contradicting" the love of Romeo and Juliet in the party scene, Act 1, Sc I, is good but is **not backed up with evidence**. The essay could have explored why Tybalt promises to be "seeming sweet" at the party but that his feelings will turn to the "bitterest gall" towards Romeo. In other words, Tybalt deliberately decides to nurse a murderous hatred for Romeo because he is insulted that Romeo has gate-crashed a Capulet party. Thus, the love scene that follows is set in the context of Tybalt's hatred; this creates suspense, underlying how dangerous it is for the lovers to fall in love.

Another scene where hatred is very evident is the famous "balcony scene". After meeting Juliet at the party Romeo goes to see her at her house and by going via the garden climbs up onto the balcony adjacent to her room. This scene has both great feelings of hate and of love as it is where Romeo and Juliet exchange vows of their love for each other and promise to get married, although they both know that by being there Romeo is in great danger as he is trespassing in the home of his families enemies.

> There is a bit of a weak point here: Act 2, Sc II is mostly suffused with love. Both the lovers are aware of how dangerous it is for Romeo to be there, but they don't dwell at length upon the hatred of the families. So here we have the candidate making a classic mistake in essays: **choosing the wrong focus**. It's important that you find **relevant quotes and evidence** for your points.

Later in the play comes the deaths of Mercutio and Tybalt, again the cause of this is both due to love and hatred. Tybalt, who has not forgotten the earlier incident when Romeo appeared at the Capulet party, threatens and insults Romeo hoping to provoke him and start a fight with him. Romeo responds calmly and doesn't get provoked, mainly due to him knowing that Tybalt is now a family member after his marriage to Juliet. A fight however is started when Mercutio, angry at Romeo's apparent cowardice takes up Tybalt's invitation for a fight and is subsequently killed. Only now does Romeo react to Tybalt in a frenzied attack kills Tybalt.

> This is quite a nice summary of Act 3, Sc I when Mercutio and Tybalt are killed but there is no quotation here. This scene is very relevant and could be explored in much more depth. We learn a great deal about the nature of the hatred in the play. Tybalt calls Romeo a "villain" because he gate-crashed the Capulet party, but Romeo claims that he loves Tybalt more than he, Tybalt, can "devise" or know. This is an extraordinary moment when the "love" generated by the lovers confronts the hatred generated by the feud. It nearly succeeds in stopping a fight and would have done if Mercutio hadn't seen it as a "dishonourable, vile submission": Mercutio, Romeo's friend, believes that Romeo is a coward and has given in. Here we see that it is ideas about masculinity which help keep the hatred between the families alive: it is a "manly" thing to fight. We see this particularly later on, when Romeo, distraught that Mercutio is dead, says that his love for Juliet has made him "effeminate"; i.e. has made him like a woman.

The final major incident involving hatred is when Romeo trying to get access to Juliet's burial tomb is confronted by Paris, who doesn't understand Romeo's urgency, stops him from entering. The two end up fighting and Paris is killed, this incident occurs due to Romeo's love for and desire to see Juliet and Paris' hatred for Romeo over the death of Tybalt.

> This potentially a very strong point but is NOT backed up by evidence. Quoting Paris's lines here would have really helped because they show that Paris automatically thinks Romeo has come to vandalize the Capulet tomb, thus showing how the feud has prejudiced so many people's minds, even Paris's, who we have learned before is a "man of wax", a perfect gentleman.

A key way in which Shakespeare creates hatred is by how he uses imagery. The reader or viewer of the play is made to like and sympathise with Romeo and Juliet, wanting their relationship to work. A major feeling felt by the audience is of the irony evident during the play. For the majority of the play the audience knows something very important which would alter the course of the play and that isn't known by the characters, these things include the audiences knowledge of Romeo and Juliet's marriage and of the plan between Friar Lawrence and Juliet. When the concerned characters do something, unaware of the vital information, the audience feels more for them. The fact that the lovers live in a world full of hatred makes the story more powerful and the audience's expectations and hopes for their success rise.

A famous quote for the play is when Juliet says 'My only love sprung from my only hate!' In this quote Juliet expresses how much she loves Romeo although is disappointed that he is such an enemy to her family. The main principle of the play is that Romeo and Juliet are meant to hate each other like most other people in their respective families' do this makes their love much more poignant as it is meant to be so forbidden.

> Here we see the candidate raising an important point; Shakespeare threads the play through with imagery that evokes and suggests hatred. Juliet's quote is a valid quote to discuss but he could **deepen his analysis**. He could analyse for example the way in which this line uses "antithesis" – the pairing of opposites – to emphasize Juliet's shock that Romeo is a Montague. Romeo is the "only" person she loves and will ever love, and he comes from a family which is the "only" thing she's been taught to hate. There is a desperation evoked in the imagery here which is underlined by the use of the verb "sprung", which gives a dynamism to the line connoting both a "spring" you might find in a mountain, and also the action of "springing" up.

'My life were better ended by their hate, than prorogued, wanting of thy love' this quote is from Romeo and is from Act 2, Scene 2 when Romeo is speaking to Juliet in the Capulet's garden. Whilst talking about Romeo being unsafe being in the Capulet houses garden this Romeo says that he would rather be killed because of their hatred than go on living, waiting for death, without Juliet's love. This quote shows that despite not knowing each other for very long, that Romeo would do very extreme things regarding his love for Juliet.

> Here we see the candidate improving his analysis of a quote; he explains it in depth, but he needs to **relate this point to the question**. He needs to talk about how this quote shows how inter-related the hatred and the love are in this play; the play operates by constantly juxtaposing love and hate. This creates the play's tension and narrative drive.

At the end of the play Shakespeare shows how the families are punished for their hatred. The two families end their long running feud only after the tragic deaths of their families. Both families at the end of the play realise that the unfortunate events only occurred due to their hatred. The Prince at the end of the play and over the bodies of the dead lovers says 'See what a scourge is laid upon your hate'. This quote would make both families feel very guilty. Although it was a good thing that the families feud was resolved it is a shame that peace came at such a cost.

> This is a good point; Shakespeare presents us with the families seemingly being punished because of their hatred for each other. However, it is love that has the final word: the deaths of Romeo and Juliet lead to the families reconciling. We could therefore, argue as many critics have done, that the play is more about love because love seems to triumph in the end. Or does it? A good answer would again come back to the question when discussing this quotation.

To conclude in Romeo and Juliet, William Shakespeare uses hatred to make the love story much more dramatic. The audience is made to feel for the main characters during key events in the play. Irony and fate are used very well in the play to make it dramatic and engaging to an audience.

> This is the beginning of a good conclusion but it needs to be a bit more detailed. When has the essay shown that hatred makes the play more dramatic? Possibly it does this when talking about Tybalt's role in the party scene and the scene where he and Mercutio die. The conclusion is weakest when it introduces a new point: it talks about "fate" which is nowhere discussed in the essay. **Avoid introducing new material** in a conclusion.

Learning points

Strengths

For the most part the essay shows that the candidate knows the story, understands the question and is beginning to argue his case.

Weaknesses

There are **factual errors** and no references: the candidate never locates quotations in specific scenes.

At key points in the essay, the candidate fails to produce **quotation** or **evidence** to back up his points.

The candidate fails at critical junctures **to relate** his points to the question.

The candidate needs to learn how to write good introductions and conclusions.

The scene-based essay

The scene based essay is probably the most common type of essay written at GCSE level. Examiners and teachers like it because it forces students to look carefully at the language of a particular scene. As we saw with the previous essay, a generalized question can cause students to "skate over" points and fail to examine the meanings and effects of the language carefully. Questions for the scene-based essay tend to be quite predictable; they generally ask: "How does the author create suspense/drama/tension in a particular scene or passage?"

There are two key words in this question: "how" and "suspense". The question is asking you "how" a writer creates interest. This means you've got to look at his techniques: **how** he makes us feel interested in the story, the characters, the themes, the language and imagery. You'll need to evaluate (or judge based on the evidence) how successful the writer is in doing this.

There are two main ways of answering this question. First, you can go through the relevant passage in "chronological order" as it were and pick out of the key ways tension is created from the beginning to the end of the scene. The advantage of this approach is that you don't really miss anything out. The disadvantage of it is that you can end up telling the story and not really answering the question. The second way is to focus upon the key techniques the writer uses:

> how the writer makes us interested in **the story**
> how the writer makes us feel sympathy or antipathy for **the characters**
> how the writer engages us intellectually with **his themes**
> how the writer dazzles and entrances us with his **language and imagery**

Personally, I think this second way of doing things is better because it stops students from "just telling the story" without actually analyzing anything. However, there is no right or wrong way of doing it.

The A* essay

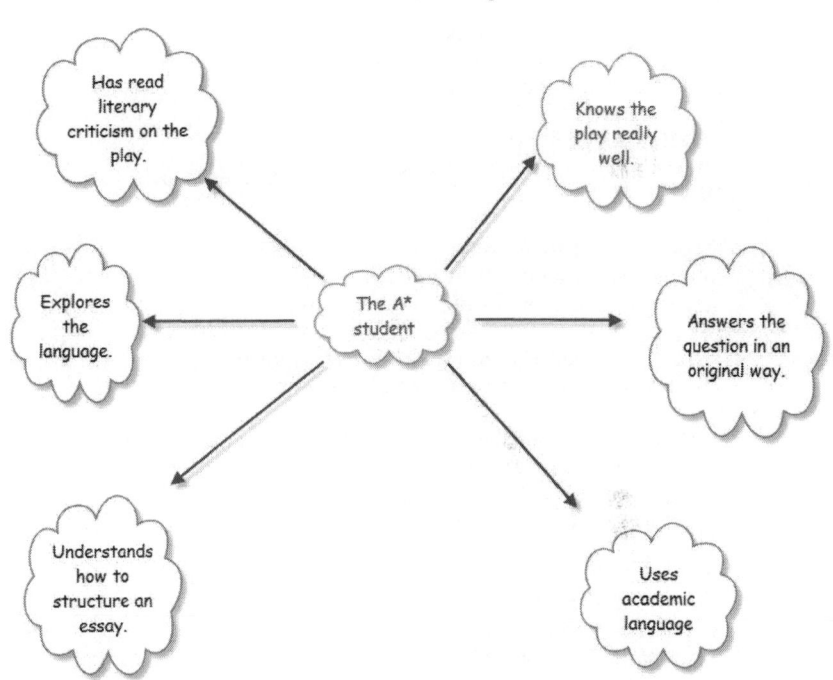

- Has read literary criticism on the play.
- Knows the play really well.
- Explores the language.
- The A* student
- Answers the question in an original way.
- Understands how to structure an essay.
- Uses academic language

Figure 17 The A* student: you can find a larger version of this diagram on **the Romeo and Juliet Reloaded website here**

The Holy Grail of many students is to get the best mark possible in an essay. Having shown you a weak essay, I want to share an essay which gained a top mark and talk briefly about why it is effective. I've decided to show you an essay which is a scene-based essay which focuses upon the last scene of the play because this means it is not only a good essay to learn from regarding essay-writing but it is excellent to revise from because it necessarily encompasses the whole play.

The title is: "How does Shakespeare create such drama and suspense in Act 5, Sc III of *Romeo and Juliet*?"

Preparation and planning

First, the candidate re-read the scene and picked out the quotes that she might use. This is important: the student started with the text. She chooses these quotes to highlight the drama and suspense:

> ROMEO By heaven, I will tear thee joint by joint
> And strew this hungry churchyard with thy limbs:
>
> PARIS here is come to do some villainous shame
> To the dead bodies: I will apprehend him.
>
> ROMEO O, here
> Will I set up my everlasting rest,
> And shake the yoke of inauspicious stars
> From this world-wearied flesh.
>
> ROMEO O true apothecary!
> Thy drugs are quick. Thus with a kiss I die.
> *Dies*
>
> FRIAR LAWRENCE Come, I'll dispose of thee
> Among a sisterhood of holy nuns:
> Stay not to question, for the watch is coming;
>
> JULIET Yea, noise? then I'll be brief. O happy dagger!
> This is thy sheath; there rust, and let me die.
>
> CAPULET O heavens! O wife, look how our daughter bleeds!
> This dagger hath mista'en--for, lo, his house
> Is empty on the back of Montague,--
> And it mis-sheathed in my daughter's bosom!
>
> FRIAR LAWRENCE Her Nurse is privy: and, if aught in this
> Miscarried by my fault, let my old life
> Be sacrificed, some hour before his time,
> Unto the rigour of severest law.
>
> PRINCE Where be these enemies? Capulet! Montague!
> See, what a scourge is laid upon your hate,
> That heaven finds means to kill your joys with love.
>
> PRINCE For never was a story of more woe

Than this of Juliet and her Romeo.

Second, the student used these quotes to get a decent plan together, which was this:

SECTION 1: The story is suspenseful. We know the lovers will die, but not HOW they will die. Tension in finding out what will happen to the other characters
SECTION 2: Sympathy and pity is generated for many of the characters: Romeo, Juliet, Balthasar, Paris (even), Friar Lawrence, the parents.
SECTION 3: The themes of love, hate and fate all explored, making think about our lives and attitudes.
SECTION 4: The language is brilliantly vivid, evoking the scene, the feelings, the distress. Use of rhyme, visual imagery, figurative language etc.
CONCLUSION: Sum up.

Having done this, the student wrote this response:

Act 5, Sc III is the climactic scene of *Romeo and Juliet*; it is the scene when all the disparate threads of the plot are brought together. Since the play is a tragedy this necessarily means that the central protagonists will die. Indeed we know from the Prologue, at the beginning of the play, that the lovers will die because they are "star-crossed" and their deaths will end the bloody feud between the families. Since we already know the ending, Shakespeare is not able to build suspense by providing the audience with any major surprises, although, as we will see, he does give us some smaller surprises along the way. Furthermore, many people in Shakespeare's audience in the 1590s would have been aware of Brooke's poem upon which the play is based and would know the ending from their familiarity with it. As a result, Shakespeare creates suspense not only by giving us an unexpected plot-twist, but by making the audience wonder exactly "how" the lovers will die and "how" the families will end their feud.

> In this first part of the essay, the student discusses the **narrative/story/plot** of the play, pointing out how **what has happened before** contributes to the suspense in the scene. The student has also shown she knows about **the sources** of the play. Notice how the introduction avoids "waffling" and gets straight to the point.

Shakespeare structures the scene so that it is "action-packed": the events themselves are enough to grip the audience. We scarcely have time to draw breath from the moment Romeo arrives at the Capulet's tomb in the dark because, after threatening his servant Balthasar that he will tear him limb from limb if he enters the tomb, Romeo then blindly fights Paris and kills him. Once he's dragged Juliet's "other husband" into the tomb, Romeo soon kills himself, at which point Friar Lawrence arrives to rescue Juliet but is scared off by the Watch, leaving Juliet to kill herself. Frenetic activity ensues as the whole town is woken by the deaths: Friar Lawrence is told to account for himself. Having listened to the Friar's story, the Prince blames the feud for the tragic deaths of the lovers. Finally, both families agree to end their enmity. Thus we can see that in a short space of time we have three deaths, an interrogation (of Friar Lawrence), an oration by the Prince, and the end of the hatred between the families. The audience is necessarily swept along by the pace of the action and this, in a large part, creates much of the drama and suspense.

> This paragraph looks at how the **structure of the scene** contributes towards it being suspenseful and dramatic. Notice how the student does **not "tell story" at great length** but highlights the key events which contribute towards it being "action-packed" as she calls it. Furthermore, she shows how the story creates suspense.

But it is more than the plot that engages the audience's interest; it is our feelings for the characters as well. Romeo has become a tragic figure at this point of the play; Shakespeare presents him as a man who is on the very edge of sanity. The fact that he threatens to kill his beloved servant, Balthasar, "joint by joint" shows how the supposed death of Juliet has unhinged him. Similarly, his wild fight with Paris – he doesn't know who he is fighting at first – reveals his passionate and mad demeanour. Far from despising him for this, we feel a deep sympathy: Romeo has been presented in the play as "fortune's fool" – the plaything of destiny. Perhaps most poignant is his speech before he kills himself. He says:

> O, here
> Will I set up my everlasting rest,
> And shake the yoke of inauspicious stars
> From this world-wearied flesh.

There is a terrible tragic irony to these words because he believes that he is defying his fate – shaking the "yoke of inauspicious stars" – by ending his life when, in actual fact, we know he is fulfilling it. His body is "world-wearied"; although he is young, he has suffered more in his short life than most will do in a life-time. His long soliloquy contrasts with Juliet's who knows she has to be quick to kill herself because the Watch is coming. We feel sympathy for her because she has been left alone by Romeo and has woken up too late to save him. In the Baz Luhrmann film, Juliet even sees the last moments of life in Romeo and he sees her before he dies, adding to the poignancy and pointlessness of his death. This however is not written into the Shakespeare play: it's very clear that

Romeo is dead before Juliet wakes up. After the death of the lovers, the focus shifts to Friar Lawrence, who is arrested and has to explain himself: his long speech explains in an honest fashion what has happened. Once again, we feel real pity for him when he says that his "old life" should be ended if the Prince finds him guilty of "miscarrying" – of doing wrong. However, a letter from Romeo to his father which the Prince reads saves the Friar from execution. The audience learns of how the Prince has suffered from the feud – Mercutio was a kinsman – and we feel the Prince's anger at the feud: "See, what a scourge is laid upon your hate". Finally, Shakespeare perhaps pulls the greatest surprise at the end when we find ourselves feeling real sympathy for the two families: we learn that Lady Montague is dead from grief at Romeo's banishment and that the acerbic Lady Capulet will die before getting old. However, both families agree to celebrate the lovers by making gold statues of them. Thus we can see Shakespeare's great achievement is to present characters who had been quite unsympathetic in a much more positive, poignant light.

> This section of the essay examines Shakespeare's **characterisations** with reference to the question. She analyses and evaluates how the characters create suspense and drama by showing that we feel a considerable amount of **sympathy** for them. Once again, as with the previous paragraph, we see her covering a lot of ground quite quickly; she doesn't provide exhaustive case studies but summarizes the key aspects of the characters quickly.

However, it is Shakespeare's use of language which is probably the most striking and gripping feature of this act. Romeo's soliloquy which he says before he poisons himself uses motifs which we have found throughout the play and this makes the audience feel the tragedy of the situation all the more deeply. When he talks about Juliet filling the tomb with "a feasting presence full of light" the iambic rhythm of the line and the evocative imagery connected with light reminds us of when he first saw Juliet and proclaimed that she "teaches the torches to burn more bright". Thus we can see how his last speech about Juliet connects with his first, but the sense of hope and optimism has gone and has been replaced by a mournful, tragic tone. The adjective "feasting" also invokes Capulet's feast when he first saw her. Yet, the speech is a sinister one because Romeo believes that Death may well have made Juliet his "paramour" – his lover – and, as a result, Romeo needs to kill himself in order to protect her. The "chop-logic" of this suggests Romeo's passionate state of mind. In contrast, Juliet's death speech is short but powerful nevertheless; she talks about the dagger being a "happy dagger" because it will bring about her death. This personification of the dagger is both surprising and alarming, making us think about Juliet's tragic situation. Perhaps the most surprising speech is that from Paris in that we learn that he too genuinely loved Juliet: he calls her a "sweet flower" – hinting at image used by Capulet when Juliet 'died' – and says he will come to her grave every night and cry: "which with sweet water nightly I will dew". Finally, we see the human side to Paris in this simple but distressing imagery; we realize his love for Juliet is genuine. Much of the imagery in this last part of the place is infused with darkness: Romeo, Paris and Friar Lawrence all refer to the gloominess and death-haunted nature of the tomb, and the Prince talks about a "glooming peace" in the last speech. In such a way, the imagery creates an overwhelmingly "black" atmosphere.

> This section discusses the **language** of the play. Crucially, you will see how the student has embedded quotation into her sentences so that, by and large, she is not quoting huge chunks of the text. She threads her points about the language together into an argument which explores the similarities and differences of the different characters' use of language.

Much of the language suggests and explores the key themes of the play: love, hate and fate. Romeo's talk about the "inauspicious stars" reminds us with its striking adjective "inauspicious" that the lovers are marked out to die. Paris's, Romeo's and Juliet's speeches all use imagery connected with love in their different ways: Paris calls Juliet his "sweet flower"; Romeo refers to Juliet as a "feasting presence of light"; Juliet talks about Romeo being her "true love". This is imagery redolent of love and is in stark contrast to the imagery connected with hatred; Paris calls Romeo a "haughty Montague" and the Prince speaks of the "scourge" – the terrible blight – of the feud. However, the imagery of love and hatred is reconciled in a dramatic way when Capulet and Montague join hands on stage. In such a way, we can see that Shakespeare ties together the two oppositional threads in the imagery by this dramatic gesture. It is all the more poignant because of the way in which the imagery connected with love and hated has been so oppositional in the play. Finally love has beaten the hatred in the play with this dramatic gesture:

> CAPULET O brother Montague, give me thy hand:
> This is my daughter's jointure, for no more
> Can I demand.

> This section examines the how **the themes and imagery** of the play are inter-connected. This is clever of the candidate because she has shown knowledge of two major areas of the play by examining them together. Her discussion of the imagery of "love" is pithy but incisive. Here she shows how the themes of the play are woven through the imagery of the play.

In conclusion, we can see that Shakespeare has created suspense and drama in a number of different ways in this final scene. First, he sets a context for the scene which means that the audience is on the edge of its seat wondering how the lovers will die and the feud will end. Second, he has made the scene "action-packed". Third, he has created characters who become much more sympathetic in this final scene. Fourth, he deployed his imagery in such a way that the key themes of the play are explored in a dramatic and engaging fashion.

> Finally, the conclusion **sums up the key points** of the play. She does not introduce any new points in the paragraph but summarizes what she has already said.

Comparing the play with filmed versions & performances

In recent years, both coursework and exam questions have required students to compare performed versions of the play with the text itself. This can be a tricky task but if you stick to a few basic guidelines, it is possible to produce an excellent response. When writing such an essay, you will need to watch your chosen performance very carefully and think hard about the things that this performance is saying to you. These are some questions you might ask when you've watched the performance:

How have the actors interpreted their characters? For example, in Baz Luhrmann's film, both Romeo and Juliet are young, modern teenagers with Romeo seemingly coming from a rougher, less wealthy background than Juliet. Romeo is presented as a dreamy but "cool" teenager who hangs around with the lads, but isn't a trouble-maker. Meanwhile, Juliet is shown to be the "sheltered" daughter of a very rich Mafioso style father, growing up in an Italian American household. If you are focusing upon a specific scene, you should think really carefully about the actors' actions and expressions, their tone of voice, and the lines that they say that are really dramatic.

How does the "mise-en-scene" (costumes, make-up, scenery etc.) add excitement and interest to the play? The Luhrmann version sets the play in a modern, violent city and replaces swords with guns. This makes the play much more engaging for modern audiences because they can see the connection between the issues in the play and what's happening in our society today. The Luhrmann version is very good at showing how the violence in the play is very similar to sorts of gang violence that we find in our society. It is always interesting to comment upon costumes and think about how they add interest to the play. For example, in the Luhrmann version, Romeo dresses as a knight and Juliet as an angel in the party scene, both images that are in the lines of the play. Thus, we can see how the director is conveying Shakespeare's imagery in a visual fashion.

How has the text been edited and what effect does this have? The best answers will look carefully about what lines have been **kept in** a scene and what have been **left out** and why. For example, in the

Luhrmann version, about two thirds of Shakespeare's lines are cut out but the really important lines are left in. Some key lines are also left out, such as most of the rhyming poem Romeo says when he first sees Juliet in Act 1, Sc V; instead we watch the two lovers viewing each other through a fish tank. One could argue that the dreamy, visual imagery of Romeo's poem to Juliet is possibly conveyed in an indirect way in the fish tank; is Juliet rather like the dove amidst the black crows as her face watches Romeo through the swimming fish? You could argue flavor of the line is conveyed in the visual image.

Consider filmic techniques if you are looking a film: the use of camera angles, the editing of the film, and the use of sound.
The primary medium for film is the visual medium: an image is the equivalent of a thousand words. A film director can conjure an entire world in a few carefully chosen camera shots, whereas a playwright like Shakespeare has to construct a scene in words: he had virtually no scenery to play with and would use dialogue and description to give the audience a sense of where the play was taking place. This is particularly the case with the "Apothecary Scene" (Act 5, Sc I) when Romeo visits a chemist for poison before going to Juliet's tomb: Shakespeare spends virtually a page having Romeo describe the apothecary's shop. A film director can show his shop and everything in it in a second or two. Film directors use techniques such as "**montage**" (having a succession of pictures of different places and people) to build up a sense of an entire world or a particular situation. They use **overhead** and **long shots** to give us the sense of an entire place or city: this is particularly the case in the Luhrmann film which has a series of very striking long and overhead shots of Verona Beach, the city where Romeo and Juliet live. They use **medium shots** to give you the sense of one place or a few characters and how they are interacting with each other. And finally, they use **close-ups** to give you a sense of a character's emotions and their reactions to the world around them.

Think about the director's overall interpretation of the play.
This is particularly important. What do you think a film director or theatre director is trying to say about the play overall? What are they saying about the specific characters? Are they portraying for example, Romeo as a selfish teenage or a wonderful, dreamy lover? Are they showing the dark side of Friar Lawrence or representing him as a man who is out of his depth?

Internet links

This publication by the OCR exam board is aimed at teachers but is very clearly written and has some excellent tips on how to discuss Shakespeare on film. It has an excellent series of prompts for writing.

The complete movie script of Baz Luhrmann's *Romeo + Juliet* can be found here.

This handout devised by PBS's Shakespeare programme is very good at helping students get good notes when analyzing a particular film extract from a Shakespeare film.

Works Cited

Belsey, C. (2001). The Name of the Rose in Romeo and Juliet. In E. b. White, *Romeo and Juliet: New Casebooks*. New York: Palgrave.
Brecht, B. (2001). The Servants. In E. b. White, *New Casebooks: Romeo and Juliet* (pp. 147-151). New York: Palgrave.
British Library. (n.d.). *Shakespeare Quartos*. Retrieved June 21, 2014, from Treasures in Full: http://www.bl.uk/treasures/shakespeare/romeo.html
Brooke, N. (1968). Romeo and Juliet. In N. Brooke, *Shakespeare's Early Tragedies* (pp. 80-106). London: Methuen.
Callaghan, D. C. (2001). The Ideology of Romantic Love. In E. b. White, *New Casebooks: Romeo and Juliet*. New York: Palgrave.
David Crystal, Ben Crystal. (2002). *Shakespeare's Words: A Glossary and Language Companion*. London: Penguin.
Eaglestone, R. (2009). *Doing English: A Guide for Literature Students*. Oxford, England: Routledge.
Eleanor Dommett, Ian Devonshire, Richard Churches. (2011). *Learning & The Brain Pocketbook*. Hampshire: Teachers' Pocketbooks.
Gibson, R. (2006). Romeo and Juliet: Cambridge School Shakespeare. In W. S. Gibson. Cambridge: Cambridge University Press.
Goldberg, J. (2001). Romeo and Juliet's Open Rs. In E. b. White, *New Casebooks: Romeo and Juliet* (pp. 194-212). New York: Palgrave.
Hodgson, B. (2001). Baz Luhrmann's Romeo and Juliet. In E. b. White, *New Casebooks: Romeo and Juliet* (pp. 129-143). New York: Palgrave.
Kahn, C. (1993). Coming of Age in Verona. In E. b. Andrews, *Romeo and Juliet: Critical Essays* (pp. 337-358). New York and London: Garland Publishing Inc.
Luhrmann, B. (Director). (1996). *Romeo + Juliet* [Motion Picture]. Retrieved from http://en.wikipedia.org/wiki/Romeo_%2B_Juliet
McMannus, B. F. (1999, November). *Outline of Aristotle's Theory of Tragedy*. Retrieved June 21, 2014, from Outline of Aristotle's Theory of Tragedy: http://www2.cnr.edu/home/bmcmanus/poetics.html
Roma Gill, William Shakespeare. (1982). *Oxford School Shakespeare: Romeo and Juliet*. Oxford: Oxford University Press.
Schmoop. (n.d.). *Romeo and Juliet Study Guide*. Retrieved June 2014, 2014, from Schmoop Study Guide: http://www.shmoop.com/romeo-and-juliet/summary.html
Smith, E. (2013, July 31). *Oxford University Podcasts Emma Smith*. Retrieved June 21, 2014, from Oxford University: http://podcasts.ox.ac.uk/why-should-we-study-shakespeare
Sparknotes. (n.d.). *Spark Notes Romeo and Juliet Study Guide*. Retrieved June 21, 2014, from Plot summary: http://www.shmoop.com/romeo-and-juliet/summary.html

The British Museum. (n.d.). *Shakespeare's Restless World*. (BBC) Retrieved June 21, 2014, from Shakespeare's Restless World: http://www.bbc.co.uk/programmes/b017gm45

White, R. (2001). Introduction: What is this thing called love? In E. b. White, *Romeo and Juliet: New Casebooks, Contemporary Critical Essays*. New York: Palgrave.

William Shakespeare, John Seeley. (1993). *Romeo and Juliet: Heinemann Shakespeare*. Oxford: Heinemann.

William Shakespeare, Rene Weis. (2012). *Romeo and Juliet: The Arden Shakespeare*. London: Bloomsbury Arden Shakespeare.

Zeffirelli, F. (Director). (1968). *Romeo and Juliet* [Motion Picture]. Retrieved from http://en.wikipedia.org/wiki/Romeo_and_Juliet_(1968_film)

About the author

Francis Gilbert is a writer who has been a secondary school teacher for more than twenty years in various London schools. He has published numerous books, including *I'm A Teacher, Get Me Out Of Here* and *The Last Day of Term* as well as a series of study guides on classic texts such as *Frankenstein, Wuthering Heights* and *Jane Eyre* -- all published on Kindle. He currently teaches part-time in a large comprehensive and is completing a PhD in Creative Writing and Education for which he writing an autobiographically-inspired novel, *Who Do You Love?*, and conducting some educational research which investigates what happens when teachers share their fiction with their pupils. The PhD has made him re-evaluate many of his assumptions about the education system. He is particularly interested in the ways in which teachers can cultivate a sense of beauty in their pupils by using all the tools of the internet, including blogging, video and audio. He frequently tries to find new ways of engaging students in difficult concepts and texts; this modern version of Shakespeare's play arose from such an experiment. You can learn more about his work by logging onto his website: www.francisgilbert.co.uk

Printed in Great Britain
by Amazon.co.uk, Ltd.,
Marston Gate.